M000251765

Reform and Transition in the Mediterranean

Series Editor
Ioannis N. Grigoriadis
Bilkent University
Ankara, Turkey

The series of political and economic crises that befell many countries in the Mediterranean region starting in 2009 has raised emphatically questions of reform and transition. While the sovereign debt crisis of Southern European states and the "Arab Spring" appear prima facie unrelated, some common roots can be identified: low levels of social capital and trust, high incidence of corruption, and poor institutional performance. This series provides a venue for the comparative study of reform and transition in the Mediterranean within and across the political, cultural, and religious boundaries that crisscross the region. Defining the Mediterranean as the region that encompasses the countries of Southern Europe, the Levant, and North Africa, the series contributes to a better understanding of the agents and the structures that have brought reform and transition to the forefront. It invites (but is not limited to) interdisciplinary approaches that draw on political science, history, sociology, economics, anthropology, area studies, and cultural studies. Bringing together case studies of individual countries with broader comparative analyses, the series provides a home for timely and cutting-edge scholarship that addresses the structural requirements of reform and transition; the interrelations between politics, history and culture; and the strategic importance of the Mediterranean for the EU, the USA, Russia, and emerging powers.

More information about this series at
http://www.palgrave.com/gp/series/14513

Joseph P. Helou

Activism, Change and Sectarianism in the Free Patriotic Movement in Lebanon

palgrave
macmillan

Joseph P. Helou
Department of Social Sciences
Lebanese American University
Beirut, Lebanon

Reform and Transition in the Mediterranean
ISBN 978-3-030-25703-3 ISBN 978-3-030-25704-0 (eBook)
https://doi.org/10.1007/978-3-030-25704-0

Cover credit: Malcolm P Chapman/Getty Images

This Palgrave Macmillan imprint is published by the registered company Springer Nature Switzerland AG
The registered company address is: Gewerbestrasse 11, 6330 Cham, Switzerland

Acknowledgements

With the publication of this title, I thank everyone who assisted in bringing this project to life. I thank the editorial team at Palgrave Macmillan.

I thank Denise Parker for her professional proof reading of this book.

I thank the academics whose comments, advice and guidance deepened my understanding of theoretical and empirical topics in the social sciences over the years; they include Bice Maiguashca, Farid El-Khazen, Irene Fernandez-Molina, Jad Chaaban, Nawaf Salam, Paul Kingston and Paul Salem, among others.

This book is based on research supported by the AUB—Issam Fares Institute for Public Policy and International Affairs Nadim Makdisi Memorial Fund. I thank the Issam Fares Institute for its support.

I am indebted to all the Free Patriotic Movement (FPM) activists whose experience in political activism constituted the primary sources for this book. I thank them for taking the time to explain vital aspects of their movement. While FPM activists spent valuable time explaining many aspects of their movement, they do not bear responsibility for the analysis fleshed out in this book, which reflects my own arguments.

I acknowledge the assistance of the archives department at the Lebanese daily *Annahar* in providing me access to hundreds of newspaper pieces featuring news on the FPM. These pieces provided reliable secondary sources to verify the existence of FPM activism throughout the period 1990–2005.

Last but not least, I thank my father Prosper, mother Lina and brother Robin for their unconditional love and support; their backing makes me who I am today. My mother's constant nudge to "go finish that book" brought this book to life.

Contents

CHAPTER 1

Introduction

The self-immolation of the Tunisian fruit-cart vendor Mohamed Bouazizi in December 2010 sparked a nationwide protest movement in his country, which quickly inspired protests in several other Arab countries that toppled long-standing dictatorial regimes. Some of the ensuing protest movements evolved into bloody civil wars, as in Libya and Syria, where the external military intervention of state and non-state actors further complicated prospects for a peaceful transition to democratic rule (Lynch 2016).

The political process generating these protests quickly became the topic of concern in several research works examining some of the influencing factors: the role of the media in the 2011 protests (Lynch 2014, Chap. 5); the political elite in prioritizing political reform while dismissing economic reforms to preserve their interests (Abdelrahman 2012); and the leaderless nature of the protests, which often transformed into broad coalitions of ideologically opposed actors that fractured the political scene and provided an advantage for the more organized actors, such as the Muslim Brotherhood (Durac 2015). Prior to the Arab uprisings of 2011, this political process hosted Islamist actors as organized forces providing breeding grounds for often violent activism (Hafez 2003; Wiktorowicz 2004; Wickham 2015) and labor movements that were infiltrated and manipulated by the regime (see Beinin and Lockman 1998; Beinin and Vairel 2011; Beinin 2015). Although dimensions of the political process varied across Arab states, different authoritarian practices were a hallmark of the Arab state system, which, in turn, decreased the access points

J. P. Helou, *Activism, Change and Sectarianism in the Free Patriotic Movement in Lebanon*, Reform and Transition in the Mediterranean,
https://doi.org/10.1007/978-3-030-25704-0_1

to government and limited avenues for political participation. Therefore, examining the composition, ideas and mobilization of social movements and other forms of protest activity became important to understand how people expressed their demands collectively outside the institutions of the state.

Perhaps Lebanon stood out from among its Arab counterparts because its political system allowed for a wide margin of political participation, with minimal intervention of national security forces in national politics. Yet, as the Syrian suzerainty of Lebanon weighed in heavily on Lebanese post-war politics in the period 1990–2005, some authoritarian practices seeped into the Lebanese political arena by diffusion (El-Khazen 2003). Lebanon's political system can be characterized as a state with fragmented institutions undergirded by elite practices mired in high levels of corruption (Leenders 2012), and as a sectarian system incentivizing people to pledge allegiance to a group of political, financial-economic and religious elites at the expense of the state (Salloukh et al. 2015), which, in turn, gains its vitality from a vast network of patron–client relations that often provide citizens with access to resources and public goods through the intercession of elites that are influential with the state (Hottinger 1961; Khalaf 1968, 2003; Cammet 2014; Helou 2015). Its domestic politics can be understood by closely examining the nature of the political and constitutional order prevailing in the country both before and after the Lebanese Civil War that began in 1975 (Hudson 1968; Picard 1996; Leenders 2012), the factors contributing to the conflagrations of the Lebanese Civil War (Salibi 1976; El-Khazen 2000; Randal 2012), and the Lebanese post-war elite who were allied with Syria (El-Husseini 2012). While this book recognizes the complexities embedded in Lebanese politics, it does not seek to adopt any of the aforementioned aspects of Lebanese politics as the focus of this study.

In fact, this book chooses to focus on the experience of the Free Patriotic Movement (FPM) in a political context governed by the dialectic of the complex nature of Lebanese politics, which on the one hand hosts democratic avenues for participation, and on the other buttresses a sectarian system with fragmented state institutions and a network of patron—client relations. This context shows that the 30-year-old trajectory of the FPM includes the early formation of the movement during the final stages of the Lebanese Civil War in 1989, its emergence and persistence as a secular freedom movement during the period 1990–2005, and a transformation into a sectarian political party following 2005.

Such a diverse and often contradictory political history can provide valuable insights into an experiment in social movement activism for many aspiring political movements and parties throughout the Middle East region. This book speaks to practitioners and intellectuals and mostly addresses those whose interests lie in collective activity, social movement and political parties, especially in the Middle East. It also makes a valuable contribution to Middle Eastern politics by illuminating the role of political activists whose backgrounds happen to be predominantly middle-class Christian, which, in turn, adds a new empirical case study to the fields of social movements and minority politics.

The FPM began taking shape when supporters, comprising largely Lebanese Christians, rallied in support of the political proposals of Lebanese army commander Michel Aoun, whose public appearances in 1989 won him popular support. Following his defeat in a Syrian-led military attack in 1990 and his expatriation to France, Aoun's supporters marched in the shadow of their leader in Lebanon, forming what became known as the FPM, which launched collective activity—that is protests, demonstrations and the distribution of pamphlets—and called for the freedom, sovereignty and independence of Lebanon, despite the many challenges imposed on the movement by the Lebanese political elite. However, this social movement not only managed to survive throughout the period 1990–2005, but even transformed itself into a political party after the return of Aoun to Lebanon in 2005. Even today, the FPM continues to exist as a powerful player in Lebanese politics, with a sizable bloc in Parliament and members serving in the Council of Ministers.

Aims

This book seeks to present an empirical analysis of a Lebanese political movement that had an important impact on the course of national politics, especially in the country's post-war scenario, as a sizable movement that was disenfranchised from formal participation in conventional politics (Parliament, Council of Ministers, positions within the state bureaucracy, etc.) in the period 1990–2005. Although this movement conveyed secular political ideas in relation to its counterparts, the sociological composition of the movement's membership was clearly tilted toward middle-class Christians, while simultaneously welcoming activists from various Muslim denominations into its ranks. Therefore, the disenfranchisement of the FPM from Lebanese politics and the expatriation of its leader, Michel

Aoun, spelled the exclusion of Lebanese Christians from actively engaging in national politics.

Despite the FPM's exclusion from national politics, the Lebanese political system was never too authoritarian to prevent the rise of opposition voices in civil society, including the FPM. With more than 20,000 troops based in Lebanon, a political elite favoring their policies and sectarianism pervading every nook and cranny of politics on the national and societal level, Syria was able to dominate and manipulate Lebanese politics, but never controlled every aspect of its existence. The political environment prevailing in Lebanon throughout the period 1990–2005 can best be described as "authoritarianism by diffusion," as suggested by Farid El-Khazen (2003), which bore witness to a number of non-transparent political practices in the country that were sponsored by Syria or its allies among the Lebanese political elite.

Ironically, the prevailing political conditions in post-war Lebanon accommodated sectarian practices, corruption and democratic avenues for participation, which, in turn, challenged the rise of opposition movements, such as the FPM, but without rendering their emergence a mission impossible. Therefore, this book seeks to explore the rise of the FPM amid a fluid and nuanced, but no doubt challenging, political environment. This work will analyze the opportunities that favored the emergence of the FPM after the expatriation of its leader, Michel Aoun, to France in 1991. It will uncover the kind of opportunities and ideas that incentivized FPM activists to partake in collective activism by organizing strikes, protests, sit-ins and so on, to voice their objection to the sectarian practices and corrupt dealings of the Lebanese political elite and to Syria's overshadowing role in Lebanon. This analysis seeks to anchor the pivotal role that civil society (members of syndicates and unions, university students and ordinary individuals across towns and villages) played in building the FPM as a social movement across Lebanon.

Another aspect this book aims to uncover is the role that FPM activists—that is, university students, members of syndicates and individuals in a number of towns and villages—played in ensuring the persistence of their movement's activism. With numerous challenges to overcome, FPM activists could not have built a movement without a semblance of organization to mobilize for activism, resources to ensure the persistence of their movement, and ideas and incentives to deepen activists' commitment to the FPM throughout the period 1991–2005. By shedding light on its operations, this book seeks to reveal the role of both Aoun and

FPM activists in forming the FPM. Typically, accounts of the movement exaggerate the role attributed to Aoun in its organization. Therefore, the analysis will strike a much-needed balance by revealing the role of various other actors.

Since this book examines the three-decade trajectory of the FPM, it will seek to analyze the institutional transformation that occurred within it following the return of Aoun to Lebanon in 2005. The institution of the FPM as a political party, the assignment of individuals to positions within the newly established party, and its participation in conventional politics (Parliament and Council of Ministers) led to a series of issues within the party that clearly characterized a transitioning social movement. Therefore, this work aims to uncover the impacts these struggles had on the shape of the party and its activities.

In addition, the book will show how the FPM turned from a movement that expressed a relatively secular political outlook and ideas to one that adopted sectarian political discourse, practices and strategies to compete against its sectarian counterparts in conventional politics; that is to say, how its members emerged victorious in parliamentary elections in the post-2005 period. They also sought to maintain their movement's position as the defender of the rights of their support base, which predominantly comprised middle-class Christians. Yet precisely why the FPM turned sectarian and how it managed to evolve in order to preserve its support base is a puzzling aspect that will be explored in this empirical account.

Rationale

The primary rationale warranting a study of the FPM is to fill a gap in the Lebanese social movement's literature. The main reason no one has analyzed the movement is because a study of it during the period 1990–2005 was almost impossible, given the tremendous challenges imposed on the FPM, which, in turn, obliged the movement to maintain a certain level of secrecy to ensure the success of its activism. Researchers who might have been willing to study the movement during the period 1990–2005 would have encountered difficulties in gathering data, since FPM activists were quite cautious about sharing information with anyone regarding their political activism within the movement for fear of being hunted down by national security institutions, such as the Lebanese army, Internal Security Forces, General Security Directorate and State Security Directorate.

Therefore, studying the FPM, which was clearly opposed to the political elite of Lebanon and the intervention of Syria in Lebanese affairs, only became possible following the withdrawal of Syrian troops from Lebanon in 2005, which provided the movement with the right to assemble freely.

Of course, an important rationale for the study of the FPM, and movement politics in Lebanon generally, is to understand how these movements interact with their broader political context. In this respect, the Lebanese state, which is driven by a complex set of disunited and fragmented institutions, a disunited and quarreling political elite, and sectarian politics, which, in turn, is manifested in high levels of post-war corruption, cannot be treated as a unitary actor as such. Since the FPM was faced with this type of fragmented state, this author was interested to analyze to what extent it was able to reject the established order on the one hand, and to what degree it coexisted within the established order on the other.

In addition to studying the interaction of the FPM with the Lebanese political system, the extent to which the movement was able to combat Lebanese sectarian politics or otherwise succumb to certain features of sectarianism constitutes an essential rationale for this research. Sectarianism is not only a power-sharing agreement that assigns members of a sectarian community to the positions designated for their specific sect within the Lebanese political system, but also a political-economic system fostered by the political elite to share in the spoils of government and then use some of those resources to mobilize the loyalty of their supporters. This book embraces the definition of sectarianism advanced by Salloukh et al. (2015, p. 3), who define it as "a modern constitutive Foucauldian socioeconomic and political power that produces and reproduces sectarian subjects and modes of political subjectification and mobilization through a dispersed ensemble of institutional, clientelist, and discursive practices." Those authors view sectarianism as a holistic political-economic and ideological system that pervades many aspects of Lebanese life, which is underpinned by clientelist patronage networks and a symbolic repertoire that incorporates large segments of society into corporatized sectarian communities. This sectarian system results in a distorted incentive structure that redirects individual loyalties away from state institutions and symbols toward sectarian communities and their political and religious elite (ibid.).

Although the FPM expressed forms of collective action that resembled many other social movements, such as protests and demonstrations, what makes a study of it extremely significant is the way it was able to run its political activity in spite of limited access to resources and exclusion from the institutions of the state, such as Parliament and the Council of Ministers. Therefore, it is possible to further appreciate the significance of this research and its aims by pinning down the precise nature of this partial exclusion from the Lebanese system, which allowed the FPM to emerge in professional syndicates, student elections on university campuses, on municipal councils and in towns and villages, while remaining officially banned as a political movement. This work seeks to clarify to what extent the Lebanese political elite consciously determined for which political positions FPM activists were allowed to strive or in which particular areas they were permitted to emerge. It will investigate to what extent FPM activists were able to build on political activities that were regarded as insignificant by the political elite, to emerge and persist as a movement throughout the period 1990–2005.

Yet another rationale for an analysis of the FPM is to contribute to the expansion of the Middle Eastern social movement repertoire by analyzing a movement with a secular political outlook, but whose active members are predominantly middle-class Christians. The logic of this complex relationship, characterized by a movement whose members are predominantly Christian on the one hand and whose political ideas are secular on the other, should be clearly examined given the sectarian features of Lebanese politics. In other words, examining to what extent the FPM was able to stand out as a secular movement or otherwise play by the rules of Lebanon's sectarian politics requires some elucidation.

Research Methodology

This book draws on 30 semi-structured interviews as primary sources of information to flesh out FPM narratives of activism, change and sectarianism during its examination of the emergence, persistence and institutional transformation phases of the movement. During the interviews the author conducted, FPM activists shared their experiences in movement activism as well as their dissatisfaction with some internal party affairs. While this author draws on the information gathered from these semi-structured interviews, no part of this work replicates the ideas, opinions or proposals of FPM activists without subjecting them to critical review.

Therefore, readers of this work should understand that this research does not constitute a movement publication that reveals the subjective voices of FPM activists, but a critical analysis of the movement that integrates these voices into an analytical framework that paints a coherent narrative of the FPM. This narrative seeks to provide valuable insights into FPM activism, change and sectarianism throughout the movement's 30-year trajectory.

The author sampled FPM activists for interviews using the snowballing technique. By pinpointing a few famous FPM activists in Lebanon, it was possible to identify some members of the core group of activists, some of whom spent an extensive period of time in mobilizing FPM activism throughout the period 1990–2005 and beyond. After interviewing some of these members, the author was able to widen the interviewee sample by gaining information on FPM activism involving other activists.

On average, the author spent 90 minutes interviewing each FPM activist. These interviews were recorded in Arabic and then translated and transcribed by the author. This process generated approximately 450 pages of typed script, which were analyzed for the dimensions of the FPM under scrutiny.

As such, this method generated important primary sources of information that contributed to the story fleshed out here. The author also relied on secondary sources of information, such as newspaper articles from the Lebanese daily *Annahar*, which covered FPM activism throughout the 1990–2005 period. Both these primary and secondary sources help explain the dimensions of the FPM in this book.

Central Argument

This book demonstrates that the role of FPM activists and Michel Aoun were the key factors that built on political change to bring about the emergence and institutional transformation of the FPM on the one hand, and to mobilize resources for the persistence of the movement on the other. FPM activists played a crucial role in dealing with the opportunities and resources at their disposal to bring the movement to life by launching rounds of activism and continuing to express their political thoughts, while also having to face the attempts of the political elite to weaken their movement. They also had to deal with the challenges imposed by the sectarian politics of Lebanon, which affected the transformation of the FPM into a political party in the post-2005 period by drawing it away from its secular political discourse toward the adoption of more overt sectarian strategies and discourse. Despite the importance of political change in bringing about the emergence and institutional transformation of the movement (an essential aspect of this analysis, no doubt), it is the role of agency—that is, FPM activists and their leader—which illuminates many aspects of the study's three lines of inquiry: emergence, persistence and institutional transformation.

The emergence of the FPM could not have occurred without the effective role of FPM activists and Aoun in seizing the right opportunities for the rise of their movement. FPM activists first saw in the rise of Aoun to the office of Lebanese premier an opportunity to wash away their grievances, chiefly because Aoun was the antithesis to the wartime chaos they had suffered. These activists continued seizing numerous opportunities in post-war Lebanon, which helped their movement emerge within universities, professional syndicates, towns and villages, before making a more visible appearance nationally. On the other hand, Aoun also played an essential role in the emergence of the FPM by framing messages and ideas that, in turn, helped to identify prevalent political issues, propose solutions and motivate individuals to action, thus having a positive bearing on the emergence of the movement. Therefore, by examining why FPM activists and Aoun acted the way they did and exercised their agency when given political opportunities, we understand why the crucial role of FPM activists and Aoun helped lead to the FPM's emergence when it happened.

The FPM's persistence also depended on the active role FPM activists played in mobilizing resources and channeling them to organize collective activity on the one hand, and on the way they structured the FPM and devised tactics to overcome attempts to weaken their movement on the other. The resources at the disposal of FPM activists may not have been substantial, but their dedication to their movement helped them structure it in a way that enabled them to persist without the need for communication (particularly in small, loosely connected and decentralized activist units). However, whether mobilizing resources, structuring the movement or employing tactics to encourage activism, the central feature of the FPM was its dedicated activists, who made sure it remained active throughout the period 1990–2005 as a social movement. As already discussed in the explanation of the FPM's emergence, the role of Aoun in framing FPM messages also ensured its persistence, chiefly by keeping activists in line with the movement's principles and goals, in addition to calling on them to adopt corrective action by persisting in their activism. Therefore, an analysis of the FPM's persistence should provide an adequate account of the role of FPM activists and Aoun in contributing to the mobilization process of the movement, because merely concentrating on the resources involved in the organization of FPM activity cannot properly convey how the movement organized its activity and overcame the challenges it faced.

The availability of certain political opportunities helped to provide a conducive environment for the FPM to participate in parliamentary elections and operate formally in the political context of Lebanon. However, although these opportunities provided an important political setting for the operation of the FPM following the Syrian withdrawal from Lebanon in 2005, they were not directly responsible for the transformation of the movement into a political party. It was the decisive agency of Aoun that played the determining role in transforming the FPM to a political party in 2005. Therefore, while political change provides conducive conditions for several aspects of movement activity, it is only by examining the conscious decisions of agency or leadership that we understand why individuals chose to act the way they did, given their circumstances.

However, because of the complexities of Lebanese politics, which is guided by an institutionally fragmented state with political elites with diverging views and sectarian politics manifested in high levels of corruption, political opportunities alone do not determine when the FPM engages in activism, especially in the post-2005 period. Perhaps in the period 1990–2005, when the FPM was partially excluded from formal participation in the Lebanese political system—that is, excluded from participation in parliamentary elections, while emerging actively within professional syndicates and on university campuses—political opportunities helped show when the FPM would emerge. However, with the FPM's formal participation in the 2005 parliamentary elections and its subsequent participation in the Council of Ministers, other factors, such as sectarian competition among the contending political parties in Lebanon, contribute to an understanding of movement politics and, thus, when those movements or political parties participated in activism.

In fact, FPM activism was often carried out throughout the period 1990–2005 to highlight the existence of a political movement that voiced its objection to the dominant sectarian political system in Lebanon, in addition to its unwavering objection to the presence of Syrian troops on Lebanese turf. It was thus directed at the political elite, many of whom were represented in Parliament, the Council of Ministers and as heads of influential political parties or movements. However, upon the return of Aoun to Lebanon in 2005 and the participation of the FPM in conventional politics, the movement found itself having to operate within the Lebanese sectarian political context. In other words, for a movement whose rank-and-file activists and leadership comprised predominantly middle-class Christians, this reality led it to compete naturally for the support of the Christian community and, as a consequence, adopt a discourse that expresses the concerns of the Christian community of Lebanon in terms of bettering their gains within the political system, while simultaneously struggling to hold on to its reputation as a movement that promoted secular ideas in the period 1990–2005. Therefore, the Lebanese political context is not a springboard for political opportunities that determines the ebb and flow of FPM activism, but rather a fluid environment in which opportunities, sectarian politics, electoral calculations and the need to maintain effective mobilization of supporters may lead movements to consider activism as a course of action.

Moreover, this analysis draws on aspects of political process theory to explain empirical questions on the emergence, persistence and institutional transformation of the FPM by referring to the theoretical concepts of political opportunity, mobilization and framing, without excluding the role of other explanatory factors, such as the agency of activists and the impact of Lebanese sectarian politics on various dimensions of the movement. As this book will reveal, agency plays a crucial role in all the stages of the FPM, thereby emphasizing the need to analyze the interaction between agency and structure together and not separately, or without dissociating one from the other. Moreover, structure, or the political context, involves more than a series of political opportunities that lead to the ebb and flow of movement activism. As evidenced by the case of Lebanon, the political context includes sectarianism as a characteristic feature that influences the course of most political phenomena, including movement activism.

Findings

This book presents important findings that contribute to a better understanding of the FPM. These reveal the role of leadership, social class, sectarian politics and ideas in the various stages of the movement.

By examining the political opportunities that FPM activists seized for their movement's emergence, this research finds that the FPM was able to emerge initially by seizing opportunities in civil society, such as elections on university campuses and in syndicates, before participating in the municipal elections of 1998. Because the sectarian strategies of Lebanon's political elite had contributed to the partial exclusion of the FPM from Lebanese politics—that is, from enjoying a presence in Parliament and the Council of Ministers, as will be demonstrated in the following chapters—activists sought other avenues for their movement's emergence. These findings are of empirical significance to scholars of Lebanese politics because, since the FPM did not enjoy a presence in conventional politics in the period 1990–2005, this is the first study that empirically tracks the developments that helped the movement emerge.

Furthermore, another crucial finding that this book uncovers is the full role of FPM activists in bringing the movement to life and ensuring its persistence throughout the period 1990–2005. This contribution is significant chiefly because the way in which these activists operated during Aoun's years in exile was largely unknown by the general public, and by many journalists too. In fact, during this author's search for pieces in the archives of the Lebanese daily newspaper *Annahar*, no article was found that describes in any detail the way these activists operated. Whether this information had been purposefully obscured by FPM activists to ensure the safety of their activism or not, the current examination of the FPM contributes to the literature of the movement by grounding it in an understanding of the role of activists, Aoun and political conditions in Lebanon throughout the movement's trajectory.

The research finds that the role played by agency in the FPM helped the movement express an ideational character, maintain its reputation as peaceful by adopting non-violent means of collective activity, and organize for collective activity despite many challenges. It uncovers how the FPM relied on the formation of small, loosely connected and decentralized activist units for the organization of activism to overcome the challenges it confronted in post-war Lebanon. Moreover, the analysis of the internal and external structures of the FPM helps to show how the movement was able to gather resources and channel them to ensure its persistence within Lebanon by maintaining a relationship with groups abroad for lobbying purposes.

This examination of the FPM also makes important contributions to the repertoire of Middle Eastern social movements generally, by highlighting the existence of a political movement whose members were mainly middle-class Christians, but whose political outlook was founded on secular ideas. In examining the movement through this lens, the results generated two outcomes. First, during the period 1990–2005 in which the

FPM was partially excluded from the institutions of state—that is, the Parliament and the Council of Ministers—it seized certain political opportunities and spaces to launch its peaceful activism against the presence of Syrian troops on Lebanese soil and the sectarian politics of the Lebanese political elite. As a result, the FPM was able to demonstrate its secular orientation by highlighting ideas that appealed to activists from both the Christian and Muslim communities of Lebanon, in spite of its membership base comprising predominantly Christians.

Secondly, when Syrian troops withdrew from Lebanon in 2005 and the FPM was able to be represented in Parliament and the Council of Ministers, the movement became more influenced by the country's sectarian politics and, as a consequence, found itself voicing a platform that aimed to achieve the demands of Lebanese Christians. Since the electoral constituencies the FPM represented were mainly Christian, the movement not only sought to fulfill its promises to Lebanese Christians, but also found itself in fierce competition with other Christian parties, such as the Lebanese Forces and the Kataeb, which, in turn, obliged the FPM to compete with these sectarian parties. This kind of sectarian competition made it adopt a more sectarian discourse and thus shift away from its previous ideas of secularism to the adoption of a bold Christian viewpoint.

Since the FPM yielded to some sectarian strategies and discourse in the post-2005 period, this study finds that the political system of Lebanon was able to reproduce sectarian modes of political subjectification and mobilization, in the words of Salloukh et al. (2015), even within the FPM, which had been established on non-sectarian ideas. However, it also finds that the FPM's predominantly Christian support base in the period 1990–2005 did not inform the movement's strategies or discourse, particularly because the FPM did not participate in conventional politics. However, with its participation in parliamentary elections and the Council of Ministers after 2005, the FPM was obliged to serve its electoral constituencies of mainly Christian voters, which included thousands of sympathizers beyond its committed activist base, who demanded social services and infrastructure projects. Due to this reality and the fierce competition the FPM faced from other Christian parties, it adopted sectarian strategies and discourse in servicing its Christian voter base. Therefore, this book shows that it is the actual participation in conventional politics that led the FPM to adopt features of sectarian politics, and not simply the composition of its support base.

As will be revealed throughout this book, this contribution to the field of Lebanese political movement literature fills an existing gap that is due to an absence of a complete analysis of the trajectory of the FPM. This contribution presents the first such work on the emergence, persistence and institutional transformation of the FPM. By filling this gap, it is hoped that these contributions will open a vent that drives further research into other aspects of the FPM and other Middle Eastern movements, which merit scrutiny in an attempt to expand the social movement repertoire and understand why and how people protest.

Book Chapters

This book deals with the topics of activism, change and sectarianism within the FPM while fleshing out the narrative of the emergence, persistence and institutional transformation of the movement. The work is divided into five chapters in chronological order, while attempting to maintain the analytical coherence of the questions researched.

Chapter 2, "The Rise of Aoun and His Movement (1988–1990)," discusses the early signs of support for Michel Aoun. It explains how personal motivations and wartime grievances experienced by the Lebanese during the Lebanese Civil War of 1975–1990 contributed to the rise of a supportive pro-Aoun movement in the period 1998–1990. It reveals why Aoun's use of simple language in speeches and his position as army commander won him the support of a segment of the Lebanese population who were predominantly Christian, but not exclusively so. It also shows how the rising pro-Aoun movement expressed secular nationalistic ideas, which sharply contrasted with the sectarian discourse of the militias prevailing during the Lebanese Civil War.

Chapter 3, "The Free Patriotic Movement's Emergence in the Complex Political Economy of Post-war Lebanon," explains why the FPM emerged in the period 1990–2005 in Lebanon following the expatriation of Aoun to France. It speaks of the movement's socioeconomic, demographic and sectarian makeup, which, in turn, explains why the middle class played an influential role in the ranks of the FPM. It shows how FPM activists blended their movement goals of freedom, sovereignty and independence with syndicate and union work throughout the period 1990–2005. This reality helps explain why the FPM emerged in civil society during the first half of the 1990s despite an official political ban on the movement, before seizing other opportunities to rise on a national scale in the latter half of the decade. Chapter 3 also sheds light on the assistive role that FPM groups in the diaspora played in leading to the rise of their movement in Lebanon.

Chapter 4, "Free Patriotic Movement Mobilization Keeps the Flame Burning (1991–2005)," deals with the same chronological time frame as Chapter 3, but tackles issues pertaining to the mobilization of FPM protests in Lebanon. It explains how FPM activists structured their activism according to small, loosely connected and decentralized cells, while maintaining only a political affiliation with the central FPM command in Lebanon and with FPM groups abroad for the distribution of news in the media. It also discusses several tactics that FPM activists adopted to incentivize their members to invest time and effort in activism. Here, too, the role of Aoun's ideas and the means of channeling those ideas in various forms of media helped keep movement activism burning, even though large-scale gatherings were not always a feasible course of action.

Chapter 5, "Risks of Party Transition and Sectarian Politics (2005–2015)," discusses the political developments that made the withdrawal of Syrian troops from Lebanon possible in 2005. It then attributes the institutional transformation of the FPM to a conscious decision taken by Aoun. However, it blames the FPM's adoption of some sectarian strategies on fierce electoral competition with other political parties in predominantly Christian electoral constituencies; here the sectarian makeup of FPM membership, discussed in Chapter 3, starts to reflect on its discourse and strategies in national politics. Chapter 5 also describes in some detail the issues faced within the FPM when transitioning from a social movement to a political party.

Chapter 6, "The General Turned President, Son-in-Law Groomed as Leader and the Dream Lost in Translation," concludes with an analysis of the political conditions prevailing in Lebanon that obliged the FPM and its leadership to defend their predominantly Christian base of support. It analyzes how the political conditions in Lebanon and the Middle Eastern region influence national politics, including the FPM's behavior. While it does fault the FPM leadership for some of the strategies adopted, it places a heavier weight on political factors in leading the FPM to adopt a sectarian discourse in the post-2005 era. Therefore, this chapter, much like its predecessors, analyzes the important role activists play in the FPM and national politics, while accounting for the role of external political factors in conditioning FPM behavior.

References

Abdelrahman, M. 2012. "A Hierarchy of Struggles? The 'Economic' and the 'Political in Egypt's Revolution." *Review of African Political Economy* 39 (134): 614–628.

Beinin, J. 2015. *Workers and Thieves: Labor Movements and Popular Uprisings in Tunisia and Egypt*. Palo Alto: Stanford University Press.

Beinin, J., and F. Vairel. 2011. "Intro." In *Social Movements, Mobilization, and Contestation in the Middle East and North Africa*, edited by J. Beinin and F. Vairel. Palo Alto: Stanford University Press.

Beinin, J., and Z. Lockman. 1998. *Workers on the Nile: Nationalism, Communism, Islam, and the Egyptian Working Class, 1882–1954*. Cairo: American University in Cairo Press.

Cammet, M. 2014. *Compassionate Communalism: Welfare and Sectarianism in Lebanon*. Ithaca: Cornell University Press.

Durac, V. 2015. "Social Movements, Protest Movements and Cross-Ideological Coalitions—The Arab Uprisings Re-appraised." *Democratization* 22 (2): 239–258.

El-Husseini, R. 2012. *Pax Syriana Elite Politics in Post-war Lebanon*. New York: Syracuse University Press.

El-Khazen, F. 2000. *The Breakdown of the State in Lebanon, 1967–1976*. London: I.B. Tauris.

———. 2003. "The Postwar Political Process: Authoritarianism by Diffusion." In *Lebanon in Limbo: Postwar Society and State in an Uncertain Regional Environment*, edited by T. Hanf and N. Salam, Chap. 3. Baden-Baden: Nomos.

Hafez, M. M. 2003. *Why Muslims Rebel: Repression and Resistance in the Islamic World*. Boulder: Lynne Rienner.

Helou, J. P. 2015. "Policy Overcomes Confessional Hurdles: A Policy Strategy Tackles Challenges in the Segmented Society and State of Lebanon." *Athens Journal of Mediterranean Studies* 1 (4): 325–340.

Hottinger, A. 1961. "Zu'ama'and Parties in the Lebanese Crisis of 1958." *Middle East Journal* 15 (2): 127–140.

Hudson, M. C. 1968. *The Precarious Republic: Political Modernization in Lebanon*. New York: Random House.

Khalaf, S. 1968. "Primordial Ties and Politics in Lebanon." *Middle Eastern Studies* 4 (3): 243–269.

———. 2003. "On Roots and Roots: The Reassertion of Primordial Loyalties." In *Lebanon in Limbo: Postwar Society and State in an Uncertain Regional Environment*, edited by T. Hanf and N. Salam, Chap. 6. Baden-Baden: Nomos.

Leenders, R. 2012. *Spoils of Truce: Corruption and State-Building in Postwar Lebanon*. Ithaca: Cornell University Press.

Lynch, M. 2014. "Media, Old and New." In *The Arab Uprisings Explained: New Contentious Politics in the Middle East*, edited by M. Lynch, Chap. 5. New York: Columbia University Press.

———. 2016. *The New Arab Wars: Uprisings and Anarchy in the Middle East.* New York: PublicAffairs.

Picard, E. 1996. *Lebanon: A Shattered Country.* New York: Holmes & Meier.

Randal, J. 2012. *The Tragedy of Lebanon: Christian Warlords, Israeli Adventurers, and American Bunglers.* Washington, DC: Just World Books.

Salibi, K. 1976. *Crossroads to Civil War: Lebanon 1958–1976.* New York: Caravan Books.

Salloukh, B. F., R. Barakat, J. S. Al-Habbal, L. W. Khattab, S. Mikaelian, and A. Nerguizian. 2015. *The Politics of Sectarianism in Postwar Lebanon.* London: Pluto Press.

Wickham, C. R. 2015. *The Muslim Brotherhood: Evolution of an Islamist Movement.* Princeton: Princeton University Press.

CHAPTER 2

The Rise of Aoun and His Movement (1988–1990)

This chapter seeks to discuss in some detail the first signs of mass support for Michel Aoun in Lebanon. It aims to show why and how individuals rushed to support Aoun and the political ideas he voiced amid the fighting engulfing war-torn Lebanon in the period 1988–1990. It reveals the makeup of the movement and those members who joined without understanding that their participation in these supportive protests were contributing to the incubation of the Free Patriotic Movement (FPM) as a visible political actor that would come to oppose government policies in post-war Lebanon.

The chapter argues that militia misdeeds and political conditions in wartime Lebanon contributed to Aoun's rising popularity. Lebanese Christians and some Muslims too rushed to support the political stances of the army commander, since the Lebanese army, as one of the few remaining national repositories of legitimacy and sovereignty in wartime Lebanon, continued to command respect from a considerable cross-sectarian segment of the country's society.

Thus, many activists interviewed in this book and others speak of grievances stemming from their negative experiences with militia practices as the driver for participation in the supportive pro-Aoun movement of the period 1988–1990. These individuals expressing support for Aoun during this time recognized that his ideas, slogans and thoughts touched on the source of their grievances, proposed solutions to their misfortunes and encouraged supporters to adopt remedial action. Both supporters

J. P. Helou, *Activism, Change and Sectarianism in the Free Patriotic Movement in Lebanon*, Reform and Transition in the Mediterranean,
https://doi.org/10.1007/978-3-030-25704-0_2

of Aoun who were disillusioned by the militias and those who merely emerged from their state of passivity supported the new political actor embodied in Michel Aoun, which led to the rise of a movement that displayed collective activity to achieve a better political alternative than the pre-existing sectarian practices of the Lebanese political elite and the prevailing chaos of wartime Lebanon.

This chapter is sub-divided into four. The first part discusses in some detail the political conditions that brought Aoun to power, the political and military moves he adopted and the formation of a supportive pro-Aoun movement in the period 1988–1990 (see Laurent 1991; Hanf 1993; P. Salem 1996; E. Salem 2003; Harris 1997). The remainder of the chapter analyzes how Lebanese individuals experienced grievances and motivations that made them more than willing to embrace political change, which they perceived as possible with the rise of Aoun on the political scene. The second part analyzes the grievances and personal motivations of some activists that incentivized their participation in this pro-Aoun movement during the period 1988–1990. The third part discusses in some detail the genuine appetite of some Lebanese individuals for political change, which provided them with the motivation to seek collective action by joining the ranks of Aoun's movement. The final part discusses how Aoun was able to invite Lebanese individuals to rally in support of his political proposals by examining the significance of the army commander's background and the way he advanced ideas.

Part I: The Army Commander Shines as Premier

The starting point will be the appearance of Michel Aoun in Lebanese politics, his political moves and the incubation of a mass movement in support of his policies. Although the rise of a mass movement in support of Aoun during the period 1988–1990 was not directly linked to the dynamics of the FPM in post-war Lebanese politics, it nevertheless helped to nurture a popular base of support for the erstwhile army general, which subsequently contributed to the rise of the FPM in post-war Lebanon.

There is clear evidence to show that activism, change and sectarianism had been a defining feature of the movement that emerged in support of Aoun even in its early stages from 1988 to 1990. Lebanese individuals whose sectarian affiliation had been predominantly Christian, but not exclusively so, knew they were supporting a Maronite army general on the basis of his secular and nationalistic ideas and discourse. However, the pervasive role of the religious institutions, political elite and institutionally sectarian political system (with the need to strike a sectarian balance in the apportionment of government positions) rendered sectarianism a challenge for the movement, even though it had very little bearing on its early formative stages. Therefore, the emerging movement had to deal with sectarianism both as a contextual challenge (state institutions, the political elite and elite practices) and as a sociological challenge of mobilizing Lebanese individuals, themselves a by-product of sectarian modes of subjectification, on the basis of non-sectarian ideas (see Salloukh et al. 2015).

Aoun's political career began with a vacancy in the Lebanese presidency. The outgoing president Amine Gemayel dismissed the caretaker cabinet of Sunni premier Salim El-Hoss and assigned Maronite General Michel Aoun to form a cabinet on September 22, 1988 (Hanf 1993, pp. 570–572). Shortly after Aoun formed his military cabinet, the Muslim ministers resigned in the face of pressure from their sectarian communities, who regarded Aoun as a Christian leader. However, this did not lead to the resignation of those Muslim army officers in service who were still supporting Aoun, nor did it dissuade Muslim activists from future participation in rallies in front of the Baabda Palace in support of Aoun, according to Pierre Raffoul (interview October 2, 2014). But with El-Hoss refusing to resign, Aoun's cabinet ruled over the Christian enclave of East Beirut, while El-Hoss maintained his authority in the predominantly Sunni West Beirut, portraying this division in sectarian terms (Hanf 1993, pp. 570–572).

Yet, Aoun's attacks against multiple sectarian militias that compromised state sovereignty won him a reputation as a non-sectarian leader. On February 10, 1989, Aoun battled the Christian-based militia of the Lebanese Forces (LF) and regained Dock Five in Beirut Harbor, one of the most important sources of state revenue (Hanf 1993, p. 572). His ensuing attempt to regain the Druze-based Progressive Socialist Party and Shia-based Amal ports of Khalde, Jiyeh and Ouzai lured him into the War of Liberation with Syria on March 14, 1989, which lasted for six months (Hanf 1993, p. 572). Financially cornered by the Hoss government and outraged at the LF for consenting to the Taif Accords of October 1989 (the Saudi-brokered peace agreement to end the Lebanese Civil War), Aoun fought a war with the LF in 1990 to extend state authority over the Christian enclave of Lebanon (ibid., p. 598).

Perhaps the obstinate stance Aoun had taken against militias in wartime Lebanon was the main reason for his popularity among a cross-sectarian segment of the Lebanese people, devastated by war and militia rule. Even when the Maronite church and 23 Christian deputies opposed Aoun by preferring a political solution to the War of Liberation, the youth of the enclave demonstrated against the church and traditional leaders, which was a novelty in Lebanon, and opted to support Aoun (Hanf 1993, p. 577).

With Aoun's promises to liberate the country and cleanse the state of corruption, he attracted a predominantly Christian population eager for order, stability and dignity, and one that was worn out by the government of the Christian LF militia (Laurent 1991). The LF militia not only shifted course from its initial cause of resisting the Palestinians and Syrians, but also developed into a state within a state, often resorting to the use of force and repression (ibid.). The levying of taxes and growing wealth of certain LF commanders increased the unpopularity of the militia. Therefore, a main contributing factor to the formation of a supportive pro-Aoun movement during the period 1988–1990 was the immense disappointment of individuals who joined his movement with the prevailing militia order.

Another issue contributing to Aoun's popularity among a segment of the Lebanese population was his firm stance against the presence of foreign troops on Lebanese soil. His rejection of the Taif Accords was due to its failure to set a clear timetable for the withdrawal of Syrian troops from Lebanon (Hanf 1993, p. 596).

Yet, Aoun's popularity also stemmed from his reputation for frankness and approachability, empathy with ordinary people and a captivating oratorical style (Harris 1997). Aoun's upbringing in the confessionally mixed town of Haret Hreik rendered him more tolerant of others' beliefs, while allowing him to develop a secular political orientation (Raffoul 1994). His pursuit of knowledge (embodied in his eagerness for books and enrollment in military courses), interest in political affairs and adherence to a strict moral code composed of integrity and transparency won him a distinctive reputation dating from his early days as a military officer (ibid.). These traits made Aoun's cohorts and friends as well as the general public admire the officer.

With his distinct reputation as a backdrop, Aoun's use of unconventional and unadorned colloquialisms during the 1989 War of Liberation attracted young people who were desperate for a hero (Salem 2003,

p. 163). In a captivating oratorical style, Aoun inspired confidence in his supporters with statements such as "You are the liberation generation, you are the nation and the national will… Tell the deputies you didn't elect them, so they've got no right to speak for you… Tell the Church the reason you're here is to speak the truth" (in Hanf 1993, p. 577; Salem 2003, p. 163). The youth heeded Aoun's messages and calls to action. In April 1989, for example, young people gathered in front of the American Embassy to protest the silence of democratic states toward Syrian-perpetrated atrocities in Lebanon.

Aoun dissolved Parliament on November 4, 1989, when it had convened to elect the first post-Taif President, Rene Mouawad (Hanf 1993, pp. 596–597). Following Mouawad's assassination on November 22, 1989, Parliament reconvened and elected Elias Hrawi, who challenged Aoun with an ultimatum before threatening to usurp power by force (ibid.). Hrawi's threat to force Aoun's abdication led thousands of Lebanese individuals to the Baabda Palace in support of Aoun. The size of the movement made the Maronite patriarch, the USA, the USSR, France and the Vatican warn Hrawi of the potentially enormous human losses that would result from an attack (Hanf 1993, pp. 596–597). Consequently, Hrawi recoiled on December 14, 1989, claiming he had never threatened Aoun with an ultimatum (ibid.).

Therefore, every time certain political developments occurred, supporters expressed their show of political support for Aoun at the Baabda Palace, which became a wide pro-Aoun movement with strong components of a personality cult (Hanf 1993, p. 597). Aoun's nationalistic campaigns influenced the gathering youth (35% of whom were under 18 and another 40% under 39) by influencing them to make secular political decisions, a shift from the sectarian options of Lebanon's political order. A survey of the Baabda demonstrators in early 1990 revealed that 96% supported a united Lebanon, 95% favored direct presidential elections, 95% opposed the Taif decisions, and 85% supported a new electoral law and disfavored existing parties (ibid.).

This emerging Aounist movement aimed to achieve an independent Lebanon free from foreign forces, end the war, create a new leadership not reliant on the corrupt machinations of the old order, and construct a positive secular image of Lebanon (Salem 2003, p. 165). It was unabashedly national and cultural in scope, spawning dozens of popular songs by famous singers like Majida El Roumi and Laure Abs. The senior Lebanese composer Zaki Nassif created music and lyrics for the movement (ibid., pp. 165–166). As a result, some nationalistic musical compositions, for example "Raji‘ yit ‘ammar Lubnan" (Lebanon will be rebuilt), became an anthem (ibid.). Musical works such as "Aounak Raji‘ min Allah," meaning "your Aoun comes from God" (Aoun meaning "help"), glorified Aoun.

The performance of poetry recitals and competitions, which became a common phenomenon at the Baabda protests, helped reassert this movement's political stances. The poet Father Simon Assaf, for example, wrote poetry that pitted Aoun against the Lebanese parliamentarians (Salem 2003, p. 166). Saiid Aql, a famous Lebanese poet, appeared regularly by Aoun's side at the Baabda festivals, promoting the idea of a free, strong and proud Lebanon. This political atmosphere also culminated in the publishing and distribution of *Al-Sahwa Al-Lubnaniya* (the awakening), a pro-FPM magazine (ibid.). The movement also generated its own distinct car horn signal, honking the rhythm on roads and in tunnels as a political show of support. In these ways, the ideational and cultural components of the FPM became pervasive phenomena that permeated music, poetry, the media, and the hearts and minds of its supporters.

Although the protests began as a spontaneous move to the Baabda Palace, Raffoul (1994), a member of the Central Bureau of National Coordination (CBNC), speaks of preparations in terms of the availability of transportation, logistics (distribution of food and water to sustain the growing crowds) and security provided by the Lebanese army to ensure the safety of the protesting crowds. Raffoul's description of this organization that was established to sustain the Baabda protests helps explain how some of Aoun's supporters gained organizational skills. However, many of those who engaged in FPM activism in post-war Lebanon had not been members of the CBNC, although they learned valuable lessons from this brief experiment.

Michel Aoun played an integral role in creating a powerful support base. Unlike supporters of other movements in wartime Lebanon, his support base was interested in abolishing sectarian practices, doing away with corrupt and traditional forms of politics, and aiming for a more representative system than the one already in place. Yet, he could not be credited for every aspect of the rise of his supportive movement, as this popular reaction must have been an expression of deep-seated grievances that were aired at the time of his assumption to the premiership.

The ensuing sections will discuss in some detail those wartime grievances and personal motivations that helped incubate this pro-Aoun movement. The next part will analyze why Lebanese individuals, who had been supporters of militias or remained passive actors throughout the Lebanese Civil War of 1975–1990, decided to break away from their previous state and join the ranks of the pro-Aoun movement.

Part II: From Despair to Activism

This section will demonstrate that certain grievances experienced by a segment of the Lebanese people led them to join the ranks of Aoun's supportive movement, which promised to rid them of the sources of their grievances: most notably, militia rule, corruption and the convoluted practices of the traditional political elite of Lebanon. These are mobilizing grievances that highlight people's disapproval of a salient issue and thus constitute a reason for brewing discontent. Such mobilizing grievances, defined as troublesome matters or conditions and the feelings associated with them, for example dissatisfaction, fear, indignation, resentment and moral shock, provide the primary motivational impetus for the emergence of social movement activity (Snow and Soule 2010, p. 23). Therefore, it can be observed that such mobilizing grievances, though experienced on a personal level, led people to act collectively by incentivizing them to join the ranks of Aoun's supportive movement. This explanation also contrasts sharply with the view advanced by some scholars, who regard grievances as relatively constant and question their role in leading to the emergence of insurgent organizations (Jenkins and Parrow 1977).

The experiences of Lebanese citizens of day-to-day affairs and multiple warring factions during the Civil War caused them to develop a shared set of grievances that distanced them from their surroundings and rendered them more conscious of the need for corrective collective action. These mobilizing grievances included disdain, disgust, distrust, fear and humiliation, inter alia, as experienced by some Lebanese people through their exchanges with various warring militias and Syrian troops garrisoned on Lebanese soil. Therefore, these particular mobilizing grievances drew people into the ranks of the Aoun movement, especially when the movement challenged the militias and Syrian troops by calling for the freedom of Lebanon and the restoration of state authority.

The failure of militias to protect and meet the expectations of their constituencies resulted in the transformation of their role, an issue that generated grievances among the Lebanese people. Because these warring militias promised to protect the confessional communities to which they belonged, their gross misdeeds during the Civil War led to popular disillusionment and a moral shock that resulted in resentment. These feelings became sufficient mobilizing grievances and cause for the subsequent consideration of political alternatives, which later translated into participation in the ranks of the FPM. Ziad Assouad, an FPM activist, pronounced a diatribe against the LF militia for failing to protect and unite its Christian constituency, which illustrates this point. He stated: "We believed these parties had big slogans but couldn't translate them… 11 out of 13 wars of these groups actually harmed Christians themselves… The only wars they launched against the Syrians were the battle of the North, the battle of Achrafieh, and the battle of Zahley" (interview October 10, 2014). This is a tangible example of how the transformation of the role of militias—namely, the LF—from protector to oppressor of their communities generated mobilizing grievances that not only contributed to fading support for the LF, but also fostered dissatisfaction among Christians, who became more inclined to join Aoun's movement.

Lebanese individuals may have viewed militias as protecting them from their sectarian counterparts at the beginning of the Lebanese Civil War in 1975, but quickly formed adverse opinions of those militias due to their deleterious practices that incited feelings of disgust, repulsion and fear. The militias did not stop short of harassing, threatening and brutally torturing Lebanese individuals who expressed a political opinion that diverged from theirs. Speaking about the LF, the dominant militia in the Christian enclave during wartime, Michel Elefteriades, an FPM activist, declared: "I used to see them getting human ears in boxes… I started explaining to other school kids about Karl Marx and the communist ideas; until one kid took a copy of a tract I had distributed about communism and showed it to his parents… His father was in the LF. The LF then took me from school… They beat me for three days and wanted to know who I was working for. That is when I began developing a keen interest in politics" (interview September 8, 2014).

As the experience of Michel Elefteriades suggests, the LF militia epitomized this characterization of intolerance, and thus generated grievances, such as hatred, among those who dared to oppose them. This is why the appearance of Aoun, who swore to rid the people of the prevailing militia order of wartime Lebanon, encouraged individuals to join the ranks of what became the FPM. If Aoun and his movement had appeared on the Lebanese political scene with proposals that did not tackle the source of people's grievances, it is highly doubtful that Michel Elefteriades and so many others would have joined the ranks of the movement.

During the Lebanese Civil War, even those Lebanese citizens who were not politically expressive of their opinions—that is, bystanders—experienced a fair share of mobilizing grievances, chiefly because the militias threatened the people's means of sustenance. Rabih Tarraf, an FPM activist, pointedly commented on the misdeeds of the militias by stating: "they slowly began fixing their own checkpoints, levying taxes, and collecting money; they transformed into an abnormal situation. People became more disgusted with them. People would be queuing for a loaf of bread when someone, due to the fact that he may be wearing the National Liberal Party, Lebanese Forces, or Kataeb outfit, would brush people aside and collect all the bread available at the bakery and leave" (interview September 11, 2014). Findings based on interviews with FPM activists suggest that many activists had not been politically active prior to the war. However, the main issue that aggrieved these Lebanese individuals was the extent to which the militia order affected their livelihoods. As a consequence, many aggrieved Lebanese people rushed to join the ranks of Aoun's movement in the period 1988–1990, since it promised to rid them of the source of their grievances.

The recurrence of similar grievance-generating experiences with several activists indicates the extent to which FPM activists perceived and suffered the same issues. In itself, the LF's forceful collection of the entire production of bread at a bakery could have been simply another of that militia's lawless deeds. However, the fact that activists recounted the story as a shocking experience or cause for grievance grants this seemingly inconsequential act extreme significance to the creation of the FPM, especially when considering that its subsequent emergence came in support of state authority and against the chaotic rule of militias. Whether these mobilizing grievances were experienced as a result of physical torture, fear, unpleasant exchanges or seemingly inconsequential events that had an impact on people's lives, it is undoubtedly their existence that rendered some Lebanese citizens more willing to embrace alternatives to the militia order, thus joining the ranks of Aoun's movement, which called for the restoration of state authority.

Even before FPM activists began questioning the legitimacy of the Syrian military presence in Lebanon in the 1990s, Lebanese individuals experienced grievances that emanated from their exchanges with Syrian troops during the Lebanese Civil War and in post-war Lebanon, which often scarred them on a personal level. A case in point was the experience of Walid Achkar, an FPM activist, with the Syrian troops based in North

Lebanon. He declared: "What used to provoke me was the way the Syrians treated us, as Lebanese, at the checkpoints. If you had stuff in your car, they wanted to know what you carried and imposed a sort of tax on you. If I was carrying stuff with me to my house in Aakar, for example, you had to offer him cigarette packets, a kilogram of tomatoes or cucumbers, or silly stuff. The way they treated us was humiliating; you used to feel the humiliation" (interview October 15, 2014). Therefore, due to the grievances that Lebanese individuals experienced as a result of such unpleasant exchanges with Syrian troops in Lebanon, many found themselves naturally gravitating toward Aoun's movement, particularly when its leadership expressed a solid political stance that opposed the presence of Syrian troops on Lebanese soil.

Indeed, the incessant reiteration of the word "humiliation" underscores the extent of the grievances that Walid Achkar experienced in his exchanges with Syrian troops in North Lebanon. These mobilizing grievances may be rooted in deeper cultural meanings that these activists, whether consciously or unconsciously, attach to certain occurrences. It may be quite unreasonable for individuals to feel aggrieved when paying taxes at a checkpoint during wartime by offering basic commodities, such as a loaf of bread or cucumbers, especially when one considers the cost perspective of exchanging a loaf of bread for one's physical security. However, Walid Achkar viewed the items as "silly" from an economic perspective and must have felt aggrieved due to the way he was treated by Syrian troops at checkpoints. In addition, the cultural significance individuals may attach to these items, for example bread, as a necessity for daily sustenance may grant the item's confiscation a meaning tantamount to the deprivation of life. In this scenario, the feelings associated with these mobilizing grievances become contingent upon those individuals' construction of the meanings they attach to their experiences.

The way FPM activists interpreted their experiences during the Lebanese Civil War highlighted a deeper connection between those interpretations, or constructed meanings, of certain experiences and the mobilizing grievances that resulted from them. This may also be illustrated in the words of Elie Hanna, an FPM activist, who stated: "We used to be annoyed when crossing Syrian checkpoints, stopping at them, waiting on the right for hours, and then seeing the Syrian soldier waving his leg for us to pass. We had this nationalistic feeling" (interview October 16, 2014). In spite of the nationalistic sentiments stirred up among activists by the presence of Syrian troops on Lebanese turf, the annoyance experienced by Hanna emanates from his interpretation of the Syrian soldier's leg-waving movement, which constitutes a serious insult in Lebanese culture. This cultural interpretation of issues can be confirmed as carrying tremendous weight in the grievance formation process that incubated the FPM, because many activists, including Elie Hanna and Walid Achkar, were merely teenagers during the Civil War. Even though activists may have shared a set of deeply felt grievances and acted collectively, they were probably able to relate more closely to personally experienced issues, as opposed to basing their political preferences strictly on national affairs, which required a close observation and monitoring of events during wartime Lebanon.

The geographic proximity of towns to more than one warring faction generated deeper, more heart-felt grievances among their inhabitants than those residing in areas where a single faction dominated. Although one may be tempted to believe that inhabitants of war-torn areas may be disinterested in participating in any political activity after suffering the taxing repercussions of war, in fact the experience of inhabitants who lived in towns along the demarcation line that separated the conflict zones of East Beirut from West Beirut, such as Hadath, Cheyeh and Ain El-Remmaneh, reveals that mobilizing grievances can make individuals more willing to adopt corrective collective activity (R. Kanj, interview September 19, 2014; R. Tarraf, interview September 11, 2014).

Interviews with FPM activists strongly suggest that the geographic proximity of towns to multiple warring factions provided individuals with an additional incentive to participate in prospective FPM collective activity. It is no coincidence that FPM activity in the aforementioned towns emerged quite forcefully because of the grievances that the population had suffered during the Civil War. This is not to say that the more abundant the grievances, the more likely movements are to spring up. However, the abundance of grievances helped make individuals aware of the high costs of remaining on the fringes and accepting the ongoing war. Moreover, this FPM case study also shows that the existence of grievances, albeit randomly distributed among a population, increases people's awareness of the difficult circumstances in which they are living, unlike the view of Klandermans et al. (2001), who argue that the effect of randomly distributed grievances is politically neutral.

At the outbreak of the Lebanese Civil War in 1975, a considerable portion of the pro-Aoun movement activists were too young to have formulated a solid opinion or comparison of life prior to the war, which debunks the utility of relative deprivation accounts in explaining dissatisfaction (see Davies 1962; Gurr 1970). Moreover, group relative deprivation accounts cannot adequately explain early shows of support for Aoun's movement (Runciman 1966; Martin 1986), since the grievances suffered by its members were not endemic to a single sectarian group in relation to another in Lebanon—that is, Christians (Maronites, Orthodox, Catholics, etc.) versus Muslims (Sunnis, Shia, Druze, etc.)—at least in the period 1998–1990. These grievances were unequivocally experienced by all sectarian groups, thereby weakening the ability of relative deprivation accounts to explain the dissatisfaction of those individuals who joined the FPM.

Therefore, mobilizing grievances best explain the grievance factors that helped to incubate the FPM by providing the initial impetus for the movement. The source of these mobilizing grievances was the misdeeds of the Syrian troops based in Lebanon and the various Lebanese wartime militias, whose immoral actions affected the livelihoods of Lebanese individuals and generated deep grievances. These grievances, the result of the interpretation of experiences and the meanings attached to those experiences, often filled individuals with feelings of hatred, repulsion, shock and disgust, which drew them away from the existing chaotic wartime order and rendered them more inclined to embrace change; namely, by joining the FPM.

As will later become clear, by identifying the mobilizing grievances of FPM activists and the sources of those grievances, this chapter clarifies precisely which ideas attracted FPM activists into the movement and exactly how those ideas were able to do so. However, the next part discusses the personal motivations of FPM activists, to explain why those motivations helped draw individuals into the pro-Aoun movement and thus contributed to its rise.

Part III: Motivations Vivify the Movement

Activists bore a set of personal motivations toward effecting social, political and economic change in war-torn Lebanon that drove them to join the ranks of Aoun's movement and thus contribute to its rise. Although social movement theory, particularly political process theory, places less emphasis on the personal motivations of activists for joining the ranks of a movement and, instead, focuses on their collective behavior, this research shows that the personal motivations of activists contributed to the FPM's emergence; these can be defined as those motivations or preferences unique to every individual activist that render them willing to pursue a certain course of action to achieve a desired outcome. In this respect, the FPM not only emerged as a reactionary movement due to the widespread grievances suffered by the Lebanese people, but also received in its ranks numerous individuals who had personal motivations for genuine political change.

These personal motivations involved an inclination to revolt against the pre-existing political establishment to advance freedom, sovereignty and independence, and to introduce reforms into the political system. Therefore, by zooming in on the personal motivations of activists, a clearer connection can be drawn between people's appetite for change in wartime Lebanon and the rise of Aoun's movement.

The family profile of activists underscores the indispensable role of education, intellectual circles and connections, usually a prerogative of the middle class, in influencing individuals to join the ranks of the FPM. Because it is generally accepted that young people can afford to spend time in collective activity of all sorts, the main issue in wartime Lebanon was why the youth by 1989 wanted to consider joining the ranks of the FPM, as opposed to the militias prevailing in the country. Although the Lebanese people were aggrieved by the misdeeds of these militias, individuals' relationships often played a role in their political orientations as well. Illustrating this point is Liwa Chakour, an FPM activist, who explained: "I was raised in a home with Saiid Aql, George Chakour and May Murr, which was a great literary and political group whose project was Lebanonization [expressing opinions and ideas that prioritized Lebanese affairs above all else]... Stemming from this point, one nurtures national feelings, the love of the land, and the love of institutions, especially the military institution that is the backbone for the construction of any nation and its protection" (interview September 29, 2014).

In the case of Liwa Chakour, the fact he was raised in a family that enjoyed connections with intellectual circles made him seriously consider participation in the ranks of a movement that fulfilled, at least in part, his political opinions. This intellectual circle expressed ideas that stressed the importance of the nation, the restoration of the state and most of all the preservation of state institutions, such as the Lebanese army. This is chiefly why Liwa Chakour found himself joining the ranks of the FPM, particularly because the movement expressed similar political views.

Family bonds also led activists to join the FPM, especially when those activists had close family members occupying positions inside state institutions. According to several FPM activists interviewed for this book, those with relatives and close friends among the ranks of the Lebanese army experienced a high level of personal motivation to join Aoun's movement. These associations proved useful in triggering participation in the ranks of the FPM, because it rendered those individuals who rushed to join the movement more aware of their personal stake in the matter. Roland ElKhoury, an FPM activist, stated: "My father was an auditor for several army institutions… When the War of Liberation occurred, most of my cousins entered the Ansar [Lebanese army unit composed of civilian volunteers to support the army headed by Aoun]. I was a child at the time so I was naturally taken by this atmosphere and the grand titles… When Michel Aoun assumed authority in 1988, we were naturally with him" (interview September 26, 2014).

The link highlighting the importance of family associations with the motivation to join the FPM is Roland ElKhoury's admission that his father, cousins and family's inclination toward the Lebanese army allowed him to be caught up by the atmosphere at the time. This underscored a clear socialization role played by the family in pointing the finger of blame at the militias for generating the chaos characteristic of wartime Lebanon, while helping to motivate family members to join the FPM movement, which upheld the aims of restoring state authority and liberating Lebanon from foreign occupation, combating corruption vested in the traditional political class of the country and promoting a secular political order as opposed to sectarianism.

Another personal motivation that led to the emergence of the FPM was activists' diverse ideological persuasions, which converged around a common national outlook. The diverse ideological persuasions of Lebanese individuals who joined the ranks of the FPM ranged from the political left to the right. In a Lebanon embroiled in civil war, this issue should have posed enormous challenges to the movement. Yet instead, it bred personal motivations among individuals that allowed for their convergence around the same national outlook. A remark by Michel Elefteriades is illustrative of this point: "I had an internationalist world view and sort of had communist inclinations back then… I had a communist vision and philosophical humanitarian view. I wanted the freedom of humans and stones [an Arabic expression implying freedom of thought and national territory], and these were presented by the General. The appearance of the General was a paradigm shift for me" (interview September 8, 2014).

The communist vision and philosophical humanitarian view that Michel Elefteriades initially subscribed to provided him with the self-motivation to engage in politics by joining the FPM. Due to this philosophical humanitarian view, he could not have preferred the militia order over the option of a strong and able state that would promote the interests of citizens and uphold human rights. His views motivated him to participate in the FPM because the movement centered on the freedom of individuals and the restoration of state institutions; this is mainly why he perceived the assumption of General Aoun to the premiership in Lebanon as constituting a "paradigm shift," or a marked turn away from chaos toward the restoration of state institutions.

On the other hand, individuals who stood at the opposite end of the ideological spectrum also enjoyed certain personal motivations that helped them join the FPM. Rock Chlela, an FPM activist and devout Christian, attributes part of his motivation to his Christian faith. He believed that "When St. Peter cut the ear off the person who came to Christ, he was told that he who takes with the sword will be taken by the sword. How could I be LF and defend Christians with the sword? He told him [meaning Christ told Peter] if my father wanted to defend me, he would have sent twelve brigades from the angels. So its symbolism was that instead of twelve brigades from the divine soldiers, he [Christ] got twelve apostles. So religiously, I had to be FPM; ethically, I had to be FPM; with the human rights charter I had to be FPM; and especially when Samir Jeajea had done all the atrocities he did" (interview October 29, 2014).

Rock sharply criticizes the brutal and violent methods of the LF militia and its leader Samir Jeajea and overtly declares his preference for the peaceful collective activity of the FPM. His Christian views not only led him to disapprove of the LF's tactics, but also provided him with the motivation to seek corrective political action by joining the FPM and engaging in its peaceful collective activity.

Whether individuals stood on the left or right of the political spectrum, the ideologies they subscribed to contained a set of common humanitarian views that motivated them to join the FPM. Since the FPM did not emphasize an ideological stance, it maintained a wide avenue for the absorption of people from all ideological persuasions, as long as they expressed their interest in solid state institutions versus militia rule, support for the cause of freedom, sovereignty and independence against foreign intervention in Lebanese affairs, and commitment to transparency and integrity to fight the corrupt machinations of the political system of Lebanon, often referred to as feudalism in a nuanced sense. Backing this argument was Michel Elefteriades, who stressed that "what makes the movement rich is that it has people from the extreme right to the extreme left… In 1989, anyone who enjoyed a good socio-cultural background was following the General" (interview September 8, 2014). Therefore, this wide margin of political goals allowed for individuals from various political persuasions and ideologies, whose political outlook found an opportunity for emergence with the FPM, to muster the self-motivation to join the movement in defense of these broad nationalistic goals.

Individuals who were genuinely motivated to reform political affairs in Lebanon and develop institutions that administered public affairs joined the FPM chiefly because they saw an opportunity to advance their reformist plans. In the case of Naaman Abi Antoun, an FPM activist, the possibility of advancing genuine political reform through the establishment of institutions to administer public affairs at local level triggered his participation in the movement (interview September 23, 2014). This indicates that he showed the motivation to introduce positive change to his war-torn society. Therefore, individuals were not only incentivized to join the FPM due to the grievances they had experienced, but also motivated by the conviction that making a positive contribution to their society was possible, despite being at war.

Elaborating on the personal motivations of activists helps to uncover why those motivations culminated in sufficient participation for the emergence of the FPM. Whether motivated by family members, ideological beliefs or a genuine interest in advancing political reforms, individuals rushed to join the ranks of the movement due to their altruistic disposition to make a positive contribution to their society. Yet, in order to better understand how individuals were attracted into the ranks of Aoun's movement in the period 1988–1990, this chapter now turns to the ideas advanced by Aoun himself.

Part IV: Aoun Quenches Thirst for Stability and Order

How did the perception of Aoun's appearance in Lebanese politics among a certain segment of Lebanese society (composed largely of Christians, but not exclusively so) lead to the formation of a membership base for his movement? The research reveals how Aoun's use of simple language in the form of slogans helped persuade and then attract those individuals aggrieved by wartime conditions into the ranks of his support movement, especially in the period 1988–1990.

Aoun's supporters regarded him as an army commander who could restore authority and confidence in state institutions, and thus they rallied in support of his proposals in 1989, holding mass demonstrations in front of the Baabda Palace. Aoun's assumption to the premiership in Lebanon helped constitute what could be regarded as the incubation phase of the FPM, because of what he represented in the eyes of his supporters; namely, restoration of state authority, termination of militia rule and the possibility of freeing Lebanon from foreign occupation.

In 1988, Aoun's rise from commander of the Lebanese army to the country's premiership conveyed the possibility of the restoration of public order because he, in military uniform, represented the antithesis of militia order and chaos, which had aggrieved the Lebanese people for over a decade. Substantiating this argument, Liwa Chakour remarked: "We had the political opportunity… The assumption of the army commander in military uniform to the premiership was the antithesis to the militia order. The military uniform was the government or state. It kept us comfortable and assured" (interview September 29, 2014). In this scenario, making reference to the "military uniform" represented a longing for the restoration of state authority, which, to an overwhelming majority of the interviewed participants and perhaps others, had become an elusive thought prior to the emergence of Aoun as premier. In addition, when Liwa Chakour refers to Aoun's rise to the premiership as a "political opportunity," he regards that rise, especially with Aoun's bold political opinions, as a conducive political moment for supporting the goals of a leader who had promised to do away with the chaos of the militia and the corrupt practices of the political class of Lebanon.

In fact, Aoun's assumption, as a military commander, of the premiership could not have been the only factor that accounted for his popularity, even though FPM activists emphasize this point; nevertheless, his democratic populist character certainly helped to attract a following. Here a populist is defined as a manipulative speaker who addresses his target audience in a direct manner through the use of clear language and simple terms and seeks to address their concerns. In this respect, Aoun epitomized the example of a populist leader by constantly framing his proposals in the form of short slogans, as explained further shortly. Therefore, this style of persuasive speech along with his firm military personality helped inspire trust among his supporters, who then rallied in support of his proposals, marched to the presidential palace in Baabda, which Aoun dubbed the people's palace, and incubated a mass movement in support of Aoun.

As a result, Lebanese individuals were attracted into the FPM because Aoun's political proposals promised to rid the people of their sources of grievance; namely, the warring militias and the Syrian military presence in Lebanon. Rabih Tarraf illustrated this point: "I began to realize that the General had guts, was daring, and used to say what we wanted to say. His speech attracted us, he had charisma, he used to speak his mind without fear and under enormous shelling, and his options were wise" (interview September 11, 2014). This study of the FPM finds that 100% of the activists interviewed spoke of a certain role held by Aoun in the emergence of the FPM. While some concentrated on his personal features and characteristics, such as charisma, an ability to inspire confidence and trust, transparency, honesty and modesty, inter alia, others, such as Roland ElKhoury, spoke of his tough and decisive military personality, in evidence when dealing with the LF militia, mentioning that "the tougher he was, the more I liked him" (interview September 26, 2014).

Through his persuasive style, Aoun managed to influence his supporters by convincing them that they possessed the ability to effect positive change. This proved essential for the formation of what can be viewed as the roots of the FPM, since Aoun's speech helped individuals move away from their politically dispossessed state toward a more active engagement in political activism. Patrick ElKhoury, an FPM activist, commented: "The situation of Lebanon—Palestinians, Syrians, and everything we lived through—nurtured the spirit of revolution in my heart. When the General appeared, this began to come out from within me… But had the General not appeared, I couldn't have been able to get it out of me. This man arrived and began getting it out of me" (interview October 1, 2014). Therefore, this clearly indicates that Aoun played a direct role in lifting Lebanese individuals out of their state of helplessness and inviting them into the ranks of the FPM.

The Aoun-inspired feeling of being able to effect change helped his supporters move from their politically dispossessed state, which had kept them on the fringes of Lebanon's political life, to being incentivized and confident individuals who joined the ranks of the FPM. These incentives emanated from the Lebanese people's perceived sense of expanding freedom. In sharp contrast to their wartime conditions, they felt, with the rise of Aoun to the premiership, that they now enjoyed the freedom of mobility that permitted them to create change. Rabih Tarraf pointedly remarked that "we felt for once that the possibility of living in a country where we enjoyed freedom was real. It felt like a bird trapped in a cage and you had never set it free in the room… So you had now freed the bird from the small cage. It felt like it could fly, like it had a wider margin to move around, it felt it possessed something someone had taken away" (interview September 11, 2014).

This sudden experience of freedom with the appearance of Aoun in the political arena of Lebanon is related to his calls to liberate Lebanon from Syrian troops and restore order by doing away with the militias; both of these points were significant sources of grievance for the FPM activists interviewed. As an army officer with a sound reputation, Aoun seemed to be a credible leader who would deliver on his promises, and this led to the rise of a movement that supported his political goals.

However, Aoun's supporters viewed their leader as credible chiefly because he was quick to act against the groups that had long constituted their main source of grievance. Pascal Azzam, an FPM activist, stated: "When there were political conditions in the country, and the General would speak, the people would march to Baabda spontaneously. You had people who would place their children on their shoulders and march to Baabda. So this depended on the occurrence of a political event" (interview October 9, 2014). For instance, Aoun's battle with the LF militia on February 10, 1989 to regain state control of Dock Five in Beirut Harbor, which was one of the most important sources of state revenue (Hanf 1993, p. 572), won his movement tremendous popular support. His ensuing attempt to extend state authority over the Khalde, Jiyeh and Ouzai ports, which were controlled by the Syrian-backed Progressive Socialist Party and Amal, lured him into the War of Liberation with Syria on March 14, 1989.

The FPM activists interviewed unanimously agreed that Aoun's strong opinions and bold moves against various militias and the foreign occupation of Lebanon by Syria and Israel, not to mention his diatribe against the Saudi-brokered Taif Accords, led Lebanese individuals who sympathized with his nationalist stance to join the FPM. The fact that "He was able to combine his words and actions together," according to Naim Aoun, an FPM activist, made Michel Aoun a model in the opinion of many supporters (interview September 18, 2014).

This reality manifested itself in several ways. First, Michel Aoun called for the implementation of United Nations' Security Council resolutions 425 and 520, which stressed the withdrawal from Lebanon of Israeli and

Syrian troops, respectively, thereby revealing that he did not display double standards regarding the withdrawal of foreign troops (P. ElKhoury, interview October 1, 2014). The main reason he had staunchly opposed the Taif Accords, the document of national reconciliation in 1989, was because it did not clearly outline a timetable for the withdrawal of Syrian troops from Lebanon. Second, Aoun's messages were directed against all militias and sought to outline broad principles of respect and preservation of state institutions, the Lebanese army and the judiciary (Z. Assouad, interview October 10, 2014). Therefore, for an aggrieved Lebanese population who had suffered intensely at the hands of militias and other anti-state elements, the rise of Michel Aoun with his vision for reviving the state brought the interviewed activists and thousands of other Lebanese individuals into the ranks of the FPM.

Whether credit should go to Aoun's personal attributes, affiliation with the Lebanese army, progressive ideas and/or bold political moves in sparking the flame of FPM emergence, it would have been hard to envisage the rise of the FPM as a movement with a progressive, secular, national and reformist outlook without the central role of its leadership. This central role played by Aoun in the emergence of the movement often drew journalists to refer to these FPM activists as "the Aoun generation, Aounists, pro-Aoun groups," which highlighted the link between his leadership and the rise of the movement.

Aoun: The Captivating Oratorical Leader

The manner in which Aoun addressed his supporters, who were predominantly Christian but not exclusively so, succeeded in attracting them into the ranks of the pro-Aoun movement in the period 1988–1990 because he framed his language in a way that touched on the source of their grievances, proposed solutions, called for corrective action and transcended the narrow sectarian rifts afflicting Lebanese society. The secular, nationalistic and all-encompassing manner in which he framed the movement's ideas cut across the sectarian rifts of Lebanese society and won him tremendous support. Conversely, McVeigh et al. (2004) show that the exclusionary boundaries of the Indiana Ku Klux Klan in the 1920s, albeit coupled with effective framing tactics, isolated a large segment of the population and prevented it from attaining broader political gains. Therefore, Aoun's ability to frame his messages in a manner that presented an inclusive platform, chiefly through his diatribe against the chaotic militia order, foreign occupation of Lebanese territory and corrupt machinations of Lebanese politics, succeeded in attracting individuals of diverse persuasions into the ranks of the FPM.

Through the instrumental use of popular slogans and stances, Aoun's framed messages resonated with the Lebanese population and played a major role in attracting individuals into the movement. A frame is a schema of interpretation that enables individuals to locate, perceive, identify and label occurrences within their life spaces and the world at large (Goffman 1974, p. 21). Frames provide an interpretive outline that simplifies and condenses phenomena by selectively encoding objects, situations, events, experiences and sequences of actions that have occurred in one's present or past environment (Benford and Snow 1992, p. 137). The use of a combination of diagnostic (problem identification), prognostic (proposing solutions) and motivational (calls to action) framing leads to the emergence of social movement activity by virtue of helping people to locate the source of blame and engage in ameliorative action (Benford and Snow 1988; Snow and Benford 2000).

Aoun's use of slogans motivated his supporters to join the ranks of the FPM, chiefly by helping them to restore confidence in their ability to effect change. Some of Aoun's populist slogans included: "You are the liberation generation, you are the nation and the national will … The state is not the people; the people are the state" (in Hanf 1993, p. 577; Salem 2003, p. 163). This motivational framing served to remind the Lebanese people by dubbing them the "liberation generation" that they carried the keys to resolve their predicament, brought about by the Lebanese Civil War. The use of this term alluded to the Syrian and Israeli occupation and the various militias dominating different parts of Lebanon as being reprehensible for compromising national sovereignty and independence, while simultaneously calling on the Lebanese people to assume a role in the liberation of their country.

Such motivational framing can generate what Snow and Soule (2010, p. 138) term "solidary and moral incentives," which inevitably influence individuals to engage in collective activity. Therefore, the slogans to which the Lebanese people were exposed awakened a sense of moral responsibility and nationalism among some that rendered them more willing to engage in collective activity to save their country. This collective activity translated into wide-scale support for Aoun's political stances, which simultaneously incubated the FPM by virtue of causing thousands to rally in support of his calls.

Aoun's motivational framing also restored his supporters' confidence in their ability to effect political change; this rendered them more willing to join the ranks of a movement that aimed to turn the table on corrupt politics, occupation and the chaotic militia order. Aoun regularly addressed the Lebanese population in an inclusive manner: although his base of support was concentrated heavily among Lebanese Christians, he did not fail to attract some Muslims to his non-sectarian discourse by calling them "the great people of Lebanon," a slogan that quickly became emblematic of Aoun and his movement. This slogan resonated positively with his supporters and contributed to the rise of the movement. Naaman Abi Antoun, an FPM activist, illustrates this point by stating: "When a person would reach Baabda on foot after hours of marching, and heard the General call out 'the great people of Lebanon', he used to feel satisfied and fulfilled. He used to feel that a part of his dignity was restored. That person would want to invest what remaining pulse he still had to support the General" (interview September 23, 2014).

Regarding this particular slogan, Liwa Chakour added: "this boosted my national ego and national feeling within me" (interview September 29, 2014). This example shows that the framing of ideas, albeit in the form of slogans in the initial phase of the movement, was able to attract individuals into the ranks of the FPM. One of the main reasons for the effectiveness of these frames lies in the fact that they were coupled with a multitude of associating factors that contributed to the rise of the movement. Some of these factors were related to the assumption of Aoun to the Lebanese premiership and what that phenomenon represented in the eyes of his supporters, as has been already analyzed.

Aoun's motivational framing was also able to resonate with his supporters and incentivize participation in the ranks of the FPM by resorting to slogans that were variations of existing literary works. For instance, Aoun used to say "pity the nation that sacrifices its youth for the sake of its elders," which was stated in a manner that resembled quotes from Gibran Khalil Gibran. By being embedded in aspects of Lebanese culture to which its citizens could relate, Aoun's framing resonated with his supporters, and especially the youth among them, inviting them to participate in the ranks of the FPM. It was no coincidence that young people formed the majority of the participants of the movement in 1989 (35% under the age of 18 and another 40% under the age of 39; Hanf 1993, p. 597) and the backbone of FPM collective activity throughout the period 1990–2005. The high level of youth participation in the ranks of the FPM clearly indicated the effectiveness of Aoun's framing tactics in persuading Lebanese individuals to assume a role in politics by participating in the collective activity of the FPM, which had a positive bearing on the rise of the movement.

Whereas Aoun's motivational framing incentivized individuals to join the ranks of the FPM, some of the slogans he advanced contained diagnostic and prognostic frames that identified the source of the problems and proposed solutions to tackle them, as well as issues leading to the rise of the FPM by clarifying its ideational character. For example, slogans such as "Tell the deputies you didn't elect them, so they've got no right to speak for you" (in Hanf 1993, p. 577; Salem 2003, p. 163) may have motivated Lebanese individuals to participate in the ranks of the FPM, but chiefly pointed the finger of blame at Lebanese parliamentarians, whose constant self-renewal of their own terms since 1972 had resulted in a largely unrepresentative Parliament by 1989.

Therefore, this diagnostic framing set out a clear target for the movement's political activity. In itself, it did not call for immediate action, but clarified the target the FPM was aiming at; namely, the country's traditional political class. The church, an influential player in Lebanese politics, also received its share of the blame when Aoun, through the instrumental use of prognostic framing, asked his supporters to "Tell the Church the reason you're here is to speak the truth" (ibid.), in reference to the Maronite church's intervention in Lebanese politics and backing of the Taif Accords that Aoun clearly opposed. These types of frames proved vital for the emergence of the FPM, not only because they attracted individuals to its ranks, but also because they clearly highlighted what ideas had led to the emergence of the movement and thus granted the FPM an ideational character.

The importance of Aoun's prognostic framing emanated from the distinct solutions embedded in the frames he put forward in the form of slogans, which helped to showcase which ideas or principles attracted individuals into the movement. For instance, a number of FPM activists interviewed in this study mentioned being attracted to Aoun's slogan of "Lebanon, too small to partition, and too big to swallow," which expressed an unambiguous rejection of the division of the country into sectarian cantons, while also rejecting the presence of foreign troops on Lebanese turf, whether those troops were the Syrian deterrent forces in Lebanon or the Israeli occupying forces in South Lebanon.

Having been aggrieved by the various militias scattered throughout the territory of wartime Lebanon and the Syrian troops deployed there,

Aoun's supporters were attracted by slogans that referred to combating the militia order and the foreign occupation of Lebanon as a potential solution. Aoun's successful framing, which became more evident as individuals became attracted to these populist slogans, helped to identify the FPM as a movement that aimed to uphold the principles of freedom, sovereignty and independence, while calling for the restoration of a capable state with features such as a strong military as opposed to chaotic militia rule, good governance in place of corrupt practices, and true democracy with competitive elections to replace the democracy of dynastic succession, in which some politicians bequeath their political status to a son or family member.

Focusing on the way in which Aoun advanced slogans to the Lebanese public risks reducing the ideas of the FPM to a few phrases if the street dynamics are not put into perspective. Aoun's framing of the FPM's messages through the instrumental use of slogans helped attract individuals into the ranks of the movement simply by indicating that it represented the antithesis of the ongoing militia order and the political chaos afflicting Lebanon during the Civil War years. Illustrating this point, Michel Eleftériades remarked: "The slogans resembled us. They were a stark difference to those presented by the LF, such as 'my country cry out, a country for a Christian nation' or 'God, the doctor [a clear reference to the head of the LF militia, Samir Jeajea], and Lebanon only'" (interview September 8, 2014). Although the FPM later set out a political platform that dealt with numerous political issues, Aoun's instrumental use of slogans clearly indicated the ideational identity of a movement emerging amid war and in a concise fashion, an issue that undoubtedly culminated in the rise of the FPM by attracting some of those aggrieved individuals who had an interest in the restoration of state authority at the expense of the militias.

Conclusion

Michel Aoun posed such a violent challenge to the status quo in Lebanon—namely, the traditional ruling groups, militias, occupying powers and policies of other international actors—that he generated momentum for concerted action among most of those disparate groups (Salem 1996). He expressed a genuine frustration with the status quo in Lebanon, and then translated that frustration into a popularly backed challenge to the traditional players of the political game in wartime Lebanon. Without Aoun's challenge, it is doubtful whether these disparate protagonists, both Lebanese and non-Lebanese, would have found cause to negotiate the agreement of the Taif Accords in the first place (ibid.).

Iraq's invasion of Kuwait in the summer of 1990 led to the formation of an international coalition of states, including the USA, Arab Gulf states and Syria, to evict Saddam Hussein from Kuwait. Aoun's position, as a recipient of Iraqi arms, became weaker due to shifting power balances in the region. As a consequence, Syria, combined with army units loyal to President Hrawi and units of the LF, drove Aoun out of the presidential palace in a military operation on October 13, 1990.

After the October 13 military assault on the Baabda Palace, Aoun and some of his close army officers sought refuge in the French embassy in Beirut, where he remained for 10 months. On August 31, 1991, he and his associates sought political asylum in France on condition of an enforced media ban on the erstwhile general. This media ban was intended to avoid political agitation in post-war Lebanon by disconnecting the lines of communication between Aoun in France and his supporters in Lebanon.

With Aoun ousted from the political arena, the Lebanese political elite and Syria, whose influence burgeoned in post-war Lebanese politics in the period 1990–2005, indulged in the fruits of post-war reconstruction. This post-war phase posed manifold challenges to the political elite of the country.

However, the convulsive reaction that Aoun triggered in the period 1988–1990 did not fade away in post-war Lebanese politics, especially with regard to his political fan base. Although Aoun was in exile in France, the reasons that had triggered the participation of many Lebanese individuals in the movement forming in support of him during the period 1988–1990, most notably the grievances and motivations, were brewing once again.

Individuals who had participated in the rallies at the Baabda Palace noticed that the former militias that had constituted their main source of grievance were actively sharing in the spoils of the state, adopting policies that had negative impacts on the socioeconomic conditions of Lebanese citizens and curbing genuine political opposition to government policies and the Syrian military presence in Lebanon. Those individuals who were disenfranchised from the political process as supporters of Aoun in the period 1990–2005 started building, whether consciously or unconsciously, the FPM from the ground up.

The next chapter turns to an analysis of how members of this movement navigated the complex political landscape of post-war Lebanese politics to form the FPM. It also examines why the movement emerged in the way that it did.

References

Abi Antoun, N. Interview by this author. 2014. Beirut, September 23.

Achkar, W. Interview by this author. 2014. Jounieh, October 15.

Aoun, N. Interview by this author. 2014. Awkar, September 18.

Assouad, Z. Interview by this author. 2014. Jounieh, October 10.

Azzam, P. Interview by this author. 2014. Beirut, October 9.

Benford, R. D., and D. A. Snow. 1988. "Ideology, Frame Resonance, and Participant Mobilization." *International Social Movement Research* 1: 197–218.

Benford, R. D., and D. A. Snow. 1992. "Master Frames and Cycles of Protest." In *Frontiers in Social Movement Theory*, 133–155. New Haven, CT: Yale University Press.

Chakour, L. Interview by this author. 2014. Jbeil, September 29.

Chlela, R. Interview by this author. 2014. Jounieh, October 29.

Davies, J. 1962. "Towards a Theory of Revolution." *American Sociological Review* 27: 5–19.

Elefteriades, M. Interview by this author. 2014. Beirut, September 8.

ElKhoury, P. Interview by this author. 2014. Dbayeh, October 1.

ElKhoury, R. Interview by this author. 2014. Jounieh, September 26.

Goffman, E. 1974. *Frame Analysis.* Boston: Northeastern University Press.

Gurr, T. R. 1970. *Why Men Rebel.* Princeton: Princeton University Press.

Hanf, T. 1993. *Coexistence in Wartime Lebanon.* London: I.B. Tauris.

Hanna, E. Interview by this author. 2014. Rabieh, October 16.

Harris, W. A. 1997. *Faces of Lebanon: Sects, Wars, and Global Extensions.* Princeton: Marcus Wiener.

Jenkins, J. C., and C. Parrow. 1977. "Insurgency of the Powerless: Farm Worker Movements (1946–1972)." *American Sociological Review* 42 (2): 249–268.

Kanj, R. Interview by this author. 2014. Beirut, September 19.

Klandermans, B., M. Roefs, and J. Olivier. 2001. "Grievance Formation in a Country in Transition: South Africa, 1994–1998." *Social Psychology Quarterly* 64 (1): 41–54.

Laurent, A. 1991. "A War Between Brothers: The Army–Lebanese Forces Showdown in East Beirut." *The Beirut Review* 1 (1): 88–101.

Martin, J. 1986. "The Tolerance of Injustice". In *Relative Deprivation and Social Comparison: The Ontario Symposium*, vol. 4, edited by J. M. Olson, C. Peter Herman, and M. P. Zanna, 217–242. Mahwah: Erlbaum.

McAdam, D. 1988. *Freedom Summer.* New York: Oxford University Press.

McVeigh, R., D. J. Myers, and D. Sikkink. 2004. "Corn, Klansmen, and Coolidge: Structure and Framing in Social Movements." *Social Forces* 83 (2): 653–690.

Raffoul, P. Interview by this author. 2014. Beirut, October 2.

Raffoul, P. G. 1994. *The Betrayal of Lebanon*. Translated by G. S. Khoury. Victoria: The Lebanese Coordination Bureau of Victoria.

Runciman, W. J. 1966. *Relative Deprivation and Social Justice*. London: Routledge & Kegan Paul.

Salem, E. E. 2003. *Constructing Lebanon: A Century of Literary Narratives*. Gainesville: University Press of Florida.

Salem, P. 1996. "Two Years of Living Dangerously: General Aoun and the Precarious Rise of Lebanon's 'Second Republic'." *The Beirut Review* 1 (1): 62–87.

Salloukh, B. F., R. Barakat, J. S. Al-Habbal, L. W. Khattab, S. Mikaelian, and A. Nerguizian. 2015. *The Politics of Sectarianism in Postwar Lebanon*. London: Pluto Press.

Snow, D. A., and R. D. Benford. 2000. "Framing Processes and Social Movements: An Overview and Assessment." *Annual Review of Sociology* 26: 611–639.

Snow, D. A., and S. A. Soule. 2010. *A Primer on Social Movements*. New York: W. W. Norton.

Tarraf, R. Interview by this author. 2014. Hadath, September 11.

CHAPTER 3

The Free Patriotic Movement's Emergence in the Complex Political Economy of Post-war Lebanon

With Michel Aoun in exile in France, his supporters in Lebanon, who were predominantly Christian but not exclusively so, were disenfranchised from the post-war political process. This ostracization weighed heavily on Aoun's supporters, as it prevented them from forming as a formal political party and marked any such assembly as one opposed to the post-war Lebanese elite and their Syrian allies. In spite of this limited political margin for formal assembly, Aoun's supporters were present in a number of political forums, gained visibility on the political scene and gradually formed the Free Patriotic Movement (FPM), albeit informally, throughout the post-war period. The FPM not only directed its criticism at the violations perpetrated by the Lebanese political elite and Syria, but also engaged in activism with the aim of affecting positive political change in a number of political, economic and social arenas, while consistently advancing non-sectarian discourse and ideas throughout the period 1990–2005.

With this challenging environment as a backdrop, this chapter seeks to explore the avenues via which the FPM emerged in that period. It also explores the impact of the FPM's sectarian and socioeconomic makeup on the movement and its activism. It delves into a brief discussion of the political-economic conditions of post-war Lebanon and how those conditions helped shape the nature of the FPM's activism.

This chapter argues that the FPM maintained itself as a movement with a secular and nationalistic agenda despite comprising predominantly, but

J. P. Helou, *Activism, Change and Sectarianism in the Free Patriotic Movement in Lebanon*, Reform and Transition in the Mediterranean,
https://doi.org/10.1007/978-3-030-25704-0_3

not exclusively, middle-class Christians because of its exclusion from formal political activity, which would have otherwise required favoring its mainly Christian voter base with public goods, social services and other incentives to ensure a parliamentary bloc. Since the FPM was operating outside conventional politics—that is to say, outside Parliament and the Council of Ministers—then it did not have to operate within the confines of this distorted incentive structure, which helped promote sectarian modes of political subjectification and mobilization. Instead, the FPM championed secular and nationalistic causes, while stressing the political values of integrity, national harmony and transparency, to name but a few. Its direct criticism of the policies adopted by the de jure governments of Lebanon earned it credibility among the middle class; that is to say, students, members of syndicates and unions, and other activists in civil society.

Therefore, the emergence of the FPM began on university campuses, in a number of syndicates and in towns and villages across Lebanon. As the movement gained ground and consolidated its presence in civil society, it became more able to seize political opportunities to emerge on a national level, such as the 1998 municipal elections and the parliamentary by-elections of 2003, than had been the case in the early 1990s.

This chapter is sub-divided into three. The first part discusses in some detail the composition of the membership, sectarian dimensions and sociological background of the FPM. The second part shows how the political economy of Lebanon affected the middle class and provided syndicates and unions with launchpads for activism against unpopular government policies. The final part shows how activists operating on university campuses and inside syndicates generated momentum for the rise of the FPM in civil society, before their participation in electoral races helped them gain national visibility toward the latter half of the 1990s. It also highlights the role of activists abroad in countries such as France, the USA and Australia in supporting the rise of the FPM in Lebanon.

Part I: Membership, Sectarian Dimensions and Sociological Background

Who were the activists who joined the FPM? The sectarian system of post-war Lebanon makes it impossible to overlook the influential role of sectarianism and simply to regard FPM activists as Lebanese citizens, or the movement's base of support as a segment of the Lebanese people, because the strategies of post-war political elites created sectarian modes of political subjectification and mobilization, as explained by Salloukh et al. (2015). Although the main base of FPM activists comprised predominantly middle-class individuals who were Christians, the political goals of the FPM, at least in the period 1990–2005, were ostensibly secular and national in scope. However, the fluid formation of social actors reveals that they were vulnerable to change depending on the social forces to which they were exposed. Therefore, an examination of the membership, sociological and sectarian backgrounds of the FPM's activists helps inform how these FPM activists were likely to behave within the complex political system of Lebanon.

In terms of demographics, a rough estimate of FPM activists exists for the period 1990–2005, but the broad base of FPM sympathizers—that is, those individuals who were not active within the movement but supported its political outlook in this period—cannot be statistically determined. Yet, different authors have attempted to offer some information regarding the makeup of the movement, specifically regarding the crowds of supporters who rallied in support of Aoun in 1989. For instance, Hanf (1993, p. 597) reveals that a survey of protestors in Baabda in 1989 finds that the majority of them were young, with 35% of participants under 18 and another 40% under the age of 39.

Regarding the size of these crowds of protestors, Harris (1997, p. 265) mentions that by December 1989 their numbers exceeded 150,000 when combined with people who joined from outside the predominantly Christian enclave of East Beirut, which implies that some participants may have been Lebanese Muslims, but without an exact estimate of their number. While confirming the diverse background of the Baabda demonstrators, Pierre Raffoul, General Coordinator of the FPM and close associate of Aoun, may have provided an exaggerated figure regarding the participants in the demonstrations at Baabda, which he also participated in coordinating. He mentions that when the Syrians threatened to shell the region, a popular gathering of 750,000 individuals marched to Baabda (interview October 2, 2014).

The number of these protestors highlighted the existence of a popular base of support for the political proposals advanced by Aoun. Whether they were in the tens or in the hundreds of thousands is not substantial evidence to demerit the movement because, in either case, thousands of individuals took the risk of demonstrating during times of war, which revealed their enormous commitment to standing for the political cause of liberating Lebanon and ending convoluted militia practices. In any event, this period marked the incubation of what became the FPM and some participants in these protests later joined in the formation of the FPM in post-war Lebanon, as evidenced in the interviews conducted with FPM activists for this book.

However, due to the immediate political circumstances of post-war Lebanon—that is, inter alia, Aoun's expatriation to France and the official banning of formal movement meetings in the first half of the 1990s—the FPM could not officially count its activists who mobilized in a decentralized manner, as will be explained in the next chapter. Yet, when these decentralized structures, which helped promote FPM activism in the period 1990–2005, became effective in planning and managing activism in towns and villages by the mid-1990s, their group leaders did become aware of how many activists existed within a given area. This is how leading activists who persisted in organizing FPM activism and played an important role in building the movement throughout the period 1990–2005 arrived at the estimate of 3000 activists for this period, before formally counting more than 60,000 members upon the FPM's inception as a political party in 2005 (L. Chakour, interview September 29, 2014). Still, FPM activism was heavily concentrated in geographic areas such as Mount Lebanon, Jbeil, Beirut and North Lebanon, where there was a strong presence of Christians and where university campuses were heavily concentrated, which allowed for the planning of movement activism.

The decision of the FPM leadership to participate in electoral races for formal office helped reveal the degree of support the movement enjoyed in Lebanon, specifically among Lebanese Christians. In the first few years of the post-war period, particularly in the 1992 and the 1996 rounds of parliamentary elections, the FPM declared its boycott of those parliamentary elections, which resulted in a low turnout of Christian voters at the polls. Following a series of important political developments, such as the withdrawal of Israel from South Lebanon in 2000 and the formation of the anti-Syrian political gathering of Qornet Chehwan, the FPM decided to support the candidacy of Gabriel ElMurr in the parliamentary by-elections in the Matn district in 2002, and to nominate its own candidate in the parliamentary by-election in the Baabda-Aley district in 2003.

The results the FPM achieved in the Baabda-Aley district asserted the political presence of the movement by revealing the number of votes its candidate earned. The FPM candidate Hikmat Dib received 25,291 votes, while his political competitor Henry Helou received 28,597 votes (Gambill 2003). Despite the fact that Helou was supported by a number of influential political parties, Dib won 73% of the Christian vote and hundreds of Druze and Shia votes (ibid.).

Dib faced several challenges, since his political competitor Helou was supported by the Shia party of Hezbollah, the Druze-based Progressive Socialist Party and several Christian parties; the fact that Helou was running to fill the post of his politically established father after the latter's death also challenged the FPM candidate (Gambill 2003). Another challenge lay in the nature of Baabda-Aley, which was a mixed-sectarian district, meaning that Shia, Druze and Christian voters all played a role in influencing the results of the elections (ibid.). The political elites' role in gerrymandering electoral constituencies, particularly by combining into a single electoral district what had been the two separate constituencies of Baabda and Aley, sought to minimize the impact of the Christian vote there; this was designed to secure the electoral interests of the post-war political elite (Salloukh et al. 2015).

Since Dib gathered 25,291 votes despite losing, the FPM was able to assert its presence as a movement enjoying popular support. It boycotted the 1992 and 1996 rounds of parliamentary elections alongside other Christian parties and politicians. This strategy of emphasizing non-participation may have resulted in a low voter turnout, but it simultaneously helped generate a new class of Lebanese post-war elite, even if they were not fully representative of their geographic constituencies or the sectarian group they were supposed to represent. However, when the FPM nominated a candidate in the 2003 parliamentary by-election, it was able to reveal its popularity in numbers; namely, 25,291 votes in the Baabda-Aley constituency (Gambill 2003).

Therefore, the FPM was able to assert its presence in the period 1990–2005, in terms of both the number of activists in its ranks and the numbers of voters who showed up at the polls. Perhaps the FPM can be faulted for not participating in more rounds of parliamentary elections to assert its popularity in numeric terms. However, the decision to participate was only made after a series of political developments, such as the Israeli withdrawal from South Lebanon in 2000, the formation of the anti-Syrian political gathering of Qornet Chehwan, and the September 11, 2001 attacks in the USA, all of which began to cast doubt on Syria's role in and policies toward Lebanon, which made FPM participation in parliamentary elections plausible. The FPM's main base of support lay within the Christian community; that is to say, that the movement's activists and supporters were predominantly, but not exclusively, Christian.

The relationship between the FPM's political proposals and the sectarian affiliation of its base of support, who were predominantly Christian, seems to be more complicated than might appear at first glance. The role of Aoun in expressing political positions and thoughts that helped ensure the nationalistic and secular orientation of the FPM in the period 1990–2005 cannot be overstated. Aoun's secular nationalism reflected the Lebanese patriotism of the army's officer corps, which did not subordinate itself with other militias during the Lebanese Civil War (Harris 1997, pp. 242–243). Yet, this reality alone cannot help explain why the FPM comprised predominantly Christian members.

The reason for the FPM's popularity among Lebanese Christians could not have lain in the fact that Aoun was a Maronite-Christian, but in his opposition to the Taif Accords and subsequently to the political practices of the political elite in post-war Lebanon. The Lebanese post-war elite, with the backing of Syria, gerrymandered electoral constituencies in the 1992, 1996 and 2000 rounds of parliamentary elections to help produce a political class who were in line with the preferences of Syria in Lebanon. While this led to distortions in the deputy representation per voter ratio across Lebanon, it fell quite hard on Christian voters, who became less able to determine their candidates in several constituencies, the Baabda-Aley district being illustrative of this point (Salloukh et al. 2015).

In the early 1990s, Parliament was increased to 128 seats from 108, the latter being the number agreed upon in the Taif Accords to establish parity between Christian and Muslim representation (Salloukh et al. 2015). To maintain parity, the 20 additional seats were divided equally between Christians and Muslims. However, the allocation of Christian seats in certain areas did not correspond with an increase of Christian voters in those areas, an example of this phenomenon being an additional Maronite seat in Tripoli and another in the Beqaa region, where members of other sects determined the representative for that position (ibid.). Even in predominantly Christian constituencies, electoral rigging and vote-buying helped to generate a political elite who did not enjoy majority representation of the voter base, meaning that they won with mainly extremely low voter turnouts (see Mansour 1992; El-Khazen 1998; Salloukh et al. 2015). Therefore, these strategies that ostracized Christian voters from the post-war political process helped them become politically committed, or at least sympathetic, to the views expressed by those actors who were also ostracized; namely, the FPM and the Lebanese Forces Party.

Nevertheless, a puzzling phenomenon revolves around the manner in which Aoun and the FPM were able to attract a membership composed predominantly of Christian individuals and some active members of other sectarian groups, without expressing sectarian opinions or giving preferential treatment to individuals based on their sectarian affiliation. This reality was made possible due to the position held by Aoun and the FPM in the power structure of Lebanon in the period 1990–2005.

In other words, with its leader in exile and partially excluded from the post-war political process—that is to say, it had no representatives in Parliament or ministers in cabinet and thus did not possess any legislative or executive authority—the FPM did not have to deal with the clientelistic practice of staffing state bureaucracies with its members, nor assign multiple candidates to run on parliamentary electoral lists. Its participation in the parliamentary by-election in 2003 required it to assign only a single candidate. The movement's activism in civil society—that is, on university campuses, in professional syndicates and in towns and villages—did not provide it with privileged access to the kind of resources a position within Parliament or the Council of Ministers would have accorded its members. Therefore, the movement did not have to grapple with the task of dispensing favors to its members.

As a consequence of this partial exclusion from the post-war political process, the FPM was able to easily express secular opinions to a predominantly Christian base of support and simultaneously attract members of other sectarian denominations into the movement, since it sought to correct the political process by calling for the withdrawal of Syrian troops from Lebanon and to combat the corrupt practices of the post-war political elite. By advancing these demands in a non-sectarian tone, the FPM attracted a membership who were predominantly Christian because it touched on the source of their grievances, and yet at the same time managed to recruit some Muslim activists, who also regarded the Lebanese post-war elite's political strategies and practices as corrupt. For example, out of the 30 FPM activists interviewed, 28 were Christians of various sectarian denominations, one was a Shia Muslim and another a Sunni Muslim. Although the sample of interviewees was not selected with the aim of being statistically representative of sectarian balances within the FPM (since that is hard to establish accurately for the period 1990–2005), it does represent a number of the core group of activists in the FPM. However, this sectarian membership of the FPM was not found to inform the movement's strategies or discourse, specifically in the period 1990–2005.

Yet, the FPM became more constrained by aspects of sectarian politics in the post-2005 period when it gained a parliamentary bloc and participated in the Council of Ministers. As a result, it found itself expressing political views in a sectarian tone to serve its mainly Christian constituency. Therefore, because the FPM existed as a social movement that did not participate within state institutions throughout the period 1990–2005, it was able to emerge and persist at this time as a nationalistic and secular movement in spite of its predominantly Christian support base.

The FPM not only reflected a predominantly Christian membership, but also one that hosted an active role for the middle class in its ranks. The definition of the middle class employed here includes those individuals who have earned a level of education, skills, professional practice and/or income that allows them, in McAdam's (1988) terms, to become biographically available to participate in movement activism, since they could afford to allocate time and effort to activism. For example, out of the 30 activists interviewed, more than 90% had taken a university degree in fields ranging from engineering to law, business, humanities and the arts, social sciences and sciences. Three activists were lawyers, six were engineers, six had business majors and three held doctoral degrees. Around 50% of the sample of interviewed activists were students and then recent graduates during their years in activism in the period 1990–2005.

This study finds that the vast number of activists came from the middle class and helped establish the FPM. As will shortly become clear, the incubation of the FPM occurred on university campuses led by students, in a number of syndicates that represented lawyers, engineers, doctors and teachers, and in towns and villages, which required skillful networking, communication and organization characteristic of a middle-class background. In fact, no information traced FPM activity to labor struggles or issues. Some movement activists launched a campaign to support greengrocers across Lebanon by selling vegetables on mobile carts, which will be explained further in the next chapter, but even this activity was organized by individuals with a middle-class profile, particularly university students (E. Hanna, interview October 16, 2014).

Therefore, the FPM can be regarded as a movement advanced by the middle class chiefly because of the essential role played by university students and members of professional syndicates in bringing it to life. This is not to say that individuals who did not enjoy this privileged status in terms of education and skills were not supporters of the FPM. However, since the FPM was conceived on university campuses and in professional syndicates, the individuals who continued playing a decisive role in the movement emerged from these institutions, which were characteristic of the middle class. Even after the FPM transformed into a political party in 2005, these individuals continued to assume leading positions within the party, in addition to welcoming those from the more financially stable elite, such as businesspeople, within the party (as will be discussed in some detail in Chapter 5).

Some activists were more financially stable than others in the movement, depending on whether they were students or working individuals. As a result, the wealthier activists constantly donated large sums of money to support FPM campaigns in the period 1990–2005. Since the activities the FPM engaged in required the personal commitment of activists and only minor resources, such as paper for distributing communiqués, spray paint to write slogans in public spaces and some offices for meetings, the sums were restricted to a few hundred dollars depending on the nature of the event. Activists either drew these sums from their own income or referred the costs to some sympathizers of the movement who were willing to dispense sums for activism. Therefore, this illustrates that the concept of the middle class advanced in this study cannot emphasize income alone as a sole determining criterion, but rather considers education and skills as essential factors too.

Moreover, members of FPM groups abroad, such as the Rassemblement Pour le Liban (RPL) in France, the Council of Lebanese American Organizations (CLAO) in the USA and the Global Front for the Liberation of Lebanon in Australia, also reflected a middle-class composition. For example, Simon Abi Ramia, a leading figure in the RPL and Lebanese Member of Parliament as of 2009, was an optometrist by education (interview November 21, 2014). Pierre Raffoul, a leading figure of the FPM in Australia and General Coordinator of the FPM after 2005, holds a PhD in humanities (interview October 2, 2014). Both these individuals confirm the presence of a wide range of expertise within the FPM in the diaspora, whether among activists or supporters in general. Another point worth mentioning is that these FPM groups in the diaspora also formed a base of attraction for FPM activists who graduated from their universities in Lebanon and traveled abroad to pursue higher education or work (S. Abi Ramia, interview November 21, 2014). Therefore, the composition of the FPM's membership base in countries such as France was influenced by new members who joined after reaching their new destination from Lebanon.

The kind of contacts and social relations that members of FPM groups in the diaspora enjoyed confirmed their middle-class background and contributed positively to the rise of the FPM. For example, Gabi Issa, who led CLAO, possessed social relationships that facilitated the scheduling of Michel Aoun's first address to the US congress (N. Abi Antoun, interview September 23, 2014). Simon Abi Ramia and Pierre Raffoul in France and Australia, respectively, both spoke of their ability, including other FPM members too, to establish important links with influential political parties and Members of Parliament, which assisted them in lobbying for their cause and supporting the movement in Lebanon. This is to say that FPM activists in the diaspora possessed the education, skills and professions characteristic of the middle class, but also enjoyed solid social relationships with members of the political and business elite (ibid.). The ability to forge strong relationships with the elite of other states and then activate those relationships to advance the cause of the FPM speaks of the sound social standing of FPM activists, one that roots them firmly in the middle class.

In spite of the existence of activists from various sectarian groups in the FPM, the movement was composed of predominantly Christian supporters. However, this predominantly Christian constituency did not inform its strategies in the period 1990–2005, chiefly because the movement did not participate within state institutions, such as Parliament or the Council of Ministers, and thus did not have to make decisions about distributing resources to its supporters. As a result, the movement was able to maintain its secular reputation by framing issues in a non-sectarian manner. In the post-2005 period, FPM participation within these state institutions obliged it to respond to the demands of its mainly Christian constituency, which made it shift away from its non-sectarian strategies toward the adoption of some sectarian strategies that served that constituency (as will be discussed in Chapter 5).

Furthermore, the FPM had a following that emerged from the middle class both inside and outside Lebanon. Apart from the approximately 3000 activists who were active in the FPM in the period 1990–2005, the movement was not able to show its popular base of support in numeric terms until the by-elections of 2003 in the Baabda-Aley district. It reflects a middle-class movement chiefly because of the activists that operated within specific institutions, such as students on university campuses and lawyers, engineers and teachers inside professional syndicates, which, in turn, helped incubate the movement and sustained it throughout the period 1990–2005.

The next part of the chapter offers an explanation of the impact of Lebanon's complex political economy on influencing the rise of the FPM in the period 1990–2005. It also discusses in some detail why the middle class reacted to the Lebanese government's policies and how that had a bearing on the shape and form of activism in post-war Lebanon.

Part II: Lebanon's Political Economy Shapes Activism

This section will show that the FPM was able to emerge in several syndicates and across civil society due to the neoliberal policies espoused by Lebanese governments throughout the period 1990–2005. These policies complied with the structural adjustment programs of the World Bank and the International Monetary Fund (IMF), but had the perverse effect of assuaging industrialists at the expense of the salaried strata of workers. While the FPM did not express a clear ideological stance on economic affairs, it tended to embrace the cause of its middle-class membership, such as school teachers, university students and lawyers, many of whom were affected by the Lebanese government's policies. Since many businesspeople refrained from expressing their support for the FPM for fear of punitive measures exacted by the Lebanese political elite sympathetic to Syria in the period 1990–2005, they remained unable to steer the movement's policy and ideological agenda. Therefore, the FPM tilted more clearly toward the interests of the salaried strata of the middle class rather than private business owners.

This reality reveals that the activism launched by the FPM was not only directed at the Lebanese political elite for their close relationship to Syria, but also driven by the economic concern that such governmental policies skewed in favor of the financial oligarchy of Lebanon were nibbling at the rights and benefits of members of the middle class and labor. While labor, in both the public and private sectors, aimed to achieve pay hikes, fringe benefits and other working conditions, members of the Association of Lebanese Industrialists and other business associations dismissed employees' demands on the grounds that fulfilling them would impose high costs on businesses, which might render them less competitive or force their closure. With these conflicting interests as a backdrop,

Lebanese governments had to mediate between various interest groups as well as uphold policies that could stabilize the national currency, promote growth, encourage foreign direct investment in the country and finance the enormous costs associated with post-war reconstruction.

Therefore, a close examination of the nature of the post-war Lebanese political economy can help shed light on the reason why the messages of the FPM resonated in syndicates and unions, universities and other parts of civil society. This lends credence to the notion that the FPM's emergence was intertwined with an effort to effect positive freedom in Lebanon, and not only calling for the withdrawal of Syrian troops.

In the immediate post-war period, political instability, flawed monetary and economic policies, as well as uncertainty about the future rendered the prospects for economic recovery quite foggy in Lebanon (Baroudi 1998). Following a period of economic decline, Prime Minister Rafik Hariri was nominated to form his first government in 1992 with a definite order of economic priorities, which included reversing the deterioration in the foreign exchange rate for the Lebanese lira, curbing inflation and launching a massive reconstruction program (ibid.). While the cabinets formed by Rafik Hariri were not preoccupied with policies to improve the livelihoods of the poor, they nevertheless believed that economic benefits would trickle down to the poorer strata of society as a result of the government's program to stimulate economic growth through private investment (Young 1996, p. 34).

The Hariri-sponsored plan for development, which was designed by the Council for Development and Reconstruction and presented to Parliament in 1993 as the Horizons 2000 plan, aimed to boost the Lebanese economy by encouraging government and private investment. According to this plan, government spending for reconstruction and infrastructural development would amount to \$13 billion between 1993 and 2002 (Young 1996, p. 34). It was met with a barrage of criticism for disenfranchising the poor in Lebanese society from a reasonable share of economic benefits, and for adopting economic principles that imposed a heavy toll on education and vocational training (Butter 1995; Young 1996, p. 35).

Therefore, the neoliberal policies espoused by the Hariri governments, and perhaps all governments formed thereafter, placed the state on a collision course with interest groups that expected official support in the form of social welfare or tax exemptions and subsidies for industrial activity. Baumann (2016) notes that neoliberalism in Lebanon implied no rolling back of state borders or restricting the role of the state to the minimal sphere of security and law enforcement, which is the conventional understanding of the philosophy. Instead, Hariri's policies were dubbed neoliberal for endorsing the economic principle of privatizing state-held enterprises, deregulating the economy and cutting spending on social welfare programs.

Perhaps the impact of this neoliberal orientation adopted by most post-war Lebanese governments was exacerbated by Lebanon's consistently negative balance of trade, which has been the case since 1990. In the post-war period, the country's imports witnessed noticeable growth necessitated by reconstruction and facilitated by inflows of foreign capital (Baroudi 2005). For all the years since 1990, exports never balanced imports, which resulted in constant trade deficits (ibid.). Some of the most egregious signs of poor economic performance appeared in Lebanon's industrial sector, whose imports of capital goods never exceeded 3% of total imports during all the years up to 2005 (ibid.), which, in retrospect, forecasted a persistent trade deficit if Lebanese industry and goods were not produced and sold with a comparative advantage in relation to their counterparts.

Lebanon's current account, calculated as the sum of the balance of trade, net income and direct payments (revealing the transfer of capital), was consistently in negative figures throughout the period 2002–2016. A current account is usually considered in balance when residents have enough to fund all purchases in the country. The people, businesses and government are the residents. According to this definition, funds encompass income and savings. Purchases include consumer spending, business growth and government infrastructure spending. Therefore, Lebanon could not fund its purchases, since it consistently experienced a negative current account balance of payments (see Table 3.1).

Alternative methods of income generation had to be explored because Lebanese governments were encumbered by the country's persistent trade deficit and vast sums were required to shore up Hariri's Horizons 2000 plan. With this economic scenario prevailing, defenders of Hariri argued that the former prime minister's infrastructural economic policies, bids for privatization, the stabilization of the Lebanese lira, cuts in taxes and the introduction of a value added tax (VAT), which was highly unpopular, were imperative for the wellbeing of the Lebanese economy and for the restoration of international confidence in the Lebanese economy (Nizameddine 2006).

Table 3.1 .

Year	*Exports of goods and services (current US$)*	*Imports of goods and services (current US$)*	*Net balance of trade (current US$)*	*Current account balance (balance of payments, current US$)*
1990	511,008,099	2,836,044,898	−2,325,036,799	
1991	587,982,910	3,748,891,033	−3,160,908,123	
1992	631,003,676	4,207,024,670	−3,576,020,994	
1993	729,016,719	5,335,122,364	−4,606,105,645	
1994	755,509,732	5,989,999,913	−5,234,490,181	
1995	1,266,386,351	7,304,200,110	−6,037,813,759	
1996	1,758,689,127	7,563,885,156	−5,805,196,029	
1997	2,289,054,888	7,490,743,748	−5,201,688,860	
1998	2,373,803,864	7,063,369,153	−4,689,565,289	
1999	2,445,876,364	6,391,244,718	−3,945,368,354	
2000	2,447,097,844	6,202,985,075	−3,755,887,231	
2001	2,754,228,856	7,051,409,619	−4,297,180,763	
2002	3,083,250,415	6,692,537,313	−3,609,286,898	−4,540,835,503
2003	3,361,194,030	7,501,824,212	−4,140,630,182	−5,138,387,089
2004	7,590,713,101	12,217,578,773	−4,626,865,672	−4,405,595,914
2005	8,050,414,594	12,464,344,942	−4,413,930,348	−2,748,000,878
2006	7,994,693,201	12,636,152,570	−4,641,459,369	−1,116,363,496
2007	9,395,024,876	15,498,507,463	−6,103,482,587	−1,604,778,256
2008	11,390,507,869	19,869,814,135	−8,479,306,266	−4,102,657,996
2009	11,955,419,928	20,294,686,989	−8,339,267,061	−6,740,936,422
2010	13,751,783,155	23,142,116,397	−9,390,333,242	−7,552,051,024
2011	14,804,320,748	25,722,307,896	−10,917,987,148	−5,407,718,159
2012	14,956,192,016	26,623,896,740	−11,667,704,724	−10,319,573,510
2013	14,641,471,871	26,925,156,435	−12,283,684,564	−11,954,333,350
2014	13,200,881,072	25,783,149,269	−12,582,268,197	−12,614,550,896
2015	13,304,875,566	23,336,338,282	−10,031,462,716	−8,645,862,033
2016	12,644,960,396	23,370,607,170	−10,725,646,774	−10,555,373,023
2017	12,236,685,012	24,039,327,402	−11,802,642,390	

Source Derived from World Bank indicators

The Lebanese government borrowed money from other states at international donor conferences hosted for the purpose of boosting confidence in Lebanon's economy, and this was on top of the increasing amounts it owed local commercial Lebanese banks. Hariri helped stage three international donor conferences known as the Paris One, Paris Two and Paris Three conferences. In the Paris Two conference in 2002, for instance, participating states were asked to support Lebanon in restructuring its domestic debts at lower rates of interest (Nizameddine 2006). Saudi Arabia, France and other states together provided $2.5 billion in soft loans (ibid.). However, as a consequence of the Paris Two conference, the Lebanese government had to fulfill the conditions of cuts in public spending and the privatization of key services, including electricity.

By embarking on this course of economic indebtedness, Lebanese economic policies were gradually becoming subservient to the structural adjustment programs of the World Bank and the IMF. In other words, a considerable part of Lebanon's budget had to be allocated for the service of debt and the interest accrued by that debt, instead of promoting potentially productive sectors of the economy. By 1999, Lebanon had been spending approximately 47% of its national budget on debt servicing and was heading toward unsustainable debt, which is debt that cannot be paid without choking the country's budget and economy, and thus renders debtor countries prey to the policies of external parties (Naiman 1999).

Even subsidies that aimed to decrease the cost of the electricity bill for the less advantaged segments of Lebanese society end up servicing the interests of the more developed parts of the country, such as Beirut with its daily power disruption of a few hours, at the expense of rural districts of South Lebanon, the Beqaa or Mount Lebanon, which experience longer power shortages (Verdeil 2018). This is not to mention the emergence of private suppliers of electricity whose operations increase corruption by encouraging the practices of lobbying, bribing and consolidating oligopolies in this hybrid sector (Stel and Naudé 2016). Such government policies, skewed in favor of political and financial oligarchies, deepen social cleavages and fail to cure the socioeconomic ills afflicting Lebanese society, except partially and temporarily with palliative remedies.

With these economic conditions as a backdrop, it can be understood why criticism of Lebanese governments during the period 1990–2005 generated political traction that mobilized discontented segments of Lebanese society, regardless of whether they participated in corrective political activism or not. Because school teachers exhibited the greatest militancy among public-sector employees, they were able to achieve their demands for a new wage and salary scale by staging strikes or by refusing to correct the official baccalaureate high school exams, which kept the fate of around 60,000 students in the dark and simultaneously pressured the government to make concessions; this was in addition to threatening to boycott the 1996 parliamentary elections (Baroudi 1998). Therefore, the role of the FPM as a movement active in a number of syndicates and unions also allowed it to highlight government failures in responding to a number of pressing social and economic issues.

As of 1996 and continuing until 2017, Lebanese governments froze wages for employees in the private and public sectors due to neoliberal policy promises made to the World Bank and IMF. The government also attempted to appease Lebanese businesspeople whose industries failed to develop a comparative edge over the quality of output produced by their trading partners (Baroudi 2000). It reduced these industrialists' obligatory contributions to the National Social Security Fund, granted them access to government-subsidized loans, and lifted all custom duties from raw material imports for industrial use in late 2000 (Baroudi 2005).

With consistently poor rankings on Transparency International's Corruption Perceptions Index, Lebanese governments never ceased to adopt policies that reflected the interests of the country's influential political, economic and religious elite. This orientation often had political officials exploiting their formal offices and overstepping their constitutional prerogatives to advance the interests of their clientele, sectarian community and political party (Leenders 2012; Cammet 2014; Salloukh et al. 2015). The Lebanese elite harnessed such a political system in which they vouchsafed favors to supporters to ensure their political longevity, but in the process they generated a mutually reinforcing corrupt system that incentivized its members to operate according to these distorted parameters.

The combined effect of the Lebanese government's neoliberal policies that disadvantaged the salaried strata, the elite's clientelistic practices, corruption and the disenfranchisement of political opposition leaders (such as Michel Aoun and Samir Jeajea) from the post-war political process generated momentum for concerted collective activism by those segments of society who felt marginalized. As such, the FPM emerged not only to call for the withdrawal of Syrian troops from Lebanon, but also to highlight the faults of this political system, which it criticized by suggesting non-sectarian proposals.

With these factors in mind, it becomes easier to understand why the FPM emerged in the way it did. It is time to describe that emergence in some detail.

Part III: The FPM Emerges from a Dispersed to a United National Movement

Because Lebanon had been governed by a political elite who adopted sectarian strategies that attempted to prevent the representation of some political competitors, including the FPM, within the country's political system—that is, within Parliament and the Council of Ministers—it is crucial to keep a vigilant eye on the political opportunities upon which activists built that resulted in the rise of the FPM in the period 1990–2005. Political opportunities are those "consistent—but not necessarily formal or permanent—dimensions of the political environment that provide incentives for people to undertake collective action by affecting their expectations for success or failure" (Tarrow 1994, p. 85). Such political opportunities may include the instability of elite alignments that impact a polity, the support of elite allies, the relaxation of state repression and the degree of openness in the institutional political system (see Eisinger 1973; McAdam 1982, 1996, Chap. 1; Meyer and Staggenborg 1996; Hipsher 1998, Chap. 7; Meyer 2007). Here the approach of social movement scholars is adopted, who advocate examining individual perceptions to understand which political events can be considered as opportunities for the rise of a movement (Kurzman 1996; Suh 2001).

Therefore, with the FPM and other Christian parties boycotting the 1992 and 1996 rounds of parliamentary elections, the movement restricted itself to operating outside formal state institutions. As a result, the FPM sought the political opportunities afforded by student elections on university campuses and nominated candidates in the elections of professional syndicates, such as those for engineers, doctors, teachers and so on. This initially limited the movement's emergence to a presence in civil society. However, when movement activists later seized the opportunity of the official ban on the FPM being lifted and participated in municipal elections and parliamentary by-elections, the movement began to gain visibility on a national level. Its activism became more publicly expressed; that is, by moving its collective activity outside the confines of university campuses to the streets and public spaces. In addition to political occurrences favoring the rise of the movement in Lebanon, the existence of sympathetic activists in the democratic systems of France, Australia and the USA, among others, helped support the activities of the FPM in Lebanon, thus contributing to the rise of the movement throughout the period 1990–2005.

Rise in Civil Society: Activism on University Campuses and in Syndicates

Following the ousting of Aoun from the Baabda Palace on October 13, 1990 in a Syrian-led military operation, the Syrian regime shored up a Lebanese political elite who gave in to their interests in Lebanon. These members of the political elite adopted a set of sectarian strategies that helped ensure their standing in Lebanese politics, supported their sectarian mobilization of supporters and helped them exclude political opponents, mainly the FPM and Lebanese Forces, from the post-war political process. As a result of the partial exclusion of Aoun's supporters from Lebanese politics—that is to say, their not being represented in Parliament or the Council of Ministers but active among the youth and members of certain professions—activists who were supportive of Aoun seized other political opportunities, such as student elections on university campuses and electoral races within professional syndicates, which inevitably led to the rise of the FPM in civil society.

With their leader in exile and officially banned by the Lebanese government, Aoun's supporters perceived university campus elections as a political opportunity to emerge as a movement (L. Chakour, interview September 29, 2014). Approximately 50% of the sample of FPM activists interviewed for this book had been involved, as either organizers or candidates, in the student-government elections held at their university campuses; moreover, the other half of the sample of interviewees regarded the student movement emanating from universities as a vital component of FPM's collective activity in Lebanon.

The young people who supported Aoun participated in student-government elections on their university campuses to promote movement activism, similar to the way in which the Chinese pro-democracy movement used university campuses for political mobilization (Zhao 1998; Snow and Soule 2010, pp. 99–100). The opportunity of student elections had a marked impact on the shape of the movement, its legitimacy and access to resources, which helped the FPM emerge in the period immediately after Aoun's exile in 1990.

Student-government elections helped young activists emerge in their respective universities and connect with counterparts across various private and public university campuses throughout Lebanon. Initially, Lebanese youth, who had expressed their support for the movement in the immediate post-1990 phase, found themselves utterly confused regarding the way they were going to engage in FPM collective activity, since the challenges imposed on the movement by the political elite isolated those activists from coordinating collective activity on a national level in the absence of an FPM central command. However, with the participation of Lebanese youth in the student-government elections held at their university campuses, the FPM began gaining political visibility, albeit while operating in loose and decentralized groups (see *Annahar*, January 29, 1997, p. 22; December 12, 1997, p. 23; April 3, 1998, p. 23; December 15, 1999, p. 19; January 26, 2000, p. 19).

Ziad Abs, an FPM activist whose university, American University of Beirut, had held student-government elections as early as 1991 in the post-war period, explained why student-government elections proved important for the rise of FPM groups across various universities in Lebanon. He stated: "We did not have communications… When we ran for elections and won—relatively speaking the engineering school and a few seats in other places, the issue was published in the papers. After it went public, we began connecting with other groups at other universities… I remember at the time, Joseph Njeim contacts me from BUC; Fadi Massaad then contacts me from NDU; Liwa Chakour contacts me from the Lebanese University. Rami Sarhan was with us in the medical school; through Rami, we communicated with Walid Achkar at Balamand University" (interview October 31, 2014).

These university campus elections also constituted an opportunity for the rise of the movement because they granted participating candidates a form of representative legitimacy usually restricted to those parties that participate in national elections. Since the FPM was a politically banned movement in post-1990 Lebanon, the victories it scored in student-government elections provided its candidates with a form of legitimacy to represent the movement both on and off campus. Antoine Nasrallah, an FPM activist whose activities began at the Lebanese University, pointedly remarked: "We ran the first student council elections at the Faculty of Law. We won 34 out of 36 seats in elections. I became head of the student council at the Faculty of Law. This issue provided me two legitimacies. I had internal legitimacy on the university campus as the head of the student council. I also had external legitimacy to speak with other parties outside the university" (interview October 6, 2014).

The external legitimacy to which Antoine Nasrallah referred was vital for the emergence of the FPM because it granted activists the ability to represent the ideas and positions of their movement within a formal institutional setting, as head of the student council for example, which helped them spread their ideas and converse with other political parties regarding issues of freedom, sovereignty and independence. Moreover, those FPM activists who gained a seat on elected student councils enjoyed, to varying degrees, the protection of their universities, which shielded the movement from attempts to destroy it, at least on campus.

All FPM activists who had participated in university campus elections believed that achieving a majority in the student government at their particular academic institution proved vital for the rise of the FPM, because such a victory provided them with formal institutional access to the university's facilities, which in turn gave them a pool of resources essential for movement activity. From the vantage point of the majority in the student government, FPM activists could determine the size of the budgets of every club on the university campus, which allowed them to favorably finance the FPM on campus, which often operated under a disguised name, for instance Social Club, Lebanese Patriotic Movement, Free Student Movement, Freedom Club and others, and also to support other clubs that shared their common values. Moreover, they gained access to photocopying facilities and office space at their universities, which helped them print pamphlets opposing the government, stow them safely and discuss their method of distribution, whether during the day or night and in which particular areas (as will be analyzed in the next chapter).

Therefore, seizing the political opportunity of student-government elections contributed positively to the rise of the FPM because it provided the movement with access to the formal institutional setting of the university, representative legitimacy as a movement enjoying popularity among young people, and a pool of resources crucial for the organization of FPM collective activity. This helped FPM activists organize collective political activities that were opposed to the Lebanese government, such as large-scale pamphlet-distribution campaigns on Army Day throughout the country in the period immediately following the defeat of Aoun in 1990, which alarmed the new political establishment by underscoring the extent of opposition to its political decisions (L. Chakour, interview September 29, 2014). It also allowed the FPM to connect more easily with its supporters among students, especially new ones, through the institutional existence of both club and student government, whose social events were a simultaneous hub for social and political FPM gatherings.

At the same time, the existence of Aoun sympathizers within the membership of professional syndicates constituted an opportunity for the emergence of the FPM and the backbone of FPM support throughout the period 1990–2005, since its ideas and reformist outlook resonated with middle-class professionals. Elections to professional syndicates proved vital for the emergence of the FPM, because they provided a political opening that the movement seized, especially in the early 1990s when such openings were not abundant in Lebanon (N. Aoun, interview September 18, 2014). Therefore, FPM activists took these opportunities to emerge within syndicates and on a civil society level, thus making the FPM's presence in Lebanon more visible and effective.

The initial political support received by the FPM in an electoral syndicate race was in the syndicate of engineers from Hezbollah in 1993. The dialog between a pro-FPM group called the Free Political Club and Hezbollah regarding the Lebanese "mithakiyya" or social charter, and the Aounist affiliations of the former, culminated in support for the FPM candidate in this syndicate. Naaman Abi Antoun, an FPM activist, remarked: "Nawaf Al-Moussawi [a Hezbollah official] said we would welcome you as the free political club to discuss the theoretical discussions regarding the Lebanese mithakiyya. But regarding your Aounist affiliations, we would have to discuss politics in our other current talks. Based on this relationship, we were able to nominate Hikmat Dib in the syndicate of engineers. Hezbollah supported the elections then" (interview September 23, 2014). In the early 1990s, both the FPM and Hezbollah shared a severe dissatisfaction with the document of national reconciliation known as the Taif Accords, which had discounted their political outlook in restructuring the post-war political order of Lebanon. As a result, the ongoing dialog between some FPM members and Hezbollah translated into a political understanding that led the latter to support the FPM candidate, Hikmat Dib, in the engineer's syndicate elections in 1993.

Whether running for positions in the doctors', engineers', lawyers' or teachers' syndicates, inter alia, FPM candidates always had a competitive edge due to their agenda that promised to safeguard the rights of union members and advance reforms to meet the interests of those members. This aspect of union work was able to draw support for FPM candidates beyond the natural affiliates of the movement. However, FPM syndicate or union members never failed to express the urgent need to attain the freedom, sovereignty and independence of Lebanon, even when working to advance the interests of their syndicates. For example, the head of the doctors' syndicate, Dr. Fayek Younnis, who was a clear FPM sympathizer, mentioned in 1996 that the purity of the FPM's nationalism did not require attestation from anyone (*Annahar*, December 31, 1996, p. 7). He condemned the concentrated campaigns against the FPM and opposition supporters on the basis of their political positions, and believed that constantly targeting these individuals did not help achieve national harmony and integration (ibid.).

Therefore, the ability to fuse both a reform agenda for syndicate work and a national political outlook helped FPM candidates emerge in various syndicates in Lebanon. Seizing the political opportunity of syndicate elections, either through the direct nomination of an FPM candidate or by swaying electoral results, helped the FPM to assert its presence in civil society and rendered it better able to pressure the Lebanese government through the institution of the syndicate. Winning syndicate elections helped nurture the rise of the FPM because those syndicate members who sympathized with their political outlook often rushed to the defense of activists, who were incriminated by the Lebanese state for their political affiliation with the movement, broadly defending freedom as a right and indirectly supporting the FPM as a political movement.

Relaxed Controls, Elite Divisions and Elections Turn the FPM National

The issue faced by the FPM in the early 1990s was that its emergence was restricted to the domain of civil society, such as on university campuses, in syndicates and in towns and villages, because the available political opportunities at the time only allowed for the emergence of the movement in these particular areas, since the movement had decided to boycott parliamentary elections. However, in the latter half of the 1990s, FPM collective activity began gaining national visibility in Lebanon due to the political opportunities the movement seized, such as relaxation of some state controls, divisions among the political elite and municipal elections. These political opportunities made possible the emergence of FPM collective activity in streets and public spaces, thus contributing significantly to the FPM's emergence throughout Lebanon.

The relative relaxation of state controls in Lebanon by 1996 helped the FPM to rise more unambiguously on a national scale. The analytical treatment of state controls is a controversial issue because of the nature of the state and the fluid meaning of this term in Lebanese politics. First, due to the existence of a quarreling political elite and volatile political alliances, the elite's employment of sectarian and clientelistic strategies to mobilize supporters and a set of fragmented institutions, the Lebanese state cannot be regarded as a unitary actor with solid political preferences (see Leenders 2012; Salloukh et al. 2015). As a result, the discussion of elite strategies to involve or exclude the FPM from political debate may provide a more accurate description of Lebanese politics, as opposed to a strict focus on the "state" as a unitary actor. In this scenario, Lebanese politics presented challenges to the FPM, but could simultaneously offer opportunities for its emergence. Secondly, the term "controls" does not mean that the FPM was fully infiltrated and manipulated by some political elites. On the contrary, had this been the case, the movement would not have been able to survive and launch collective activities throughout the period 1990–2005 in Lebanon.

In post-war Lebanese politics, state controls included the five-year media ban imposed on Aoun, the detainment of FPM activists for crossing red lines in terms of organizing for mass collective activity on the streets (those red lines were determined by the Lebanese political elite and Syria and changed constantly depending on prevailing political circumstances), and other elite strategies that aimed to maintain the dominance of the political elite while excluding members of the opposition. Despite all these challenges, FPM activists took advantage of their emergence in a number of avenues in civil society to coalesce as a national movement.

Although some semblance of organizational structure representing Aoun and his movement had existed since 1992, the actual public opening of an FPM office in 1996 marked a significant leap forward. The five-year media ban imposed on Aoun upon his expatriation to France had expired by 1996, leaving the media freer to consider interviewing the FPM leader. Moreover, some FPM activists believe that the Lebanese political elite had taken a conscious decision to decrease their checks on the movement, believing that a movement active in civil society, universities and syndicates, and whose activist membership comprised university students, could not inflict harm on the interests of the de jure government backed by Syria (A. Aoun, interview March 12, 2014).

This relative decrease of controls influenced the FPM's organizational form by culminating in a central command that allowed activism to emerge on the streets. FPM activists agree that the opening of an office provided the movement with a greater avenue for the organization of collective political activity. FPM activism, which had been restricted to universities, syndicates, towns and villages, albeit operating in a clandestine manner, now had the political opportunity of relatively greater openness. This was embodied in the opening of an FPM office, which marked the right moment to step up the magnitude and political impact of the movement's protests by going public.

This relative political openness leading to the first official FPM headquarters presented the movement with an opportunity that allowed for more coordination between the newly established central command and the decentralized groups operating in various parts of civil society, such as universities, syndicates, towns and villages. Although political conditions by the latter half of the 1990s allowed for the emergence of a central FPM command in Lebanon, the movement maintained the organization of activists in small, decentralized groups for mobilization purposes, as will be further explained in the next chapter.

This decrease in state controls influenced the rise of FPM activism on the streets because it provided latitude for the organization of large-scale protests. It became more evident when an interview with Aoun from exile, scheduled to appear on the Lebanese channel MTV, was banned by Lebanese state forces on December 14, 1997, an incident that caused enraged FPM activists to transport their activism from its concentration in universities and small groups to larger-scale collective activity on the streets and in public spaces (see Zourob, December 15, 1997, p. 8; Hajjar, December 17, 1997, p. 9). Due to the magnitude of the protest, which was unusual for post-war Lebanon, Samir Kassir, a renowned Lebanese journalist, credited this demonstration with the achievement of breaking the state prohibition on protests that had prevailed since the beginning of the post-war era (December 19, 1997, p. 1), believing that it would have an impact on Lebanese politics.

However, it was the activists' perception of relative political openness that provided the main opportunity leading them to open an FPM office, coordinate more closely and subsequently take to the streets in such numbers following the banning of Aoun's interview. Without the political opportunity of the relaxation of state controls, the organization or structures that facilitated the emergence of the movement on the streets could not have enjoyed the liberty to take shape in the first place. Therefore, the FPM's ability to emerge on the streets is inextricably linked to the degree of political openness that Lebanon experienced toward the latter half of the 1990s.

Moreover, divisions among the political elite, such as the break between Michel and Gabriel Murr resulting from their diverging political orientations, presented an important opportunity for the rise of FPM activism. In the late 1990s, a rift began to form between Michel Murr, Interior Minister, and his brother Gabriel, the owner of Murr Television (MTV). The reason behind this disagreement lay in Gabriel's development of business ties with Premier Hariri, Michel Murr's nemesis (Abdelnour 2003). As a result, MTV began airing reports critical of the government and interviewing popular opposition figures, becoming the first media station to interview Michel Aoun in 1997 (ibid.). In August 2001, MTV broadcast tales of torture and beatings of FPM activists by internal security forces, which had launched a massive campaign against the movement (ibid.).

In April 2002, the death of MP Albert Moukheiber transformed the by-election to fill his vacant parliamentary seat into an inter-family showdown between Gabriel and Mirna Murr—Gabriel's niece and Michel's daughter. Receiving the backing of the FPM and other opposition groups, Gabriel won the elections, but had his short-lived position quickly rescinded under the pretext that his electoral campaign violated media laws, thus highlighting the ability of his brother Michel to maneuver and manipulate the political system (ibid.).

The Murr family division had a positive impact on the emergence of the FPM by providing the movement with relatively more coverage on MTV in comparison with what its activity had received in the first half of the 1990s, and also with more support from Gabriel Murr. Since Gabriel possessed a high level of technical expertise, given his ownership of MTV, he provided some media assistance to the FPM. Roland ElKhoury, who was an FPM activist at Notre Dame University (NDU), mentioned that "The first interview with the General from Paris on a university campus in Lebanon occurred in NDU. Gabriel Murr helped us organize the technical issues of the interview. This was in 1999" (interview September 26, 2014).

Moreover, FPM activists who participated in organizing the famous anti-regime protests on August 7, 2001 testified to the role MTV played in communicating their message to the broader Lebanese population, which produced a synergic effect. Considering that the political division within the Murr family coincided with the state's relative relaxation of repression of the FPM, the movement seized both opportunities to increase its standing on a national level between 1997 and 2001. In addition to these opportunities, Gabriel Murr's victory in the by-elections for the vacant parliamentary seat in 2002, albeit short-lived, confirmed the extensive presence of the FPM and its supporters among Lebanese Christians, since the movement had supported Gabriel in his electoral campaign in the Matn district, which was home to a predominantly Christian voter base. These political opportunities provided the movement with greater freedom of mobility during this period, allowing FPM activism to emerge more visibly in various parts of Lebanon.

In addition to relaxed controls and divisions among the elite, the opportunity to run FPM candidates in both the municipal elections of 1998 and the single-candidate parliamentary by-elections of 2003 contributed to the emergence of the FPM on a national scale. Although the movement did not participate effectively within state institutions till 2005, this opportunity allowed it to gain visibility nationally. After the FPM attempted to seize these particular opportunities, it became a movement that not only expressed political thought on the streets, but also one that resorted to institutional tactics, such as municipal elections to voice political concerns.

By seizing the opportunity to participate in municipal council elections throughout Lebanon in 1998, the FPM witnessed its first rise on a nationwide scale that came via public office. Given the inclination of the government to rig election results in favor of its preferred candidates, the exact number of victorious FPM and opposition candidates remained a contested issue. However, the FPM emerged more unambiguously in this particular electoral race because it showcased its ability to nominate candidates in a multitude of municipal councils across Lebanon and put forward a reform platform for municipal elections, defying pro-government voices that attempted to portray it as a movement lacking popular support. Moreover, with the promulgation of the official results of victorious candidates in the municipal electoral race, it would have been close to impossible to hide the FPM inclinations of the victorious candidates from the local community that voted for them, since the community's prior knowledge of the candidate must have entailed some information regarding their political leanings.

Seizing the opportunity of municipal elections proved vital for the FPM's emergence because the movement proposed a modern reformist platform that made people aware of its positive contributions to political life in Lebanon, and thus incentivized individuals to join its ranks. Hiam Alkoussaifi, a journalist reporting on FPM activity, analyzed its 16-page reformist platform for municipal elections, believing that it positioned the FPM as a green movement rather than a strictly political one (February 13, 1998, p. 6). The FPM's municipal platform outlined a definition of municipalities and their essential role, conditions of municipalities, municipal priorities, the prerogatives of municipal councils and their presiding members, and the principles and personal qualifications of the members and heads of municipal councils. It also concentrated on municipal initiatives for the preservation of identity, the environment as a human right, expedited environmental measures, the transformation of waste for municipal benefit, municipal health measures, infrastructure and development works, social affairs, cultural affairs, sports affairs, productive sectors, budget and income and municipal administration.

The FPM platform for the municipal elections of 1998 clearly demonstrated that it was not strictly a political opposition movement, but one that bore a clear reform agenda that succeeded in attracting people into its ranks. George Hadad, a lawyer and FPM activist, commented: "Environmental and development topics are at the forefront of our platform. We don't politicize this operation, but the development aspect cannot be separated from politics because the authorities confiscate municipal money and that's a political action. We want to return this money so municipalities can be able to resolve their problems" (Alkoussaifi, February 13, 1998, p. 6). The majority of FPM activists interviewed for this study consider participation in the 1998 municipal elections as an important point in the history of the movement, because it was its first participation in elections held within the formal setting of the state, albeit only within local institutions. Since FPM candidates were now vying for positions on municipal councils, they could more overtly discuss projects that aimed to preserve Lebanese identity from the overwhelming influence of Syria, development issues pertaining to infrastructure and the environment, and ways to fight the corruption that festered in state institutions.

Even in subsequent rounds of municipal elections, such as those in 2004, the FPM advanced a 22-page election manifesto that dealt with a comprehensive list of developmental and political issues. It outlined ways to deal with pressing environmental concerns, heritage preservation and, more importantly, the allocation of an annual budget for municipal councils, which, in turn, annoyed the existing political elite, as this call for a decentralization of authority threatened to weaken their control over the affairs of municipalities (Raad 2004). The movement responded to political comments that dismissed it as simply aimed at Syria and nothing else by advancing a reformist platform in municipal elections, which contrasted sharply with the random electoral campaigns of the traditional political class.

In the 1998 round of municipal elections, the FPM chose to form alliances with candidates whose aim was to combat corruption, promote transparency and integrity, and hold an unyielding stance regarding Lebanese sovereignty, freedom and independence (Frangiyeh, May 1, 1998, p. 6). These topics were among the main factors that had initially triggered individuals to join the ranks of the FPM. Therefore, since municipal elections had provided the political opportunity for the emergence of the movement within the setting of a state institution, the possibility of being able to implement the FPM vision led activists to perceive the municipal elections of 1998 as an important opportunity for the rise of their movement, albeit within the confines of municipal councils.

The FPM also seized the opportunity of nominating Hikmat Dib, an FPM activist, as their candidate for the by-election to fill the parliamentary seat left vacant due to the death of MP Pierre Helou in the Baabda-Aley district in 2003. Hikmat Dib did not win the elections due to the political elite's redrawing of the Baabda-Aley electoral district to minimize the impact of Christian voters, who were believed to be supportive of the FPM. Yet, the FPM was able to compete with Henry Helou, son of the late parliamentarian, despite his backing by Hezbollah, the Progressive Socialist Party and a number of Christian parties, as explained earlier in the chapter. By revealing the extent of the FPM candidate's popularity—that is, 25,291 votes for the FPM candidate along with 73% of the Christian vote in the district, in comparison with the victorious candidate's 28,597 votes—the movement gained greater political visibility, which positioned it as an increasingly influential player in Lebanese politics (Gambill 2003). In order to nominate a candidate for parliamentary elections in Lebanon, political movements require considerable sums of money to pay for electoral campaigns, advertisements and other campaign-related costs. The manner in which the FPM gathered these sums from various individuals highlighted the commitment of FPM activists and supporters to their movement, and made sure these resources were channeled adequately to capitalize on the political opportunity of parliamentary elections.

The FPM case also emphasizes, especially in the period following Aoun's expatriation from Lebanon, the importance of political opportunities, such as student-government elections on university campuses and elections taking place at professional syndicates, in the rise of the movement within civil society. However, in the period following 1996, the relaxation of state controls, divisions among influential members of the political class, support provided by the elite and participation in municipal elections were important political opportunities that helped the FPM emerge more evidently on a national scale, from a presence that had been almost strictly confined to civil society.

Activists Abroad Support the FPM at Home

The active role of Aoun's supporters in countries such as France helped build the roots of a supportive movement abroad to assist in the FPM's emergence in Lebanon. This proved to be vital, considering that foreign states provided a suitable avenue for freedom of expression and assembly. When examining the FPM, the analysis needs to encapsulate the activity of the movement in countries such as France, the USA and Australia, which hosted large Lebanese communities that sympathized with the cause of the FPM.

The democratic political order in France provided a wide margin of freedom for the rise of the FPM, also known as the RPL in France. First, the support extended by a number of the French elite made possible the rise of the FPM in the country. Figures such as Frédéric Deniau and Jack Barro, who facilitated activities including the logistics of the FPM in France, helped to facilitate the rise of the movement (S. Abi Ramia, interview November 21, 2014). Secondly, the emergence of the RPL in France helped shed light on the activities of the FPM in Lebanon, including the arrests of activists, and conveyed the information to human rights organizations and other international parties (ibid.). Upon his arrival in France, Aoun found an organizational structure that assisted him in voicing his opposition to the political state of affairs in Lebanon, albeit from a distance. Thirdly, FPM members in Lebanon, especially in the period 1990–2005, took advantage of the democratic political order in France by traveling there to attend large FPM conferences that could not be held in Lebanon. This included the 1994 Lebanese National Conference, at which the decision was taken to spread FPM activism from syndicates to the streets of Lebanon (Ghanem ElBonn, June 9, 1994, p. 4; June 13, 1994, p. 5; June 14, 1994, p. 4; *Annahar*, June 11, 1994, p. 3). Therefore, the emergence of the FPM inside Lebanon was inextricably linked to its rise outside the country because of the democracy enjoyed by countries such as France, which provided a forum for FPM activists to meet.

The political weight of the Lebanese diaspora was also an essential factor that was able to bring about the rise of the FPM outside Lebanon. In Australia, for example, the Lebanese community did not strictly rely on support provisioned by the elite, but actively participated in Australian national parliamentary elections, on both provincial and federal levels, to promote those candidates who agreed to support the Lebanese cause represented by the FPM. By helping candidates to electoral victory on the federal level, the FPM in Australia was able to break the travel ban on Aoun by convincing the government to send him a formal invitation to visit Australia in 1998 (see *Annahar*, June 15, 1998, p. 4). Pierre Raffoul, a close associate of Aoun and an active member of the FPM in Australia, remarked: "We saw we could promote parliamentarians on the federal level to Parliament in around 7 or 8 places. On the local level, we could promote a lot of MPs to Parliament; I'm talking about 35 or 40 members... We ran a study and discovered that in 6 states, we could influence the elections of 8 members to Parliament on the federal level. So we told the two main parties in Australia, the Labor party and the Liberty party, that we wanted to invite General Aoun to Australia... So the Liberty party agreed to send General Aoun a formal invitation if they received our support in elections. They won the elections and invited the General" (interview October 2, 2014). Thus, the political weight of the Lebanese diaspora in Australia, which played a decisive role in legislative elections, had important ramifications for the FPM in Australia and in Lebanon.

The active role of FPM activists in bringing about the emergence of FPM groups in France, Australia, the USA, the UK and Canada, inter alia, contributed to the rise of their movement on a global scale. This widespread presence of FPM groups on a global level helped shed light on the existence of a vibrant political opposition to the Lebanese political elites who designed strategies to keep the opposition under control in Lebanon, by making sure it did not gain significant representation inside Parliament or the Council of Ministers. The political opposition in Lebanon not only included the FPM, but also other political parties who were ostracized from the post-war political process; this included the Lebanese Forces party. Of course, the fluid formation of the political opposition incorporated parties, such as the Commoners Movement of Najah Wakim, whose main emphasis was critiquing the economic policies of the Hariri governments. The FPM converged with some members of these opposition parties to run against government-sponsored lists, particularly in the municipal elections in Beirut in 1998.

Conclusion

Although the FPM did not emerge as a sectarian movement, it attracted a membership composed of predominantly middle-class Christians and hosted some activists from other sectarian groups. This sectarian composition did not inform its discourse in the period 1990–2005, particularly because the movement was partially excluded from state institutions. This partial exclusion meant that the FPM was not represented in Parliament and the Council of Ministers and thus was able to advance a secular political agenda without having to adopt the strategies of the political elite, which were sectarian. An important event was its participation in the 2003 parliamentary by-election in Baabda-Aley district, which enabled the movement to reveal the size of its following in Lebanon. In addition, most of the FPM activists operating in Lebanon had a middle-class profile because of the areas in which they emerged, namely students on university campuses and lawyers, engineers and teachers within their professional syndicates. FPM activists in countries such as France, Australia and the USA also reflected a middle-class background because of their qualifications and the social relationships they enjoyed with members of the political elite, which is an important indicator of their social standing.

This chapter also revealed that the neoliberal policies adopted by most post-war Lebanese governments in the period 1990–2005 negatively impacted the salaried strata of Lebanese society. Members of these salaried strata were registered in syndicates and unions where the FPM enjoyed a base of support. Because of these complex political-economic conditions, the FPM exploited policy shortcomings to direct its diatribe against de jure Lebanese governments and to emerge as the defender of just causes on several fronts, which also had a bearing on the shape of the movement.

The analysis helped to elucidate why the FPM had initially emerged in civil society, through student-government elections held at university campuses and elections within professional syndicates, and why it subsequently emerged more clearly on a national level when a relative relaxation of state repression, coupled with divisions among the political elite, the support of a select elite and the movement's participation in municipal elections, became visible. When the FPM was constricted to seizing the political opportunities of student-government elections at universities and elections at professional syndicates, for example, its rise was confined to avenues within civil society, which allowed the movement to emerge in the form of loosely connected and small, decentralized groups in the absence of an FPM central command in Lebanon. In contrast, when the FPM seized the opportunities afforded by the relative relaxation of state repression, divisions among the political elite, municipal elections and so on, it was able to form a central movement command and emerge on a national level; this had a marked qualitative impact on the nature of its collective activity executed.

The supporters of Michel Aoun in countries such as France, Australia and the USA worked to form FPM groups in the diaspora. These FPM groups played an essential role in lobbying for the cause of the movement internationally and supporting it in Lebanon. Therefore, the role of agency in contributing to the rise of the FPM cannot be understated.

While this chapter revealed the sociological composition of the movement, the political-economic conditions of post-war Lebanon that had a bearing on the shape of the FPM and the avenues in which it emerged, another important factor yet to be explored is the mobilization effort of FPM activists. Amid these challenging political conditions in post-war Lebanon, one must appreciate that FPM activists devised strategies, shaped organizational structures and provided incentives to encourage participation in FPM activism throughout the period 1990–2005. Such concerns will be the topic of exploration in the next chapter.

References

Abdelnour, Z. K. 2003. "Dossier: Michel and Elias Murr, Former and Current Lebanese Interior Minister." *Middle East Forum and United States Committee for a Free Lebanon* 5 (6).

Abi Antoun, N. Interview by this author. 2014. Beirut, September 23.

Abi Ramia, S. Interview by this author. 2014. Beirut, November 21.

Abs, Z. Interview by this author. 2014. Beirut, October 31.

AlKoussaifi, H. 1998. "Liana AlHawiya fi Khattar WaMinajli I'adat AlKarrar ilal-Baladiyya AlTayyar AlAouni Yakhoud Alintikhabat biBarnamaj Aasri. 'Because Identity Is in Danger… and to Regain Municipal Decision-Making Aounist Movement Runs for Elections with Modern Platform'." *Annahar*, February 13, 19972 ed.: 6.

Annahar. 1994. "Shkhsiyat Intadabat Chamoun liTamthiliha fi Mou'tamar Paris. 'Personalities Delegated Chamoun to Represent Them in the Paris Conference'." *Annahar*, June 11, 18853 ed.: 3.

———. 1996. "Nakib AlAttiba': Safa' AlTayyar AlWatani La Yahtaj Shahada. 'The Head of the Doctors' Syndicate: the Purity of the Free Patriotic Movement's Nationalism Does Not Require Attestation'." *Annahar*, December 31, 19633 ed.: 7.

———. 1997. "AlTayyar AlWatani AlHurr Fawz Sahek fi Kouleyat AlHandassa. 'The Free Patriotic Movement a Sweeping Victory in the Faculty of Engineering'." *Annahar*, December 12, 19922 ed.: 23.

———. 1997. "Fawz Toulab AlTayyar Alwatani AlHurr. 'The Victory of the Students of the Free Patriotic Movement'." *Annahar*, January 29, 19657 ed.: 22.

———. 1998. "AlTayyar AlWatani AlHurr Youhane' Faezih. 'The Free Patriotic Movement Congratulates Its Victors'." *Annahar*, April 3, 20014 ed.: 23.

———. 1998. "Aoun Intakala ila Melbourne AlAalam Yousa'idouna iza Saadna Anfousina. 'Aoun Moved to Melbourne the World Helps Us If We Help Ourselves'." *Annahar*, June 15, 20070 ed.: 4.

———. 1999. "Fawz AlToulab AlTayyar fil'ouloum AlIktisadiya fijami'at Alkoudis Yousef. 'The Victory of the Movement's Students at the University of Saint Joseph'." *Annahar*, December 15, 20528 ed.: 19.

———. 2000. "AlAouniyoun wa Mounasiruhoum Fazou bi Koul AlMaka'ed fil AlIntikhabat AlTalibiya lilAdab-2. 'The Aounists and Their Supporters Won All the Seats in the Student Elections of the Arts-2'." *Annahar*, January 26, 20561 ed.: 19.

Aoun, A. Interview by this author. 2014. Beirut, March 12.

Aoun, N. Interview by this author. 2014. Awkar, September 18.

Assouad, L. 2015. *Top Incomes and Personal Taxation in Lebanon, an Exploration of Individual Tax Records 2005–2012*. Master Analyse et Politique Economiques. Paris: Paris School of Economics.

Baroudi, S. E. 1998. "Economic Conflict in Postwar Lebanon: State–Labor Relations Between 1992 and 1997." *Middle East Journal* 52 (4): 531–550.

———. 2000. "Business Associations and the Representation of Business Interests in Post-war Lebanon: The Case of the Association of Lebanese Industrialists." *Middle Eastern Studies* 36 (3): 23–51.

———. 2005. "Lebanon's Foreign Trade Relations in the Postwar Era: Scenarios for Integration (1990–Present)." *Middle Eastern Studies* 41 (2): 201–225.

Baumann, H. 2016. "Social Protest and the Political Economy of Sectarianism in Lebanon." *Global Discourse* 6 (4): 634–649.

Butter, D. 1995. "How Hariri Pulled Lebanon from the Abyss." *Middle East Economic Digest*, October 27: 3.

Cammet, M. 2014. *Compassionate Communalism: Welfare and Sectarianism in Lebanon*. Ithaca: Cornell University Press.

Chakour, L. Interview by this author. 2014. Jbeil, September 29.

Eisinger, P. K. 1973. "The Conditions of Protest Behavior in American Cities." *American Political Science Review* 67 (1): 11–28.

El-Khazen, F. 1998. *Lebanon's First Postwar Parliamentary Election 1992: An Imposed Choice*. Oxford: Center for Lebanese Studies.

ElKhoury, R. Interview by this author. 2014. Jounieh, September 26.

Frangiyeh, T. J. 1998. "Masoul Fi AlTayyar AlHurr fi AlBatroun: Haleefouna man Tatawafar fihi AlNazaha waKhasmouna man Bakiya Aala alMafaheem AlKadeema. 'An Official in the Free Movement in Batroun: Our Ally Is He Who Has Integrity and Opponent Who Stuck to Old Understandings'." *Annahar*, May 1, 20035 ed.: 6.

Gambill, G. C. 2003. "FNC Triumphs in Baabda-Aley." *Middle East Forum and United States Committee for a Free Lebanon* 5 (8–9).

Ghanem ElBonn, B. 1994. "AlMou'tamar AlWattani AlLoubnani fi Paris Youkhtatam AlYoum wa 600 Yousharikouna Fih. 'The National Lebanese Conference in Paris Concludes Today with 600 Participants'." *Annahar*, June 13, 18854 ed.: 5.

———. 1994. "ashiyat AlMou'tamar AlWattani fi Paris Arkan AlMouarada AlLoubnaniya ila Ayn?. 'On the Eve of the National Conference in Paris the Pillars of Lebanese Opposition Heading Where?'." *Annahar*, June 9, 18851 ed.: 4.

———. 1994. "Mou'tamar AlWattani AlLoubnani Khtama a'malahu bi Qarrarat wa Mawakef. 'The Lebanese National Conference Concluded Its Proceedings with Decisions and Stances'." *Annahar*, June 14, 18855 ed.: 4.

Hajjar, G. 1997. "Itlak AlMo'takalin Khafafa AlGhadab Wa Iddrab AlAyyam AlThalatha Yantahi AlYoum. 'Releasing Detainees Decreased Indignation and the Three-Day Strike Ends Today'." *Annahar*, December 17, 19926 ed.: 9.

Hanf, T. 1993. *Coexistence in Wartime Lebanon*. London: I.B. Tauris.

Hanna, E. Interview by this author. 2014. Rabieh, October 16.

Harris, W. A. 1997. *Faces of Lebanon: Sects, Wars, and Global Extensions*. Princeton: Marcus Weiner Publishers.

Hipsher, P. L. 1998. "Democratic Transitions as Protest Cycles: Social Movement Dynamics in Democratizing Latin America." In *The Social Movement Society: Contentious Politics for a New Century*, edited by D. S. Meyer and S. Tarrow, Chap. 7. New York: Rowman & Littlefield.

Kassir, S. 1997. "Al'an Bada'at AlSiyyassa. 'Now Politics Begins'." *Annahar*, December 19, 19928 ed.: 1.

Kurzman, C. 1996. "Structural Opportunity and Perceived Opportunity in Social-Movement Theory: The Iranian Revolution of 1979." *American Sociological Review* 61 (1): 153–170.

Leenders, R. 2012. *Spoils of Truce: Corruption and State-Building in Postwar Lebanon*. Ithaca: Cornell University Press.

Mansour, A. S. 1992. *Al-Lnqilab 'Ala Al-Taif. "Overturning Taif"*. Beirut: Dar Al-Jadid.

McAdam, D. 1982. *Political Process and the Development of Black Insurgency, 1930–1970*. Chicago: University of Chicago Press.

———. 1988. *Freedom Summer*. New York: Oxford University Press.

———. 1996. "Conceptual Origins, Current Problems, Future Directions." In *Comparative Perspectives on Social Movements: Political Opportunities, Mobilizing Structures, and Cultural Frames*, edited by D. McAdam, J. D. McCarthy and M. N. Zald, Chap. 1. New York: Cambridge University Press.

Meyer, D. S. 2007. *The Politics of Protest*. New York: Oxford University Press.

Meyer, D. S., and S. Staggenborg. 1996. "Movements, Countermovements, and the Structure of Political Opportunity." *American Journal of Sociology* 101 (6): 1628–1660.

Naiman, R. 1999. "Millennial Middle East: Changing Orders, Shifting Borders." *Middle East Report* (Middle East Research Information Project [MERIP]) (213): 13–15.

Nasrallah, A. Interview by this author. 2014. Dbayeh, October 6.

Nizameddine, T. 2006. "The Political Economy of Lebanon Under Rafiq Hariri: An Interpretation." *Middle East Journal* 60 (1): 95–114.

Raad, N. 2004. "FPM Unveils Comprehensive New Election Manifesto." *The Daily Star*, April 15. Accessed November 22, 2018. http://www1.dailystar.com.lb/ArticlePrint.aspx?id=2014&mode=print.

Raffoul, P. Interview by this author. 2014. Beirut, October 2.

Salloukh, B. F., R. Barakat, J. S. Al-Habbal, L. W. Khattab, S. Mikaelian, and A. Nerguizian. 2015. *The Politics of Sectarianism in Postwar Lebanon*. London: Pluto Press.

Snow, D. A., and S. A. Soule. 2010. *A Primer on Social Movements*. New York: W. W. Norton.

Stel, N., and W. Naudé. 2016. "'Public–Private Entanglement': Entrepreneurship in Lebanon's Hybrid Political Order." *Journal of Development Studies* 52 (2): 254–268.

Suh, D. 2001. "How Do Political Opportunities Matter for Social Movements?: Political Opportunity, Misframing, Pseudosuccess, and Pseudofailure." *Sociological Quarterly* 42 (3): 437–460.

Tarrow, S. 1994. *Power in Movement*. New York: Cambridge University Press.

Verdeil, E. 2018. "Electricity Subsidies: Benefiting Some Regions More Than Others." Lebanese Center for Policy Studies (LCPS), September 16. Accessed November 17, 2018. http://www.lcps-lebanon.org/featuredArticle.php?id=163.

Young, M. 1996. "Stability and the Poor." *The Lebanon Report* (2): 24–34.

Zhao, D. 1998. "Ecologies of Social Movements: Student Mobilization During the 1989 Prodemocracy Movement in Beijing." *American Journal of Sociology* 103 (6): 1493–1529.

Zourob, M. 1997. "Tathahoura Aouniya Ila Makar AlMTV Baaed Mane' Zuhour Aoun. 'An Aounist Protest to the MTV Headquarters After Prohibiting Aoun's Appearance'." *Annahar*, December 15, 19924 ed.: 8.

CHAPTER 4

Free Patriotic Movement Mobilization Keeps the Flame Burning (1991–2005)

The Free Patriotic Movement's (FPM) ability to call for political change in the form of sustained collective activism throughout the period 1991–2005, despite Michel Aoun's exile in France, points to the movement's organizational effort. This reality illuminates the role of FPM activists in keeping their movement alive in the face of challenges from the political elite and Lebanese state institutions, such as the Lebanese army, General Security, Internal Security Forces and State Security. While Aoun's position in the movement inspired many activists to join or remain committed, this alone could not explain how activists gathered the resources imperative for activism, formed activist groups, devised tactics to mobilize for collective activities and communicated with the media and international organizations, since Aoun in exile remained unaware of the minute details involved in organizing activism in Lebanon.

This chapter aims to examine the way the FPM ensured its continued existence on the one hand, and overcame the challenges advanced by the Lebanese political elite on the other, by closely examining the movement's mobilizing structures, tactics and framing techniques throughout the period 1990–2005. Since the FPM faced multiple challenges from the Lebanese political elite who sanctioned the detainment of FPM activists, no account of FPM persistence could be complete without an adequate analysis of the strategies used to meet these challenges. Therefore, this chapter will investigate how the FPM ensured the continuance of its col-

J. P. Helou, *Activism, Change and Sectarianism in the Free Patriotic Movement in Lebanon*, Reform and Transition in the Mediterranean,
https://doi.org/10.1007/978-3-030-25704-0_4

lective activity, while devising strategies to overcome the challenges posed by the Lebanese political elite and national security institutions.

The chapter argues that internal mobilizing structures, which comprised secret, loosely connected and decentralized units, ensured the persistence of FPM activism by gathering resources and shielding the movement from state crackdowns. External mobilizing structures allowed the movement to persist because they helped to influence public opinion by gathering support from international organizations, the media and the Lebanese diaspora. To overcome challenges imposed by Lebanese national security institutions, the FPM applied a number of mobilizing tactics that encouraged activists to break their fear barrier and persist in FPM activism in spite of hardships. The FPM's framing of ideas helped locate the source of blame, proposed potential solutions and motivated activists to action, thereby highlighting the ability of the movement to interact with salient political topics, demonstrating the applicability of its principles to political situations and thus ensuring the continuance of the movement.

This chapter is sub-divided into three. The first part shows how the adoption of internal mobilizing structures that depended on small, loosely connected, decentralized activist units helped to shield the FPM from the crackdowns led by national security institutions, such as the Lebanese army, Internal Security Forces, and General Security Directorate, while mobilizing for collective activity. It also reveals the intense commitment on the part of FPM activists that allowed them to devise innovative techniques to gather resources for their collective activity. Then it reveals how the adoption of external mobilizing structures helped the FPM in Lebanon to spread its messages to international organizations and the media, which, in turn, helped it ensure the persistence of its collective activity.

The second part describes in some detail the nature of the challenges that the FPM had to face in the post-war Lebanese political system, before elaborating on the mobilizing tactics it applied to ensure the persistence of its activism. Finally, the chapter discusses how the framing of ideas by Aoun and FPM activists helped to locate the source of the blame, proposed solutions to political issues and motivated individuals to persist with activism, which, in turn, had a positive impact on the movement's collective activity by ensuring its continued existence throughout the period 1990–2005.

Part I: National and International Efforts Sustain the Movement

The means of the FPM adopted to mobilize resources for collective activity reflected intense commitment on the part of the movement's activists, chiefly because they had limited access to resources. Interviews with FPM activists show that the task of garnering resources essential for the persistence of their activism was not easy and must have involved a high level of commitment. The fact that the FPM continued organizing activism throughout the period 1990–2005 given the challenges imposed by the Lebanese political elite speaks to the importance of activists' commitment in time and effort, even to the extent of risking detainment by the authorities.

Whereas Lebanese political patrons exploited their patron–client network of social services to keep their supporters in line with their political stances (see Hottinger 1961; Khalaf 1968, 2003; Johnson 1986; Helou 2015), the commitment of FPM activists to the cause of their movement was not nurtured by material rewards; on the contrary, it even led those individuals to contribute what nominal resources they possessed for the sake of organizing collective activity.

In spite of the severe institutional fragmentation of the Lebanese state, which required the adoption of a nuanced approach toward various security institutions, such as the army, the General Security Directorate and the Internal Security Forces (Salloukh et al. 2015), the decision to detain FPM activists whenever their activism was demonstrated on the streets, whether in small groups or in large demonstrations, was taken by Lebanon's post-war elite, who enjoyed a close relationship with Syria. Even though the sectarian affiliation of an officer or his sympathy for Aoun may have led to better treatment of FPM activists in detention, it did not stop the security units of those officers from actually arresting FPM activists in the first place, chiefly because this decision was taken by the political elite. As a result, some democratic avenues in Lebanon's political system allowed for the emergence of the FPM, as demonstrated in the previous chapter, but the political elite made sure that FPM activism remained in check by resorting to the detainment of the movement's activists. While the nature of detainment (the associated treatment, days spent in detainment and the pretext used to charge activists) may have fluctuated in the period 1990–2005 depending on political circumstances, which were subjectively determined by the political elite, the mobilizing structures and tactics adopted by the FPM helped to ensure its persistence throughout this period.

This section of the chapter argues that FPM activism persisted due to the adoption of mobilizing structures that centered on small activist units in a decentralized manner, allowing individuals to carry out collective activity without communicating with their peers in other units, a situation that also helped to shield the movement from infiltration attempts. These activists mobilized a steady flow of resources to sustain their movement's activism by collecting personal contributions, organizing fund-raising events and personal initiatives, which simultaneously underscored the commitment of these activists to the cause of the movement given the multiple challenges they had to face. They also sustained FPM activism throughout the period 1990–2005 because of the external mobilizing structures or links fostered with other networks, such as international organizations, human rights organizations and the media, to spread messages of violations against activists; mention should also be made here of the FPM groups in the diaspora who supported their counterparts in Lebanon.

Groups in the Movement

The formation of FPM activist units across Lebanon occurred in two different but largely overlapping forms, in the shape of pyramids and cluster-like organizations, which ensured the persistence of activism by avoiding the paralysis of collective activity in case of crackdowns by national security institutions. In both the pyramidal and cluster-modeled units, activists had no communication with their counterparts operating in other units; this provided them with an avenue for autonomous decision-making and simultaneously minimized the risk of external infiltration of the units. However, even if the Lebanese military intelligence or other state security institutions managed to infiltrate activist units via some of their members, the autonomous arrangement of those units ensured the persistence of FPM activism, since the detainment of some members of some units did not paralyze the ability of others to carry out collective activity. According to the majority of the interviewed activists, these closed pyramid and cluster units restricted any exchange of information regarding the activism of the unit to its members, which helped to ensure the secrecy of collective activity.

Since the political circumstances in Lebanon prevented the formation of a central FPM command prior to 1996, the spontaneous emergence of various FPM groups throughout Lebanon seemed to draw those groups into adopting a pyramidal, cluster-like, or some variable combination of both models for the organization of collective activity in a largely uncoordinated fashion. For example, Michel Elefteriades' pro-FPM group MUR (United Movements of Resistance), which carried out collective activities in the early 1990s, fashioned its movement's units according to the pyramidal model: the head of a group distributed information to certain individuals, who in turn led other groups of individuals, each of whom led others in a repetitive pattern (M. Elefteriades, interview September 8, 2014). This structuring of activist units did not emanate from deliberation among FPM members, but involved a great deal of personal initiative, since the decentralized form of the movement provided activists with a wide margin of mobility.

In contrast, Mansour Sfeir explained how he formed units according to the cluster model. He stated: "At one point during 1991, we had around fifty rings in Kiserwan. They extended from Meyrouba, Hrajel, Fareya, to Ajaltoun and... Some rings operated with three individuals while others contained twenty. We tried not to expand them. They didn't know one another. I knew them all. I was the contact point. Those working with me didn't know everyone else. I had purposefully organized it in this fashion to avoid uncovering the groups in case of some arrests. I didn't want the arrested person to tell about the rest" (interview September 30, 2014). He mentioned borrowing the idea for these organizational units from the Bolsheviks, while stressing that he had initially operated in the early 1990s without communicating with other FPM counterparts in Lebanon.

This arrangement of small, loosely connected and decentralized units had not only been the form of organizational unit utilized by activists in towns and villages across Lebanon, but also by those student activists who operated from university campuses. FPM student activism constituted the backbone of the movement's collective activity, but alarmed the political elite when their activism was demonstrated on the streets, and thus became the target of detainment in order to keep FPM activism under control. Therefore, students designed their activist units in a loosely connected fashion that would not affect the frequency of their collective activity in case some members of those units were arrested. Toni Harb, an FPM activist, pointedly remarked: "I personally began forming units at the university faculties... I used to work on one person. I would find that 'burned head' [meaning daring person]. I would then ask that person to get another; the other person to get another person and so on. In this way, we began forming small units in every university. At the beginning, they wouldn't know one another. When I saw that their numbers were convenient, like four or five, I would gather them together" (interview October 30, 2014). This form of organizational unit helped FPM student activists to mobilize for major activities and distribute pamphlets both inside and outside their universities, while maintaining a degree of operational secrecy to ensure the persistence of their movement.

The unfolding events of August 7, 2001 illustrated the effectiveness of these decentralized activist units in organizing continuous rounds of collective activity, even after several FPM activists had been arrested by Lebanese authorities for participating in protest activity. On August 5, a group of FPM activists decided, without formal approval from their central command, to protest against the Maronite Patriarch's reconciliation with Druze-chieftain Walid Jumblatt, since the latter had been responsible for displacing large Christian communities from the Shuf region during the Lebanese Civil War. According to the interviewed activists who took part in these events, the instrumental media coordination of this protest with the Lebanese channel MTV granted the protest fair coverage on the evening news and reached sympathetic audiences who had long been deprived of audiovisual coverage of FPM activity. Rushing to contain these protests, Lebanese military intelligence arrested the participants in these protests immediately, at least those who were visible on camera.

On August 7, a large meeting of the FPM's central command, which sought to explore methods of freeing the activists who had been arrested two days earlier, was also crushed when military intelligence threw its 70 participants behind bars. However, this large-scale crackdown of leading movement activists did not manage to cripple the FPM's ability to carry out collective activity due to the existence of small, decentralized activist units. These units mobilized for protests in front of the Palace of Justice only two days later, showcasing the resilience of FPM mobilization (R. Tarraf, interview September 11, 2014).

Therefore, the formation of a central FPM command helped to centralize the decision-making process regarding the time and location of protests, but left small, decentralized units with the capability and means to determine their own independent moves, which contributed to the persistence of collective activity. If the small, decentralized units with their autonomous decision-making capacity had been absorbed into a larger organizational structure, the Lebanese authorities could have easily weakened the movement on August 7, 2001 with their concentrated crackdown on its central command. Yet, since these small units maintained a wide margin of mobility and the ability to decide on their protest activity without referring back to central command, the Lebanese authorities were unable to weaken the movement, even after arresting many of its leading figures. The majority of activists interviewed for this study recognized the importance of having shied away from organizing the FPM in a formal institutional fashion; that is to say, with declared organizational bodies, individuals in clear organizational roles and centrally controlled mobilization units.

However, the success of FPM mobilization resulted from the decentralized manner in which its activists coordinated the resources at their disposal to generate collective activity, because this coordination method helped shield the movement from Lebanese state crackdowns, regardless of whether they were carried out by the Lebanese army, General Security, Internal Security Forces or the State Security Directorate. The cassette distribution effort, for example, was coordinated by both the FPM in France and activists in Lebanon to spread Aoun's messages to supporters in Lebanon. Patrick ElKhoury, an FPM activist, would receive the cassettes via someone traveling to Beirut from France. He would record around 200 copies of each cassette, which contained a 20-minute speech by Aoun, on a double-tape machine. In his meeting with other prominent FPM activists such as Ziad Abs, Naim Aoun and Liwa Chakour, he would hand them copies of the cassettes for them to follow the same pattern of recording and distribution to their units (P. ElKhoury, interview October 1, 2014). Activists did not stop short of distributing these cassettes on the streets and at meetings of professional segments of society, such as a lawyers' conference.

The FPM in France would first send the cassette of Aoun's recorded speeches with two or three different people traveling on flights to Beirut to make sure that FPM activists received a copy, in case the passenger transporting those cassettes was caught by General Security officers at Beirut airport. As a result, several activists in Lebanon would receive the cassettes and engage in producing copies for distribution. Through this system, FPM activists transmitted Aoun's political messages to their counterparts and to a wide segment of movement sympathizers, whose main exposure to the ideas of the exiled leader had been through recordings or the print media.

This decentralized information distribution system fostered FPM mobilization for two main reasons. First, this system ensured the transmission of information, albeit in the form of recordings and other material imperative for activism, from Aoun in France to FPM activists in Lebanon. Even if officers of the General Security Directorate managed to confiscate some of the movement's material transported by a traveler at Beirut airport, someone else was bound to succeed in getting the material past them. Second, since activists operated in a decentralized fashion, those receiving the cassettes worked on producing copies for distribution without being aware of how many tapes their counterparts were producing. Therefore, every activist making copies of cassettes believed they bore the responsibility of distributing them to the widest possible segment of society. This inspired a sense of responsibility that helped to boost mobilization efforts and strengthened activists' commitment to the collective activity of the movement.

With time, FPM activists gained experience in the organization of collective activity, which allowed their activist units to coordinate collective activity on the streets in a more effective manner. Whether distributing cassettes, pamphlets or the weekly *Lebanese Bulletin* issued by Aoun in France, activists designated individuals within working units across various geographic areas to transmit the FPM's messages to the widest segment of sympathizers. Patrick ElKhoury pertinently stated: "Let's say we decided to distribute it in Achrafieh. We would form groups in two or three different locations and distribute the bulletin... We would decide to divide Achrafieh into four parts. Accordingly, we would assign groups and place 4 here, 7 there, another 5 here... The following day, we would assist the Matn, Kiserwan, and other areas" (interview October 1, 2014). Executing collective activity by resorting to these working units ensured the persistence of FPM activity, because arresting activists that belonged to one working unit did not affect the flow of operations of others; namely, mobilizing resources, planning activity and executing collective activity by organizing activists into units.

In fact, if only a few members of a unit were arrested, the same unit could persevere in the organization of collective activity without the need to apply major changes to its action plan. By understanding the collective activity they were carrying out—that is, pamphlet distribution, protests, demonstrations and so on—every FPM activist enjoyed a margin of freedom that allowed them to decide on the best way to continue carrying out collective activity if members of their activist unit were detained by the

Lebanese authorities. Since members of one unit usually did not know where other units were operating or which activists constituted those units, this arrangement shielded the movement from large crackdowns, even when some activists were detained and interrogated.

The countless pamphlet distribution campaigns, protests, demonstrations and sit-ins organized by the FPM throughout the period 1990–2005 not only proved the movement's ability to mobilize its forces, but also underscored the importance of these decentralized organizational units in promoting collective activity. It was thanks to these units that FPM activists were able to organize collective activity on annual preset occasions, such as the anniversary of Aoun's War of Liberation on March 14 and the memorial of Aoun's ousting from the premiership on October 13, regardless of the way in which the Lebanese state subsequently dealt with that activity. For example, the large-scale protest organized by FPM activists on March 14, 2001 against Syrian stations in Lebanon illustrated the effectiveness of these units in coordinating collective activity.

Thus, Mario Chamoun, an FPM activist who operated closely with students, commented: "In 2001, on March 14 we decided to demonstrate in front of the Syrian stations in Lebanon. This was the biggest and most effective event in my opinion... We did not inform the exact whereabouts of our demonstration... We sent out a press release and listed all Syrian stations. We listed around twenty or thirty stations of the Syrian intelligence. On that day, the Lebanese army deployed on [the] ground and closed all of Lebanon's streets... In the last 30 minutes, we sent SMS messages to all our groups across different universities and we were able to mobilize them all to the Lebanese University in Fannar, where the Syrian army used to occupy part of the campus" (interview October 15, 2014). Nonetheless, to flesh out a complete understanding of FPM mobilization, the analysis should stretch beyond the mere organization of activist units to a discussion of how activists gathered and channeled resources for the organization of collective activity.

Resources Fuel FPM Activism

FPM collective activity, whether distributing pamphlets, spray painting political slogans in public spaces or organizing protests, occurred due to the unflinching commitment of activists to mobilizing resources and coordinating those resources to produce the synergies of collective action. For university students who had to pay exorbitant fees and individuals who had to support a family, they faced the additional load of paying for the cost of material for their activism, such as paper, spray paint and photocopies, inter alia. This section explores how FPM activists mobilized resources for activism, and argues that it was the commitment of individuals to the cause of the FPM that ensured the movement's persistence throughout the period 1990–2005.

An account of how these activists financed their movement cannot be separated from their enormous commitment to its cause. Since 90% of the sample of interviewed activists stated that 100% of the FPM's resources were self-financed, it was activists' personal initiatives, innovative methods and reliance on movement sympathizers that helped to mobilize and coordinate resources for the organization of FPM collective activity.

On a personal level, FPM activists' commitment to the cause is what made them willing to sacrifice resources to organize collective activity. When university students spent their pocket money of $50 to purchase print material, spray paint and other items, they revealed a dedication to the political message of the FPM that called for the freedom, sovereignty and independence of Lebanon. Their commitment did not end with the financial contribution they made, but usually involved a direct role in the planning and execution of collective activity both inside and outside their university campuses. Elie Hanna, an FPM activist, remarked: "For activities we ran outside NDU [Notre Dame University], we used to resort to our own pocket money. If someone's father provided him with $50 for pocket money, for example, we used to buy paper, spray paint, scarves, and hats for distribution" (interview October 16, 2014).

With time, FPM student activists, especially those who operated in private universities, became more aware of the financial vicissitudes that might have a negative impact on FPM mobilization, and thus sought to assist their less financially capable counterparts at public universities in order to ensure the persistence of movement activity. Roland ElKhoury, FPM activist in charge of the FPM student dossier for the Kiserwan–Jbeil province, stated that "students of the Lebanese University, for example, couldn't participate in protests if transportation wasn't provided for them. They probably wouldn't be able to pay the 5,000 lira [$3.33] transportation fee. So, it prevented them from getting to protests. Therefore, we had to rent buses for them" (interview September 26, 2014). These examples illustrate the genuine commitment FPM activists bore toward advancing the mobilization effort of their movement by showing how they were willing to give up their own resources to promote FPM activism. Many such contributions played a vital role in ensuring the persistence of the movement's activity throughout the period 1990–2005.

The creativity of FPM activists also drew them to devise innovative methods of fund-raising in order to finance their movement's collective activity and simultaneously circumvent state surveillance. In a short-lived attempt during the early 1990s, some FPM activists devised a system in which the individual performing a service or selling a product to another activist would pay a tax of 1%. The tax collected would be placed in a bank account to subsequently finance the costs of FPM collective activities (N. Abi Antoun, interview September 23, 2014).

Because individuals who considered financing FPM activities would have suffered punitive measures at the hands of the Lebanese authorities, FPM activists had to tap unexpected sources of finance in a subtle manner to finance the movement; for example, borrowing on credit in the form of a personal bank loan, without declaring the real purpose for the loan, to finance collective activity or the opening of an FPM office. Patrick ElKhoury stated: "I took a loan of fifteen million liras [$10,000] and paid it back in installments over a three-year period to open an office... But I had to deal with the costs of printing pamphlets, pictures, office supplies, water, purchasing printers and fax machines, and other things" (interview October 1, 2014). Several FPM activists sacrificed their own money and resources to promote the collective activity of the movement. This personal initiative that required the sacrifice of time and resources reflected their commitment to the cause of the movement, and demonstrated how the FPM was able to persist in the organization of collective activity.

FPM activists also requested assistance or donations from some financially secure individuals who were sympathetic to their cause, but who could not express their political opinions freely for fear of the reaction of the Lebanese political elite. Although around 90% of the activists interviewed for this study believed that 100% of the FPM's resources were self-financed, some activists, such as Ziad Abs, believed that donations existed, but did not exceed 20% of the movement's resource base (interview October 31, 2014). Commenting on the issue of resources, he stated: "We would do our study and see that the event cost $2000. So Liwa [another FPM activist] would return to check whether he could ensure money from his contact. I used to know people... For example, I know someone that provided us with 60,000 cassettes... I know someone that printed our pamphlets free of charge. Someone else gave us watches so that Patrick would place the General's picture on them. So, there were people and they were prominent figures, but they wanted to remain anonymous and discreet" (ibid.). The mobilization efforts of FPM activists reveal that the movement's resources were not strictly centered on money, but included the dispersion of material resources from some FPM sympathizers as well. These resources were more accessible to those activists who enjoyed good connections with the business elite, who sympathized with the cause of the FPM.

FPM student activists, for instance, also ran fund-raising events that helped raise money for the organization of collective activity while simultaneously serving to create bonds of friendship among activists. At NDU, FPM activists had organized barbecue nights and Argileh (water-pipe) nights, in which activists participated and welcomed other non-affiliated individuals as well (E. Hanna, interview October 16, 2014). A number of FPM student activists had mentioned raising funds by renting out a movie theater from among those that would agree to provide the movement with a share of the sum of ticket revenues. George Choucair, an FPM activist, explained how these events helped finance the collective activity of the movement: "We held a party at a pub in Sersok; it was open drinks for $20 per person. We gathered $700 from the event and used the money to pay for print material for distribution" (interview October 16, 2014). The organization of such activities brought individuals closer together and helped gather money, albeit nominal amounts, to finance collective activity. These activities positively affected activists by providing them with the impetus to persist in the organization of activism, since the discussion of common and shared experiences in movement activism often strengthened an individual's bonds with the FPM.

Another crucial resource was the free space of many private and public university campuses across Lebanon, because they served as mobilization centers for FPM activism by providing activists with a secure environment to plan and execute activism away from state crackdowns. In social movement jargon, free spaces are those places that ensure a safe environment to plan and organize collective activity away from state surveillance, such as private offices, homes, churches and university campuses. This phenomenon explains why more than 50% of the sample of activists interviewed for this research had been FPM student activists at their universities.

Student activism within the FPM was not an exception to the rule in the social movement repertoire. Numerous studies on US social movements underscore the essential role that university campuses and students played in mobilizing for movement activity: for example, in the women's movement (Freeman 1975; Taylor and Whittier 1992), the civil rights movement (Morris 1981; McAdam 1988), the divestment from South Africa movement (Hirsch 1990; Soule 1997) and the conservative movement on college campuses (Munson 2010). Students have also been considered a vital constituency for social movement activity, the example of the pro-democracy movement in China being a case in point (Zuo and Benford 1995; Calhoun 1997; Zhao 1998). McAdam (1988), for example, contends that students are more likely to participate in activism because they have fewer family commitments, responsibilities and work duties. Therefore, students can afford to spend more time in activism than those encumbered by other commitments.

In line with the numerous studies on social movements that emphasize the important role of students in contributing to the organization of activism, FPM activists also invested considerable effort into winning a majority on the student-government body at their universities, since that position helped them gain vital access to a pool of resources that would assist them in the organization of collective activity both on and off campus. From the vantage point of the majority in student governments, FPM student activists were able to finance their collective activity on campus, which often included simple tasks such as printing communiqués or distributing movement news. Yet, since universities contained thousands of students within a confined space, these seemingly inconsequential activities often had a powerful impact on student mobilization. Commenting on the importance of student councils (student government) as a body to organize and mobilize students within the Lebanese University, Antoine Moukheiber, an FPM activist, stated: "It was not tough in the first two years: 1991 and 1992. We took advantage of this situation by organizing it. When we ran meetings, we had around a thousand students. Out of 7000 students, we had 1000 students in our meetings... The soil was fertile and you needed someone to grab the ground... We grabbed it quickly and went to form the student council inside the Faculty of Sciences, and Tanious [another FPM activist] presided over the council" (interview October 31, 2014).

When Antoine Moukheiber describes the political landscape at the Lebanese University as being "fertile" in 1991–1992, he is referring to the existence of a wide segment of Lebanese youth that supported Aoun and the principles that subsequently constituted the FPM. Therefore, student activists played an essential role in mobilizing vital resources for FPM activism, in addition to converting bystanders or sympathizers into activists, an issue considered vital for sustaining movement activity (McCarthy and Zald 1977).

FPM student activists cleverly exploited their position on the university student council by dispensing services that benefited the student body at large and, through the distribution of those services, accumulated resources to finance FPM activism. They imposed an enrollment fee of 5000 or 10,000 Lebanese liras ($3.33 or $6.66) that had to be paid by students to the student councils (L. Chakour, interview September 29, 2014). These fees helped finance the activities of the student council that, in turn, supported the activities of the FPM on university campuses. Methods of income generation often benefited the student body at large, such as the inception of a photocopying center at the Lebanese University. Elaborating on that project, Liwa Chakour stated: “I found a photocopying center on university campuses. We got machines. While students paid 50 liras (¢3.3) outside campus for a single page, they would pay just 30 liras (¢2) on campus. The cost of a single page would be around 20 liras (¢1.3) and the remaining money would be a good source of income for us [us refers to the student government in which FPM consistently enjoyed a majority]. This income would help finance student activities elsewhere” (ibid.). Therefore, FPM student activists on university campuses took initiatives that resonated positively with the majority of students, whether FPM or not, and, in this way, ensured a flow of vital resources and coordinated collective activity that culminated in the persistence of the FPM throughout the period 1990–2005.

Based on an analysis of the interviews conducted with FPM activists, the free space of universities, including homes and some private offices offered by FPM members, such as Naji Gharios, Hikmat Dib, George Hadad, Patrick ElKhoury and Ziad Abs, inter alia, constituted an important resource for the persistence of FPM activism by assisting in the planning of collective activity while shielding activists from state crackdowns. In those meetings, activists would determine how they were going to carry out some of their collective activity, whether it would encompass sit-ins, demonstrations or protests, or whether they were simply going to distribute communiqués. The nature of the agreed collective activity depended largely on what FPM activists believed was possible, given their predictions regarding the reaction of the political elite or prevailing political circumstances. As FPM activism began to gain visibility, communication between the heads of various FPM units began to increase. Therefore, when FPM activists sat in on meetings of their activist units, they began to know when and how they were to assist their cohorts in the movement in certain collective activity across Lebanon. This is chiefly how large protests, for example the student protest toward the Syrian stations on March 14, 2001, were organized.

External Groups Sustain FPM Activism at Home

The FPM's public presence or image in the media and its ability to mobilize public opinion were dependent on the relationship between its central bureau nationally on the one hand, and international organizations and the media on the other. Its ability to influence public opinion and sway sympathetic audiences depended on the links activists maintained with human rights networks, such as the Foundation for Human and Humanitarian Rights and Amnesty International, and on their relationship with the media. Thus, activists interacted with the political conditions prevailing in Lebanon to develop movement structures that could help sustain FPM activism throughout the period 1990–2005.

The development of some of these movement structures helped to formulate a central FPM command that planned certain collective activity and had representative legitimacy as the political body representing Aoun's stance in Lebanon. In 1994, for instance, the institution of the 12-member coordinating committee headed by General Nadim Lteif was officially recognized as the representative of Aoun's movement in Lebanon. The FPM youth viewed this arrangement as grossly misrepresentative of their effective role in the mobilization of movement activism from university campuses across Lebanon, which had constituted the backbone of the movement. Accordingly, by 1996, an executive committee with associated sub-committees was established, absorbing the youth into the central decision-making offices of the movement (N. Aoun, interview September 18, 2014).

Although this book retrospectively refers to the movement as the FPM for consistency purposes, that actually became the official name for all activist units at an activist meeting of movement cadres with Aoun in France in 1996. At this meeting, participants decided to fuse the names of two student activist groups, the Free Student Movement and the Lebanese Patriotic Movement, to form the FPM (Z. Abs, interview October 31, 2014; Mouawad, April 21, 1996, p. 16). This action testifies to the extent of the influence of the youth movement and the active role student activists played in contributing to the persistence of movement activism throughout the period 1990–2005 in Lebanon. In fact, the FPM had drafted the first organizational structure in 1998, which remained more or less the same till 2005, when the movement was declared a party.

By the mid-1990s, FPM activists, especially the youth among them, began meeting with their movement cohorts from around the world in France every two years, in what became known as the Lebanese National Conference (LNC). The 1994 LNC conference in France had been the starting point at which activists officially took the decision to launch and organize the movement in towns and villages in Lebanon in a more effective manner, though it had begun to emerge spontaneously earlier. The link between the FPM in Lebanon and its counterpart in France had become vital for the mobilization of public opinion, because this relationship granted the movement's messages the multipliers needed to draw sympathetic audiences and to highlight the violations perpetrated by the Lebanese authorities. Tony Harb commented: "We aimed to send our message out to three places: local public opinion, international public opinion and specialized international opinion, such as human rights organizations and Amnesty International" (interview October 30, 2014). In fact, the Rassemblement Pour le Liban in France, the Council of Lebanese American Organizations (CLAO) in the USA and the Global Front for the Liberation of Lebanon in Australia, among many other FPM groups in the diaspora, worked with the FPM in Lebanon to lobby for the movement's cause and spread news of human rights violations taking place within Lebanon.

Since the RPL in France were in close proximity to Aoun, they played the most effective role in mobilizing public opinion, assisting him in lobbying for the freedom of Lebanon and communicating movement messages to the media and foreign states. The reason they were able to carry out these tasks was due to their instrumental organization, division of tasks and activist commitment that contributed to the persistence of the movement in France throughout the period 1990–2005. Simon Abi Ramia, an FPM activist who was the head of the RPL in France, stated:

> Every time something happened in Lebanon, we would bring it to the attention of human rights organizations. We had relations with 30 or 40 organizations; Amnesty, Human Rights Watch, and Middle East… In France, we had relations with Journalists without Borders, Federation of Human Rights, and everywhere. What we did is that we were smart organizational units… Every person had an operating team that was in charge

> of a dossier; political lobbying had a team and so did media, relationships with human rights organizations, students and the youth, and logistics. We were organized in a scientific way. It was in contrast to the movement in Lebanon that was organized in a random way. (Interview November 21, 2014)

Because FPM activists attended meetings in France every two years, they came to know the RPL team that operated with Aoun in France. When certain detainments or human rights violations, such as freedom of expression or the right to association, were carried out by the Lebanese authorities, the FPM in Lebanon promptly notified its counterpart in France, who immediately took to spreading news of these violations to human rights organizations and the international press. The FPM was successful in swaying public opinion and winning the support of international organizations. Amnesty International, for example, issued reports condemning the use of military courts to prosecute FPM student activists (Amnesty, April 25, 2000), thus showing how the FPM was able to channel its messages to international organizations.

The role of FPM counterparts abroad stretched beyond the mere distribution of information and news about the movement in Lebanon, to include lobbying foreign states for the cause of the freedom, sovereignty and independence of Lebanon. Some FPM members discussed the role played by the CLAO in convincing the US Congress of the urgency of liberating Lebanese politics from the overwhelming influence of Syria. Gabi Isa and Tony Hadad, both members of CLAO, played an essential role in lobbying Congress, culminating in the US invitation to Aoun to speak to Congress (*Annahar*, June 26, 1997, p. 6; P. Raffoul, interview October 2, 2014).

Following his initial visit to speak to Congress, Aoun launched a series of attempts to persuade the USA to adopt more stringent measures against Syria's presence in Lebanon, culminating in the passing of the Syria Accountability and Lebanese Sovereignty Restoration Act. Though this Act held Syria responsible for meddling in Lebanese affairs, it mainly focused on Syria's links with non-state actors, such as Hezbollah, Hamas and the Islamic Jihad, among others, which the USA classified as terrorist groups (Syria Accountability Act 2003). Therefore, this convergence of interest between the FPM and the USA, despite ending with Aoun's return to Lebanon in 2005, helped to bring about a reorientation of US policy toward Syria, partly due to the lobbying efforts of CLAO, which constituted the initial nexus between Aoun and the US Congress.

By virtue of their association with and membership of various human rights networks and organizations, both in Lebanon and abroad, FPM activists succeeded in portraying the challenges imposed by the Lebanese political elite against activists as a clear violation of the human rights of freedom of expression and the right to association, which influenced public opinion in a powerful manner. In fact, most of the activists interviewed as part of this research explained that the detainment, torture and trials of activists at military courts had constituted gross violations of international standards and the Universal Declaration of Human Rights. Naaman Abi Antoun, an FPM activist, illustrated this point: "our relationship with human rights organizations came via the Foundation for Human and Humanitarian Rights... Our position as human rights activists also gave us an important relationship with the outer world... I participated in several human rights conferences. We used to call for political freedoms in Lebanon... The FPM gave human rights a fair share in its struggle" (interview September 23, 2014).

Because the FPM broadly construed the challenges to it as a violation of freedom and the right of association, the movement attracted the political support of some rightist and leftist Lebanese parties as well as international organizations. This formed an important bulwark for the FPM, especially when some of its activists were detained. It exerted more pressure on the Lebanese government, since multiple political factions were objecting to its treatment of political activists; namely, of the FPM. In addition, by carrying the banner of human rights, the FPM defied Lebanese factional politics and persisted as a progressive secular movement. Had it failed to highlight these issues, it would have been eventually portrayed as another sectarian movement, since Lebanon classified movements based on the sectarian background of their popular base, which was predominantly Christian in the case of the FPM.

Although media censorship of FPM news had limited the movement's ability to influence public opinion, activists constantly attempted to mobilize the media and journalists for better news coverage. George Hadad and Ramzi Kanj, both FPM activists in charge of the movement's media dossier, continually worked on receiving wider coverage in the press in order to influence public opinion. Speaking about the importance of press coverage for FPM activism, Ramzi Kanj commented: "But for sure, when we had journalists covering our events, that was great. When we received press coverage, human rights organizations, syndicates, the lawyers, the professions would all move in support of us. They used to object too.

Our relationship with human rights and their relationship with the UN and the USA and other countries supported us. When reports were published from here and went to the USA, France, and the UN, this used to create some good attention" (interview September 19, 2014). Therefore, the network with the media and international organizations proved vital for the mobilization effort of the FPM. Because of the restricted access its activists had to the media in Lebanon, the relationship they forged with external organizations helped them spread the movement's messages and news of human rights violations perpetrated by the Lebanese government.

The relationship between the FPM in Lebanon and its counterparts in France, the USA and Australia, inter alia, and the close links forged with the media, human rights organizations and other international organizations proved vital for persuading public opinion. Since the FPM portrayed the detainment of its activists as a violation of the human rights of freedom of expression and the right to association, it managed to attract a sympathetic segment of public opinion that viewed these rights as inalienable, and thus sympathized with the FPM in its quest to attain them. The various Amnesty reports reprimanding the Lebanese government for torturing detainees and resorting to the use of force against protestors are an indication of the FPM's ability to channel its news to the right target audience and thus affect public opinion. The important role played by the Foundation for Human and Humanitarian Rights in raising awareness of political freedoms and declaring the illegality of detaining peaceful political activists also reveals how the FPM employed its good relationship with organizations to support its collective activity (*Annahar*, September 25, 1998, p. 6).

To sum up, the FPM was able to organize collective activity and mobilize resources in Lebanon due to its small, decentralized activist units. These activist units operated incognito from the central FPM command in Lebanon and with minimal direct interaction. They could mobilize resources as well as carrying out and often persisting in collective activity, even when some of their members were arrested by the Lebanese authorities.

The FPM central command, which began to play a more effective role in the latter half of the 1990s, called for collective activity on certain political occasions, but never carried out the organizational tasks for the event centrally. Organizational issues were always left to the decentralized activist units to determine as they deemed necessary.

However, the importance of the central command in Lebanon was that it formed structures to mobilize public opinion by means of fostering good relationships with international organizations, human rights organizations and the media. These external mobilizing structures helped to spread the movement's messages and influence public opinion, which also helped the movement to sustain its collective activity by focusing on political activism and freedom of expression as a human right. Therefore, the relationship between the FPM on the one hand, and certain international organizations and the media on the other, helped attract attention to its cause, which, in turn, contributed to the persistence of the sustained collective activity that characterized the movement. In fact, the role of both the internal and external mobilizing structures of the FPM was crucial for the continuance of the movement's collective activities, because each played a designated role that ensured the continuity of organizational and political action. The next section turns to the tactics the FPM applied to ensure the persistence of its collective activity, despite the many challenges designed by the political elite of Lebanon to weaken the movement.

Part II: Tactics to Strengthen Activism and Face Challenges

This part of the chapter sets out to demonstrate that the FPM employed tactics to strengthen the movement's solidarity and activists' perseverance in activism in spite of the manifold challenges advanced by the Lebanese state. Some of these state-imposed challenges included censorship of the media, prosecution of peaceful activists in military courts and the brutal treatment of political activists, to name but a few. These challenges were intended to sway individuals away from political activism but, obviously, did not deliver the intended effect.

In fact, the tactics the FPM employed managed to strengthen activists' persistence in collective activity. These tactics included placing first-time activists in the front lines of protests, supporting those activists and their families if they were arrested for their involvement in FPM activism, trying to keep student activists away from long prison sentences, especially during school terms, and exposing activists to the speeches and ideas of Michel Aoun, among others, all of which had the intended effect of strengthening activists' persistence in the FPM's collective activity. We can appreciate the impact of these mobilizing tactics after examining the challenges to FPM activism produced by the Lebanese political elite, and then discussing the tactics that maintained FPM activism.

Challenges to Activism

The Lebanese political elite aimed to keep protest movements, such as the FPM, under control; that is to say, to prevent them from mass mobilization throughout the period 1990–2005 by means of detaining and sometimes mistreating protestors whose political opinions critiqued the political elite's sectarian strategies, corrupt political practices and relations with Syria, which was viewed as an occupying power by the FPM. Several primary and secondary sources suggest that various national security institutions, such as the Lebanese army and General Security, regularly detained FPM activists for carrying out collective activity, sentenced them to prison, tortured them and made several attempts to demobilize their movement (*Annahar* 1994–2001). Despite this, by analyzing these repressive tactics, this section elucidates the vicissitudes confronting FPM persistence, which will lead to a deeper appreciation of the strategies and tactics applied by the FPM to ensure the continuance of its collective activity.

Following the ousting of Aoun from the premiership on October 13, 1990, the post-war Lebanese political class, with the political backing of Syria, rushed to restrict the number of media outlets (television, radio, newspapers) that had proliferated during the Lebanese Civil War, frequently without a license. In principle, this move was intended to organize the rather jumbled condition of the Lebanese media. However, in reality it ended up concentrating the ownership of the Lebanese media in the hands of individuals who were sympathetic to Syria and the new post-war political class, notwithstanding a few exceptions (see Dajani 1992, 2005; Kraidy 1998; Melki 2007; Y. Dabbous 2010, 2012; D. Dabbous 2013). The Lebanese broadcasting law that was endorsed by Parliament in 1994 reduced the number of television stations to a select few and regulated what had been a chaotic media scene established during the Civil War (Dabbous 2013).

By restricting the number of media channels in post-war Lebanon, post-1990 Lebanese governments granted opposition movements who were ostracized from the post-war political process, especially Aoun's FPM, a very restricted avenue for the expression of their political opinion. These media restrictions, coupled with the five-year media ban imposed on Aoun, burdened the FPM with a heavier load. In April 1993, for example, the Lebanese government shut down Nida Al-Watan, a Christian television channel and newspaper, which interviewed Aoun in defiance of the government-imposed ban (Harris 1997, p. 289).

In a show of strength, Lebanese governments did not budge in the face of attempts to interview the exiled FPM leader. Because the bold move of interviewing Aoun had been associated with enormous costs, television stations shied away from making such a move throughout the 1990–2005 period. MTV, which broke the rule by interviewing Aoun in 1997 and then began providing a platform for the expression of opinions critical of Syria and the Lebanese political elite, subsequently bore the brunt of a government-enforced shutdown in 2001 due to the channel's clear political preferences, which were aligned with the FPM and a number of other parties that were also critical of Syria and the political elite. Against this background of such a restrictive media scene, the manner in which FPM activists exploited their connections with some individuals in media institutions to gain more coverage, such as the August 7 events described in some detail earlier in the chapter, can now be appreciated more deeply.

On the other hand, Lebanese governments did not stop short of referring peaceful activists, who were often detained for distributing political pamphlets calling for increased freedom, to trial in the military court in a clear attempt to decrease FPM activism. Although this treatment of activists was considered illegal on several fronts, some of the political elite attempted to shame FPM activists by persuading public opinion that the individuals on trial planned to "incite sedition, disturb civil peace, disturb relations with a neighboring state, and threaten national security inter alia." George Hadad, lawyer and FPM activist, mentioned: "The military route for prosecutions is illegal in Lebanon. The judges in military courts know very little about laws. The worst thing about it is that the intelligence forces control the military courts. At one point, the judge of the military court was a military pilot in his sophomore year at law school... The legal text between his hands allowed him to execute people. They used to fill in decisions according to a check list" (interview September 17, 2014). Therefore, the transfer of activists to military courts was regarded as another means of repression, to incite fear and disincentivize Lebanese individuals from participating in FPM activism.

The military courts in Lebanon also engaged in the practice of fabricating false charges to put FPM activists on trial, with the aim of quelling their activism. The majority of the interviewed activists in this book who had been tried for their activism confirmed that they were tried in the military court. For instance, a group of FPM activists, including Naaman Abi Antoun, Jose Afif and others, distributed a pamphlet on the occasion of Independence Day on November 22, 1992 that called for the freedom of

Lebanon from foreign occupation (N. Abi Antoun, interview September 23, 2014). As a consequence, these activists were charged under Article 157 of the military penal code, which deals with the printing and distribution of information through the media (Amnesty, January 14, 1993). Jose Afif was charged under Article 285 of the penal code, which deals with unauthorized entry into enemy territory and unauthorized commercial contact with enemy nationals or residents (ibid.). The decisions of the military court defamed FPM activists by attempting to fabricate false charges of collaboration with Israel, a long-standing enemy of Lebanon.

Because the FPM was committed to liberating Lebanon from the Syrian military presence, called for increased transparency in political affairs and declared its opposition to what it regarded as a corrupt ruling political class, members of the Lebanese political elite used their connections inside state bureaucracies, such as various security institutions and the judiciary, to slander the reputation of FPM activists throughout the period 1990–2005. This defamation was not restricted to news that harmed the reputation of FPM supporters and sympathizers, but included the fabrication of accusations that could easily culminate in prison sentences for the individuals charged (N. Abi Antoun, interview September 23, 2014). In 1996, Pierre Atallah, a journalist who sympathized with the FPM, had been charged for distributing political pamphlets and was convicted for "spoiling relations with a neighboring state, slandering the reputation of the army, and debunking the order of the military and submission to hierarchy, and communicating with the agents of the Israeli enemy" (*Annahar*, December 31, 1996, p. 7). In 1994, a group of FPM activists including Hikmat Dib, Houda Yameen, Mouna Shkeyman, Lina Ghreyeb and others were detained by the Lebanese authorities for writing and distributing a pamphlet that encouraged people to protest in response to two articles published by *Herald Tribune* (*Annahar*, September 28, 1994, p. 5). As justification for the arrest, the military court invoked Article 295 of the military penal code, which declared the following as an illegal act: "carrying out, during wartime or during expectation of war, an advertisement that aims to weaken national feeling or incite racist or confessional prejudices" (ibid.).

Although FPM activists, supporters and sympathizers may have cast doubt on the authenticity of the claims fabricated by the Lebanese state, these claims, which often included some reference to Israel or sedition, were used as solid evidence to justify the detainment and prison sentences of activists calling for the liberation of Lebanon from foreign troops.

By attempting to slander the reputation of FPM activists, the Lebanese authorities not only tried to throw activists behind bars, but also endeavored to dissuade the broader public from joining the movement.

Indeed, the Lebanese political elite attempted to discourage activists from persisting in activism with the FPM not only by adopting the strategy of referring them to trial in military courts, but also by sanctioning the use of violence against protestors. These protestors, who had university students and peaceful civilians within their ranks, had not physically attacked state property or employees, but merely expressed political ideas that disagreed with the political inclination of the de jure government of Lebanon. George Hadad confirmed the peaceful nature of the FPM: "We always depended on peaceful tactics. We had ethically clean people. I dare anyone to say we broke a traffic light or a single tile from the sidewalk" (interview September 17, 2014).

Yet, the repertoire of violence adopted by the security units policing FPM protests included the use of water hoses, tear gas, truncheons and gun butts against peaceful activists to break up protests. These violent tactics against FPM activists increased the cost of participation in FPM collective activity, thus rendering the decision to participate or the task of recruiting individuals to a protest fraught with challenges. In this scenario, the free-rider problem risked weakening the intensity of FPM activism if those less committed members believed that their more enthusiastic counterparts could organize collective activity on their own (Olson 1965).

The Lebanese political elite sanctioned the use of some violent tactics with the aim of at least containing FPM activism. Several of the interviewed activists confirmed their mistreatment by different units of national security institutions, such as the Lebanese army, General Security, the Internal Security Forces, as well as the Syrian forces based in Lebanon. Physical beatings, slaps, handcuffed detention and enforced signing of false charges became regular experiences for FPM activists from 1990 to 2005 in Lebanon. In addition, some activists testified to their exposure to psychological torture, such as being forced to confess while listening to the sound of people being tortured outside the interrogation room, only to subsequently discover that the security forces had been playing sound tapes.

However, these national security institutions hoped that by defaming, humiliating and torturing detained activists, they would be able to discourage others from participating in FPM activism. This kind of mistreatment made it difficult, if not impossible, for any individual to overlook the costs of participation in FPM activism. Nonetheless, the fact that FPM collective activity was sustained throughout this period in spite of multiple challenges makes the FPM's persistence and the tactics that contributed to it worthy of scrutiny.

Tactics for Activism

It can be argued that the FPM was able to sustain its collective activity despite government-imposed challenges due to its implementation of mobilizing tactics that maintained activists' commitment to the movement's cause. These tactics remained peaceful in nature chiefly because the FPM leadership—that is to say, Aoun—constantly insisted on maintaining peaceful forms of collective activism in expressing the movement's messages and opinions. Some of these tactics included placing first-time activists in the front lines of protests, supporting those activists and their families in the event that they were arrested for their involvement in FPM activism, trying to protect student activists from long prison sentences especially during school term, and exposing activists to Aoun's speeches and ideas, all of which had the intended effect of strengthening activists' persistence in the movement's collective activity.

The reason the FPM was able to maintain its status as a peaceful movement was due to the role of Michel Aoun who, from his exile in France, stressed the importance of adopting peaceful tactics of collective action and clearly eliminated consideration of all violent tactics from the movement's collective action repertoire. This highlights how the FPM was able to remain a peaceful movement in the face of state repression and crackdowns. George Hadad described the first phase of Lebanese state repression in the early 1990s as a "bone grinding" period in which the Lebanese political elite and the national security institutions displayed zero tolerance toward FPM activism (interview September 17, 2014).

A study of Islamist movements shows that the application of indiscriminate and reactionary state repression against movement members can draw them into adopting violent tactics in response to state repression (Hafez 2003, 2004, Chap. 1). Although the Algerian state's reaction to Islamists was far more ferocious than the treatment the FPM received from the Lebanese army or other national security institutions, two of the activists interviewed for this research tabled the topic of forming armed units at their meeting with Aoun in France. However, Aoun was diametrically opposed to all proposals to transform the peaceful nature of the movement into a confrontational militant movement that carried arms against the state. As a former army commander, he probably understood the chaos such a proposal would inflict on the Lebanese political arena and within Lebanese society. Therefore, he consistently stressed the importance of adopting peaceful tactics to express the FPM's political message and clearly restricted the movement's repertoire of collective activity to peaceful forms of expression, such as pamphlet distribution, sit-ins, demonstrations, protests, talks, workshops and so on.

More importantly, Aoun's role in determining the action repertoire of the FPM revealed that his charismatic authority was able to determine the collective repertoire of the movement and its future course, even from his position in exile. According to the majority of activists, whenever they consulted Aoun on certain matters, their leader's judgment was binding on activists, who adhered to it diligently. Although they enjoyed the freedom to determine the time, location and size of a group they were going to lead in collective activity, they often consulted Aoun on major issues, especially matters that affected the course of the movement in its entirety. Since mere censure or abandonment of an activist unit by the influential leader risked weakening the commitment of individuals to that unit, FPM activists adhered to the decisions taken by Aoun.

On the other hand, FPM student activists applied the tactic of placing new activists on the front lines during protests to encourage them to play an active role in movement activism. This helped to ensure the movement's persistence in two essential ways. First, positioning new activists on the front lines of a protest allowed individuals to perceive themselves as playing a leading role in the execution of FPM collective activity. In doing so, they became more willing to strengthen their commitment to FPM activism, which reflected positively on the persistence of that collective activity over time. Secondly, the position they held on the front lines exposed them to the possibility of being detained by the Lebanese state authorities, which subsequently resulted in their active participation after being released from detainment. As Liwa Chakour commented: "When we held a protest, I would ask our cadres to place the new students in front… By having them arrested, these students would feel hurt by the security institutions. It was a sort of baptism. When these people were baptized by the security institutions, they would be committed to our group 100%. They persisted with us in the struggle" (interview September 29, 2014). Therefore, the terrible experiences individuals witnessed in their encounters with the Lebanese authorities actually strengthened their commitment to FPM activism.

Even if such tactics led to the imprisonment of FPM activists who were expressing their political opinion peacefully, those very same activists would leave prison even more determined to pursue activism, since they would have overcome the fear barrier associated with the possibility of being arrested. Tony Harb stated this concisely: "If an activist was arrested, he would leave jail and participate in more activities. Because the fear barrier would be broken once a person was arrested, they would leave jail and be labeled champions. He would become an achiever and resister so he would have these nice characteristics [implying commendable or inspiring traits]. He would then participate forcefully and with incentive" (interview October 30, 2014). Because the repertoire of FPM collective activity included only peaceful means, such as pamphlet distribution, sit-ins, demonstrations and protests, the Lebanese state always lacked the political pretext that persuaded or resonated with society to detain activists for indefinite periods of time. Therefore, the more the FPM activists were imprisoned simply for demanding freedom, sovereignty and independence, the more they felt emboldened by their righteous cause to participate in collective activity.

FPM activists also relied on the tactic of encouraging individuals to persist in movement activism by performing heroic tasks, which other FPM activists might be inspired to emulate and accordingly contributed to the persistence of the movement's activism. In no way were FPM activists reckless or kamikaze-like individuals who cared very little about their lives. However, they grew conscious of the fact that in order to persevere with activism for the freedom of Lebanon, they had to make sacrifices that would inspire others to follow suit. Patrick ElKhoury stated: "We were conscious of what we were doing; we were ready to receive the blows in order to encourage others to join us… We used to enter prison, sacrifice, and leave with more determination. We were role models for people; we used to encourage people… People would say that's Patrick; he was imprisoned" (interview October 1, 2014). Although these sacrifices did not generate a snowball effect that exponentially increased the size of the movement, they did help to maintain activism or the persistence of collective activity throughout the period 1990–2005, chiefly by setting examples for others to follow.

FPM activists also applied the tactic of keeping students out of prison during their study terms, often by resorting to handing themselves in to Lebanese authorities in their place. Because the imprisonment of individuals who had just settled into a new job or students who were sitting exams at university risked weakening the intensity of FPM activism for a period, FPM cadres or leading activists often took the bold decision of going to jail to keep their counterparts with job or study commitments free. Commenting on this phenomenon, Naim Aoun stated:

> In April 2000, there were some detentions at the time… Three people were arrested before their exams. They wanted to destroy the movement because they arrested them before exams. I didn't want us to lose momentum… I felt there was a sort of impasse in freeing the guys. I felt this was unacceptable because it would have demoralized our movement for some time. So I took the decision—and Ziad Abs as well—to go to jail… We remained in prison for some time—approximately 20 days—and it created a big hassle. We amplified the problem. (Interview September 18, 2014)

FPM activists had grown conscious of the importance of making sacrifices to maintain a steady rate of activism. Considering that not all activists shared extensive experience of collective activity, veteran activists had to bear a heavier load in relation to new movement activists to sustain their collective activity. With time, activists became more adept at devising tactics to keep individuals out of prison, escape police during protests and ensure the uninterrupted flow of activism.

The ability to keep students out of prison involved negotiation tactics that FPM activists eventually came to master. The officers of the various national security institutions, such as the Lebanese army or the Internal Security Forces, came to know who was leading FPM protests; that is, part of the core group of activists interviewed here. When student protests occurred, such as those in April 2000, these officers were more interested in detaining the leading figures within the FPM, as opposed to ordinary students who simply participated in protests without having an immediate role in the organization of that collective activity. Perhaps these officers believed that by detaining leading FPM activists, they would be able to weaken the movement's activism for some time. As a result, veteran FPM activists, such as Naim Aoun and Ziad Abs, were able to negotiate the release of students by handing themselves in. In so doing, these leading activists knew that they were amplifying the situation, because the media, sympathetic journalists and international organizations were more likely to react to the detainment of leading figures within the movement, and thus help ensure their release after a few days.

Another important factor that facilitated the FPM's negotiation with Lebanese authorities, especially officers of national security institutions, was the membership of some FPM activists in syndicates. Those who were lawyers and enjoyed membership in the lawyers' syndicate helped negotiate with the Lebanese authorities for several reasons (A. Nasrallah, interview October 6, 2014). First, lawyers possessed skills that allowed them to strategize and negotiate with officials in a professional manner by making reference to Lebanese law, which contained essential democratic elements that allowed for freedom of expression. Secondly, by enjoying membership in a body such as the lawyers' syndicate, these activists also gained the support of non-affiliated individuals who rushed to defend their colleagues in the event that FPM lawyers were detained (ibid.). Therefore, lawyers possessed the ability to both negotiate with the Lebanese authorities to help release their counterparts and mobilize the support of the syndicate.

In addition, professional syndicates, such as those of lawyers and engineers, never held back from expressing bold stances that helped ensure the persistence of FPM activism. They often issued communiqués that condemned the government's actions against FPM protestors. Since they were professional bodies, they had better access to the media and their voice was heard more loudly. FPM activists were active members of professional unions. This reality helped the FPM to put pressure on the Lebanese government to release detained activists. Moreover, members of the lawyers' syndicate enjoyed relatively greater immunity because of their membership in a larger body that could be mobilized. Therefore, FPM lawyers always took up the defense of activists who were detained merely for distributing a communiqué, demonstrating or protesting in a peaceful manner (A. Nasrallah, interview October 6, 2014).

Whether it was the FPM central bureau, leading FPM activists or activists who were part of a syndicate who were engaging in negotiation with the Lebanese authorities, these actors never negotiated to explore the potential participation of the FPM in government, but were strictly focused on releasing FPM activists from detainment in order to ensure the persistence of their movement's activism. This must not mislead readers into believing that a robust relationship between the movement and members of the political elite existed throughout the whole period 1990–2005. On the contrary, had there been a solid relationship between the FPM and the political elite of Lebanon, members of the political elite would not have constantly attempted to concoct strategies to exclude the FPM from participation inside Parliament, illustrated in the practice of gerrymandering electoral constituencies to minimize the impact of Christian voters who were expected to be supporters of the FPM, as revealed in the 2003 Parliamentary by-election results in the Baabda-Aley district (Gambill 2003).

Yet, with time, members of the FPM became better able to negotiate with the Lebanese authorities. The ability to negotiate was an accumulated skill on behalf of FPM members who became more effective as FPM activists found themselves negotiating with the Lebanese authorities on several occasions. These accumulated skills helped activists to ensure the persistence of the collective activity of their movement, chiefly because activists became almost certain that their detainment would not last for an indefinite period, meaning that their cohorts and the supportive system they helped establish put pressure on the Lebanese political elite to order the release of detained activists. Therefore, by entering into some negotiations with the Lebanese authorities, the FPM was able not only to carry out activism, but also to ensure that its activists were released after being imprisoned for organizing collective activity, which was a significant factor that contributed to the persistence of FPM activism throughout the period 1990–2005.

However, even though those FPM activists had to face some prison sentences ordered by the Lebanese political elite, who displayed very little tolerance of forms of political activism that critiqued their politics, the tactic of defending those imprisoned activists and supporting their families during their short periods of imprisonment built a feeling of trust among FPM members that made them willing to continue devoting their time and effort to activism, which ensured the persistence of the movement's collective activity. When activists were detained, their movement cohorts would visit their families in a clear expression of support. Describing the extent to which FPM activists stood by the families of detained activists, George Hadad compared the phenomenon to a "site of pilgrimage," in reference to the movement's solidarity and the number of individuals who showed up to express their support (interview September 17, 2014). This reality forged a feeling of solidarity within the ranks of the FPM, because detained activists knew they were not abandoned. Activists even strengthened their commitment upon realizing that their movement cohorts took equal risks in expressing collective activity and backed those who were caught.

Another tactic resorted to by FPM activists was reminding individuals of the ideas of General Michel Aoun, which helped ensure the persistence of FPM activism. Focusing on the ideas of freedom, sovereignty and independence, good practice versus corruption, democracy and equal opportunity as opposed to manipulated representation taking the form of political succession, FPM activists were able to mobilize the youth on the basis of these ideas, which had been initially expressed by Aoun during his premiership. Speaking about how he used to mobilize individuals into the FPM, Liwa Chakour stated: "I got videos of the General's speeches in Baabda. In our student club, we had a big screen… So upon reaching university, we would introduce the students to the speeches of the General. In a couple of years following 1990, most of the students were young and didn't know much about the General. Through this way, we would nurture a national feeling among the students… it sparked a sense of national feeling and motivation" (interview September 29, 2014). Aware of the rampant corruption in post-war Lebanese governments and of the dominant role of Syria in Lebanese politics, a vast number of young people naturally gravitated toward Aoun's expressed ideas, since they named and promised to redress the faults of the Lebanese political system.

The specific tactic of communicating with Aoun during his years in exile encouraged FPM activists to persist in activism within the movement. It often led individuals to deepen their involvement in the organization of FPM collective activity. Antoine Moukheiber stated: "We began telling the guys in the areas to gather the people because we will ensure a call with the General. This used to give us a great incentive for movement. When they heard the General, their morale and excitement increased" (interview October 31, 2014). According to him, the talks with Aoun helped ensure the persistence of the FPM not only by virtue of strengthening the commitment of activists to collective activity, but also by encouraging them to take on leading roles in the organization of collective activity. He commented: "The talks with the General were very useful for us. This also made a large cadrification" (ibid.). This reveals that activists' personal communication with Aoun, listening to his speeches, conversing over the phone and even possibly visiting him in France, incentivized them to move from their activist state to play a larger role in the organization of FPM collective activity.

FPM tactics of organizing collective activity that was intertwined or coincided with issues of national concern helped create synergies that made Lebanese society sympathize with FPM activism throughout

Lebanon. For instance, Syrian workers and merchants, who were allowed to work in Lebanon without a work permit or paying taxes, competed with Lebanese workers and merchants, since they provided their labor at a lower price. In order to point out this flaw in the Lebanese political-economic system, FPM activists decided to work as greengrocers on Labor Day by locating vegetable carts at ten different locations across Lebanon. Elie Hanna stated: "On Labor Day, we also launched an event… I went to the bean cart and asked him where the beans were from; I told him I wanted to teach my brother the profession. We agreed on how to sell the vegetables. We located ten different locations; we placed points in Achrafieh, Hadath, Gallery Samaan, and other places. We were losing money to Syrian vegetable carts" (interview October 16, 2014).

FPM activists organized these activities from their own resources and were able to deliver synergic effects by attracting the attention of society at large. Commenting on the impact of these activities, Rabih Tarraf, an FPM activist, stated: "People would buy our products quickly. By twelve midday, we would have nothing left on our cart… We were rejecting the Syrian vegetable seller who competed with Lebanese stores… Lebanese shop-owners would come to buy our products to show the people that we were right… It was known that we are Aounists. We had the Lebanese flags with us" (interview September 11, 2014). Therefore, the nature of FPM collective activity centered on highlighting the faults of the Lebanese political system by virtue of tackling political-economic faults and stressing the importance of prioritizing Lebanese goods and services over foreign, especially Syrian, competition.

Since the Lebanese political elite attempted to keep opposition movements docile, especially those who were critical of the post-war political elite's strategies and the presence of Syrian troops in Lebanon, it is quite difficult to measure clearly the impact of FPM activism on the non-activist population, whether supporters or foes of the FPM, in the period 1990–2005. However, interviews with FPM activists reveal that the Lebanese people were quite responsive to the activities and messages of the FPM. Commenting on how people responded to the FPM activists' pamphlet-distribution campaigns, Elie Nemnom, an FPM activist, mentioned: "Imagine, they waited for the people to exit the movies and began dropping the pamphlets on them from above. You know how it feels when you drop wheat for the army. It was as if you were providing these people with bread, with spirit. In Jounieh, it was the same thing… People would leave their tables and pick up the pamphlets" (interview September

9, 2014). Many of the interviewed activists mentioned receiving friendly hand gestures or supportive car honks by individuals driving by in their cars when they were distributing pamphlets, cassettes or pictures of Aoun on the streets.

Moreover, the way in which FPM activism moved from its concentration in small, decentralized groups to larger protests by the latter half of the 1990s clearly shows the success of FPM tactics in drawing individuals to the streets, thus contributing to the persistence of the movement and to increasing the size of FPM protests. Therefore, FPM tactics helped transform sympathetic individuals into supporters of the movement, and often even into activists who bore the brunt of challenges imposed by the Lebanese political elite and persisted in organizing movement activities against all odds.

By virtue of incentivizing individuals to persist in the organization of FPM activism, these tactics help to achieve McCarthy and Zald's (1977) strategic tasks of mobilizing supporters, neutralizing and/or transforming mass and elite publics into sympathizers, and achieving change in targets, which ensured the persistence of FPM activism throughout the period 1990–2005. Whereas collective behavior scholars concentrate on solidary incentives in promoting mobilization (Blumer 1957; Smelser 1962; Park 1967) and resource mobilization scholars place a heavier weight on individual material incentives (McCarthy and Zald 1973, 1977), some revisionist social movement theorists stress the importance of purposive incentives for the mobilization of movements (Wilson 1973; Gamson 1975; Fireman and Gamson 1979). Fireman and Gamson (1979) argue that activists invest effort in a social movement because they believe in its goals and understand that self-sacrifice is essential when working for a political cause, as was the case with many FPM activists. However, this author agrees with Hirsch (1986), who criticizes the unbalanced approach of the aforementioned scholars and believes that a combination of incentives can promote movement mobilization. Indeed, this author embraces the approach of scholars who resort to various incentives to explain the mobilization of movement activism (Meyer 2007, p. 50; Snow and Soule 2010, pp. 134–135).

FPM activists emphasized tactics that facilitated the organization of the movement's collective activity by means of incentivizing individuals to persist in movement activism. By participating in FPM activism, individuals were exposed to a set of solidary incentives that simply encouraged them to persevere in the movement's collective activity. Solidary incentives are rooted in the affective and emotional attachments that make one feel part of a group, and only affect those individuals who participate in collective activity (Meyer 2007, p. 50). The feeling of partaking in activity alongside people who share similar beliefs is a powerful motivator that encourages further participation in collective action. This is mainly why a discussion of incentives in the persistence phases of a movement is crucial, given that solidary incentives often appear after individuals have already participated in the movement; that is, especially after the movement has already emerged. Therefore, solidary incentives allow individuals to continue contributing their time and effort to the organization of activism, which reflects positively on the persistence of the movement.

The tactics of placing new activists on the front lines of protests or showing a willingness to be imprisoned helped to ensure the persistence of the FPM by means of generating solidary incentives. When individuals saw their cohorts taking risks in movement activism, they were often incentivized to emulate their actions in support of the political cause. In addition, the support that FPM activists extended to those individuals imprisoned for their activism helped foster a sense of trust within the movement. Activists imprisoned for their activism, in turn, persisted in FPM activism immediately after their release from prison. Therefore, this indicates the effectiveness of the FPM's tactics in sustaining the movement's activism throughout this period in spite of the challenges it faced. The next section offers an explanation of how the framing of ideas helped to ensure the persistence of the FPM's activism throughout the period 1990–2005.

Part III: Framing Ideas Ensures Persistence

The way FPM ideas were framed helped ensure the persistence of the movement by revealing how it translated principles into actual political phenomena through locating the source of blame and calling for corrective action. A frame is a schema of interpretation that enables individuals to locate, perceive, identify and label occurrences within their life spaces and the world at large (Goffman 1974, p. 21). The use of a combination of Snow and Benford's (2000) diagnostic framing (problem identification), prognostic framing (proposing solutions) and motivational framing (calls to action) is what helped the FPM react to salient political issues in Lebanese politics and underscored the existence of a vibrant political movement that could formulate a clear stance in all fields. Since Aoun and

FPM activists interacted with political issues in Lebanon, they were able to influence individuals to persist in movement activism by constantly highlighting the wrongdoings of the Lebanese political system and providing the solution in the form of calls to activism.

FPM activists played a major role in contributing to their movement's persistence throughout the period 1990–2005 because of the manner in which they continued to express the movement's ideational character, which centered upon the ideas or principles of transparency, nationalism, integrity, freedom, sovereignty and independence, among others. They concentrated on conveying the ideas and political stances of their exiled leader to a wide segment of his supporters in Lebanon.

Even though Aoun was in exile in France, he constantly registered his stances according to the most politically salient topics in the political order of Lebanon. For instance, he consistently rejected dropping the border with Syria and pointed to the importance of disarming Palestinian refugee camps in Lebanon (*Annahar*, September 9, 1995, p. 4; September 27, 1995, p. 6; Assaf, August 23, 1997, p. 4). Therefore, Aoun helped stretch the FPM's calls for sovereignty beyond mere statements to explanations that were situated in the reality of the Lebanese political order, especially ones to which people could relate. His position, covered daily by journalists in *Annahar* and in his weekly publication the *Lebanese Bulletin*, helped to keep FPM activists in line with the political orientation of the movement.

FPM activists absorbed this political orientation and conveyed their thoughts through various means, such as public displays (spray painting on walls and protests) and print publications. The most important aspect of this ideational expression is that it contrasted sharply with the version put forward by all the de jure Lebanese governments who were heavily influenced by Syria, a sworn enemy of Aoun and the FPM. As a consequence, this movement analysis kept the flame of FPM activism burning throughout the period 1990–2005, chiefly by providing an alternative version to the prevalent and dominant political state of affairs in Lebanon.

The FPM's collective activity of spray painting graffiti in public spaces expressed its ideas and influenced activists and society at large in two clear ways. First, the slogans spray painted on public walls reflected both solid principles and the movement's orientation on a salient political issue. Slogans such as "Aoun's returning," "No to Syria" or "No to occupation" reflected activists' commitment to the liberation of Lebanon and their demands for increased freedom. These slogans surfaced in the early

1990s, but became consistent demands that reflected the stable principles of the movement throughout the period 1990–2005; that is, until the withdrawal of Syrian troops from Lebanon in 2005. Slogans such as "Boycott elections" or the public display of blacking out pictures of the Lebanese president or prime minister for yielding to the political influence of Syria largely depended on the temporary political salience of the topic, and thus reflected the movement's ability to react to any and all issues taking place in Lebanon. Of course, some slogans and public displays also reflected a degree of creativity, such as Ziad Abs' slogan to boycott the 1992 parliamentary elections: "You are Lebanese so you are my brother; the bird doesn't give birth in a cage to not bequeath slavery to his offspring, boycott the elections!" (interview October 31, 2014).

Secondly, the mere existence of graffiti in public spaces incentivized activists to compete with their counterparts in populating public spaces with the movement's slogans. A majority of the interviewed activists informed this author that while attempting to spray paint movement slogans in public spaces, they often discovered that their counterparts had already covered those walls. Therefore, the work that one activist unit carried out often incentivized others to follow suit and compete with the active units. For example, the spraying of graffiti in public spaces by the FPM group MUR encouraged the FPM activist unit of Roland ElKhoury to increase its activism in order to compete with its counterpart.

This research revealed that the content of the messages scribbled in public spaces helped locate the source of blame (diagnostic framing), which usually centered on the Syrian forces in Lebanon and politicians who allied themselves with Syria and supported its military presence in the country. It also highlighted solutions to Lebanon's predicament in the form of prognostic frames, which were embodied in the famous slogan of "Aoun's returning." The importance of these scribbled messages is that they, at one point, seemed to present an important public platform for freedom of speech in Lebanon; thus, FPM activists made use of that space to express their political opinions freely and influence others to follow suit. Using an iconographic analysis of wartime posters in Lebanon, Maasri (2009) argues that the portrayal of deceased or disappeared Lebanese leaders in a larger-than-life image in posters helped strengthen mobilization for the cause of the movement or community to which they belonged. Since Aoun was alive and active, albeit in France, activists were more interested in the actual analysis he proposed. Therefore, in the case of the FPM, populating public spaces with movement slogans had a positive impact on the persistence of activism, simply by confirming the existence of the FPM as a vibrant movement with active supporters in Lebanon.

By analyzing the ideas fleshed out in the FPM student publication *Samizdat*, the weekly *Lebanese Bulletin* drafted by Aoun and interviews in the famous Lebanese newspaper *Annahar*, Aoun's motivational speeches helped to translate principles into political embodiments and thus ensured the persistence of activists within the political orientation of the FPM. For instance, in response to Lebanese politicians who claimed the loss of the FPM in the municipal elections of 1998, Aoun launched a fierce diatribe against the censored media that misreported the elections' true results.

However, Aoun presented his words in a fiery and motivational manner that could not but have attracted the attention of movement activists. He stated:

> They wish for the failure of the FPM and thus wrote about its failure. They wish for the end of the FPM, and thus wrote about its termination… Therefore, they wrote at the beginning that the phenomenon of Aoun is a lie, then it became a creation of the intelligence and subsequently it deteriorated… The FPM gauges its success through its presence across all the Lebanese territories, and through bearing national ideas that struggle to liberate Lebanon and its citizens. It also challenges all the political sectarian and feudal people, financial mafia, and the authorities… The FPM has no voice in Lebanon, but is the voice of the conscience of every Lebanese and no one can silence it, and even if it lacks a station in Lebanon. (*Annahar*, June 13, 1998, p. 4)

By dubbing the Lebanese government a "financial mafia" and the FPM the "conscience" of Lebanon, Aoun clearly accuses the government of financial misappropriation and calls on FPM activists to persist in their political struggle to fix the predicaments of the political system. In other words, Aoun motivated FPM activists to persist in their activism by informing them that they bore a duty to elucidate the faults that lie in the political order in Lebanon.

Aoun often made reference to parts of the Bible and thus had a powerful impact on his audiences, because situating the Lebanese people's political state within a biblical message helped his points to resonate sharply with them, especially when considering that the FPM's base of support was predominantly Christian individuals. With clear reference to the political misdeeds of the Lebanese ruling class, Aoun stated: "Conscience followed Cain after he had killed Abel, to all the hideaways. He couldn't hide from it. The FPM is the conscience of Lebanon and no one can separate conscience from the self. And as for the conscience of Cain, it is going to follow all those that killed their brother or attempted to kill him" (ibid.). Infused in this message is a subtle call for FPM activists to concentrate on combating corruption, which was embodied in the political class that governed Lebanon. For activists who already understood the aims of their movement, these messages that took the form of motivational framing of speeches served to strengthen or confirm their commitment to the political orientation of the FPM.

Commenting on the role of Syria and the de jure Lebanese government in absenting Lebanon from the Middle East peace talks with Israel, for example, Aoun's message to the participants of the 1996 LNC in France criticized Lebanese politicians and called on the FPM to persist in its activism. He declared: "They negotiate on our behalf and they tie the fate of our negotiations with the fate of others… Ignorant virgins are only the ruling class that believe and wait at the doors rushing to enter, and without oil in their lanterns… No, not at all, do not be hopeful, but be like those wise ones. Prepare yourselves for something totally different. Fill your lanterns with oil, your minds with wisdom, and hearts with faith, persistence, and hope" (Atallah, February 19, 1996, p. 4).

Aoun's situating of political messages in biblical frames served to locate the source of the blame (diagnostic framing) and his calls to adopt ameliorative action (motivational framing)—such as dubbing the FPM the conscience of Lebanon or asking people to fill their hearts with hope, persistence and faith—served to ensure the persistence of the FPM by asking activists to carry on with their duty to liberate the political system from its faults. This motivational framing fulfilled the specific task of requesting that activists persist in the FPM's struggle because, as Oegema and Klandermans (1994) show in their exploration of the reasons for the low turnout for a Dutch peace movement, participation in social movement activity occurs if activists are asked to participate; that is to say, if they are mobilized into activism. Therefore, in addition to the mobilization efforts of FPM activists on the ground in Lebanon, Aoun's calls to persist with activism against the corrupt political class and the Syrian and Israeli occupation of Lebanon led activists to strengthen their commitment to FPM activism throughout this period.

Considering that FPM activists were predominantly Christian, but also included activists from other sectarian affiliations, geographic areas and political persuasions across Lebanon, the FPM remained faithful to its principles and called for the political rights of all the Lebanese people regardless of their confessional affinities. Aoun, for instance, not only placed his political messages within a biblical framework, but also referred to parts of the Koran when registering a political point, which helped his messages resonate with Lebanese citizens of both Christian and Muslim faiths. At the same time, Aoun stressed the importance of the FPM's principles of integrity as opposed to speaking of parochial confessional interests. During a press conference held in France in preparation for the 1998 municipal elections in Lebanon, he stated: "I am against confessional duopolies, and our stances should remain nationalistic and represent both Christians and Muslims. It is not my ambition to be a Christian or Muslim leader, but to combat the evil that exists in government today" (Sassine, May 21, 1998, p. 6).

Whether in press conferences, written messages to the Lebanese people or speeches given by phone (*Annahar*, April 7, 1998, p. 4), Aoun regularly emphasized the importance of combating corruption alongside the liberation of Lebanon from foreign occupation, which portrayed the FPM as a movement with a positive contribution to the Lebanese political system as a whole. Aoun may have resorted to passages from the Bible or the Koran in his political speeches, but only with the aim of rendering the impact of his political messages more culturally significant to the Lebanese people. His use of this language did not detract from the importance of the secular positions he adopted, nor the progressive political ideas he attempted to advance in the period 1990–2005. Therefore, FPM activists continued to regard their movement as one that upheld secular political orientations and to express their beliefs according to those FPM principles.

The FPM's collective activity persisted in attracting sympathetic audiences because the movement did not display double standards regarding the implementation of its principles and political stances. Although the political messages of its collective activity had sharply criticized the presence of Syrian troupes on Lebanese turf, which the FPM insisted on referring to as the "Syrian Occupation" of Lebanon, the movement also celebrated the Israeli withdrawal from Lebanon with great jubilation, because the withdrawal removed the occupation from part of Lebanese national territory.

The clear censure of Israel in a communiqué distributed by the FPM to celebrate the Israeli withdrawal from Lebanon bears witness to the movement's actual political stance on the topic. The communiqué read:

> With iron and fire you hit, our children you kill, our light you block, our structure you destroy. The dialog of humans seems impossible with you but the answer became clear: what all the diplomacies of the world failed to persuade you to recognize, the unity of our people was able to enforce upon you. You had no choice but to depart. Nothing was left for your arrogance except to be crushed in the face of the greatness of the Lebanon's population. Depart because your planes don't scare us, our will for survival is stronger than your capability to destroy. So if you destroyed stone, we have built a unified population that despises you… So leave us and you will be haunted by the cries of joy that will permeate Lebanon from its North to its South. And the victory of our people over the occupying army of the Israeli enemy will remain an example for all the victimized populations and a glimmer of light for the rise of a new global dawn. (*Annahar*, May 9, 2000, p. 23)

This sharp rebuke aimed at the Israeli forces revealed the genuine stance the FPM adopted toward all forms of occupation of Lebanese soil. It actually translated the FPM's principles of freedom, sovereignty and independence into palpable political positions that were made quite evident to FPM activists and the Lebanese population as a whole.

The political positions and ideas expressed by Aoun and the FPM helped ensure the persistence of the movement chiefly by showcasing how it translated its principles into real collective activity. Through the speeches and writings of Michel Aoun, it became quite evident how the principles of integrity, freedom, sovereignty and independence, inter alia, were applied by the FPM in various political, economic, social and educational fields (*Lebanese Bulletin* 1997–2001; *Samizdat* January–March 2004). The FPM had not strictly organized collective activity for the sake of highlighting its oppositional stance toward the Lebanese government in office, but reacted to the salient political issues at hand in order to present its vision of political issues that were in line with the broad principles of the movement. Whether the FPM highlighted the intense corruption festering in government or protested against the political intervention of the political elite in the affairs of the Lebanese University (*Annahar*, June 5, 2001, p. 19; Barada, June 7, 2001, p. 17), the movement always positioned itself as a defender of just causes, thus ensuring its political credibility among its supporters and sympathetic Lebanese audiences at large.

Conclusion

By and large, the persistence of the FPM was dependent on mobilizing structures, tactics to ensure sustained activism and the framing of ideas. It hosted two types of mobilizing structures: internal and external. The internal mobilizing structures, which coordinated collective activity in Lebanon, comprised small activist units organized according to a pyramidal or cluster-like arrangement, in which members of the unit communicated with their leader, but without necessarily knowing one another. This arrangement allowed for operational secrecy, minimized the risk of state infiltration and repression, and ensured the persistence of the unit's collective activity, because the detainment of a single activist did not assist state authorities in tracking down other activists. These activist units relied heavily on the commitment of their members in mobilizing resources, for instance money, paraphernalia (printers, paper, cassettes, inter alia) and office space for meetings, in order to plan and execute FPM activism. University campuses in Lebanon proved to be an important mobilization center for activism because, as pointed out by McAdam (1988), students are less encumbered by work and family commitments; thus, they can afford to spend more time actively engaged in activism.

Fostering external mobilizing structures, on the other hand, assisted the FPM in gaining political visibility and spreading its messages to international organizations and the media. Individuals associated with Aoun had begun forming some movement structures just before 1994 in Lebanon. However, it was the formation of the LNC in France in 1994, placing General Nadim Lteif as its representative in Beirut to coordinate the efforts of activists, that led to the compass of movement activism being extended in cities, towns and villages. However, the underrepresentation of youth in the decision-making positions of the organization led to the formation of a more representative structure in a meeting with Aoun in France in 1996. The formal name of the FPM was adopted in this meeting, though the name is used retrospectively here because the movement had existed earlier, albeit operating in a loosely connected and decentralized form. Furthermore, FPM activists broadly construed their political struggle in human rights terms and thus attracted sympathetic audiences beyond their movement's following. By instrumentally channeling news of detainments of FPM activists to Amnesty International, Human Rights Watch and the Foundation for Human and Humanitarian Rights, these organizations were enabled to portray the FPM's cause as a struggle to regain Lebanese citizens' right to freedom of expression, thereby assisting in attracting a sympathetic audience for the FPM.

The FPM resorted to the tactics of placing first-time activists on the front lines of protests, supporting those activists and their families if they were arrested for their involvement, trying to keep student activists away from long prison sentences especially during school terms, and exposing activists to the speeches and ideas of Aoun, among others, all of which had the intended effect of strengthening activists' persistence in the FPM's collective activity. These tactics centered on ensuring the consistent participation of individuals in collective activity in order to sustain movement activism in the long run. Therefore, participating in protests and displaying a degree of resilience in returning to participate in activism after being imprisoned for affiliation with the FPM generated solidary incentives that encouraged many to persist in collective activity. It also helped break the fear barrier associated with detainment by the Lebanese authorities, which contributed to the persistence of FPM activism by virtue of rendering those once detained activists more resilient and willing to make sacrifices for the long-term goals of the freedom, sovereignty and independence of Lebanon. Through his conversations with FPM activists, Aoun played a major role in motivating individuals to persist in activism and to assume leadership roles in the movement. Aoun also played a decisive role in maintaining the peaceful orientation of the FPM and rejected all forms of armed activity proposed by some activist units when faced with tremendous challenges.

The FPM also persisted throughout this period due to the manner in which it expressed its ideas and the way Aoun kept activists in line with the political orientation of the movement through his expressed thoughts. The graffiti FPM activists scribbled in public spaces reflected broad movement principles, such as Lebanese freedom and sovereignty, by calling for the withdrawal of Syrian troops from Lebanon, and revealed the FPM's position or reaction to other salient political developments, for example boycotting national parliamentary elections, which were largely perceived by the FPM as rigged.

However, the display of slogans and other graffiti in public spaces often led various activist units to compete with one another, since the loosely shaped form of these units often meant they had to operate without communicating with their counterparts; this competition ensured the persistence of FPM collective activity. Aoun regularly framed the movement's aims as promoting integrity and transparency in political affairs. He resorted to the use of metaphors, biblical stories and references from the Koran in order to situate his political points in a cultural frame to which Lebanese citizens, the overwhelming majority of whom were either Christian or Muslim, could relate. Although his speech persuaded individuals to strengthen their commitment to the FPM, he always emphasized the importance of progressive ideas and secular political options as part of the movement's political outlook. Another reason activists persisted in their activism with the FPM is that the movement did not display double standards when dealing with political principles.

After exploring the reasons for the persistence of the FPM throughout this period, this book now turns to the institutional transformation of the FPM from a social movement into a political party. These reasons are currently absent from the literature on Lebanese political movements and thus require further exploration. Moreover, the institutional transformation of the FPM into a political party had impacts on the movement in many ways that generated mixed feelings and opinions among FPM activists themselves. Therefore, why the FPM was transformed into a political party and how successful that transformation was are the topics to be explored in the next chapter.

References

Abi Antoun, N. Interview by this author. 2014. Beirut, September 23.

Abi Nader, W. Interview by this author. 2014. Jounieh, October 15.

Abi Ramia, S. Interview by this author. 2014. Beirut, November 21.

Abs, Z. Interview by this author. 2014. Beirut, October 31.

Achkar, W. Interview by this author. 2014. Jounieh, October 15.

Amnesty International. 1993. "Legal Concern/Fear of Torture." Amnesty International Report, January 14, MDE 18/01/93 ed.

———. 2000. "Use of Military Court Against Student Demonstrators a Violation of Rights." Public Statement, April 25.

Annahar. 1994. "Mawkoufu AlTayyar AlWattani Ouhilu 'ala Al'askariya. 'The Patriotic Movement Detainees Were Transferred to the Military'." *Annahar*, September 28, 18945 ed.: 5.

———. 1995. "Almounasekiyya Alaama Lilmouta'amar Alwatani Nazeh Assilah Alfalastini Niha'iyan. 'General Coordination for the National Conference

Destroying Palestinian Arms Permanently'." *Annahar*, September 27, 19247 ed.: 6.

———. 1995. "Aoun: Itha Sharaka Altayyar Alwatani FilSouta Sayounathef Albikaa min Almoukhayyamat Alirhabiyya. 'Aoun: If the Patriotic Movement Participates in Government It Will Clean the Bikaa from the Terrorist Camps'." *Annahar*, September 9, 19232 ed.: 4.

———. 1996. "Takhleyat Khair waKhamsa Akhareen wa Istimrar AlTahkeek FiMalaf AlTa'aamol. 'Releasing Khair and Five Others and Continuing the Investigation into the Collaboration Dossier'." *Annahar*, December 31, 19633 ed.: 7.

———. 1997. "Daawat Aoun Tahawoulon Jathri Fi AlCongress AlAmeriki. 'The Invitation of Aoun Radical Transformation in American Congress'." *Annahar*, June 26, 19777 ed.: 6.

———. 1998. "Aoun Yad'ou AlBatrouniyeen Ila MouWajahat AlIktaa AlSiyassi Wal Malli. 'Aoun Calls on the Batrounees to Confront Political and Monetary Feudalism'." *Annahar*, April 7, 20017 ed.: 4.

———. 1998. "Aoun Yaroudu aala AlQa'ileen biKhisaratihi Yatamanoun Nihayatana wa Yakhdaoun Anfousahum. 'Aoun Responds to Those Who Claim His Loss They Wish for Our End and Trick Themselves'." *Annahar*, June 13, 20069 ed.: 4.

———. 1998. "Mouassasatan liHoukouk AlInsan Tastankiran AlIstid'aat. 'The Institutions of Human Rights Condemns the Detainments'." *Annahar*, September 25, 20158 ed.: 6.

———. 2000. "Toulab AlTayyar AlWattani AlHurr Waza'ou bayanat Tahtafel bi Zawal AlIhtilal. 'The Students of the Free Patriotic Movement Distributed Communiqués in Celebration of the Demise of Occupation'." *Annahar*, May 9, 20644 ed.: 23.

———. 2001. "AlTayyar AlWattani Tahadatha 'an I'tiqalat li Anssarih. 'The Patriotic Movement Spoke of Detainment of Supporters'." *Annahar*, June 5, 20967 ed.: 19.

Aoun, A. Interview by this author. 2014. Beirut, March 12.

Aoun, N. Interview by this author. 2014. Awkar, September 18.

Assaf, Z. 1997. "Raddan Aala AlDaawa Ila Iskat AlHoudoud. 'Responding to the Calls of Dropping Borders'." *Annahar*, August 23, 19828 ed.: 4.

Assouad, Z. Interview by this author. 2014. Jounieh, October 10.

Atallah, P. 1996. "Almou'tamar Alwatani Alloubnani FiBarees Ikhtatama Youmein min Aljalasat. 'The Lebanese National Conference from Paris Concluded Two Days of Sessions'." *Annahar*, February 19, 19368 ed.: 4.

Azzam, P. Interview by this author. 2014. Beirut, October 9.

Barada. 2001. "Fi Taharoukin Houwa AlAkbar li Mouwajahat Damj Fourou' AlJami'a AlLoubnaniyya. 'In the Largest Move to Confront the Merger of the Branches of the Lebanese University'." *Annahar*, June 7, 20969 ed.: 17.

Blumer, H. 1957. “Collective Behavior.” In *Review of Sociology: Analysis of a Decade*, edited by J. B. Gittler, 127–158. New York: Wiley.

Calhoun, C. 1997. *Neither Gods Nor Emperors: Students and the Struggle for Democracy in China*. Berkeley: University of California Press.

Chakour, L. Interview by this author. 2014. Jbeil, September 29.

Chamoun, M. Interview by this author. 2014. Beirut, October 15.

Chlela, R. Interview by this author. 2014. Jounieh, October 29.

Choucair, G. Interview by this author. 2014. Beirut, October 16.

Dabbous, D. 2013. *Regulating Lebanese Broadcasting: A Policy Analysis*. Saarbrücken: Lambert Academic Publishing.

Dabbous, Y. 2010. “Media with a Mission: Why Fairness and Balance Are Not Priorities in Lebanon’s Journalistic Codes.” *International Journal of Communications* 4: 719–737.

———. 2012. “Teaching Investigative Journalism in the Arab States.” Policy Brief, Beirut: Workshop: UNESCO Investigative Journalism at Lebanese American University.

Dajani, N. 1992. *Disoriented Media in a Fragmented Society: The Lebanese Experience*. Beirut: American University of Beirut.

———. 2005. “The Re-feudalization of the Public Sphere: Lebanese Television News Coverage and the Lebanese Political Process.” New Media, International Conference for Contemporary Middle East Studies. Denmark: University of Southern Denmark.

Elefteriades, M. Interview by this author. 2014. Beirut, September 8.

ElKhoury, P. Interview by this author. 2014. Dbayeh, October 1.

ElKhoury, R. Interview by this author. 2014. Jounieh, September 26.

Fadel, M. Interview by this author. 2014. Dekwaneh, November 20.

Fireman, B., and W. Gamson. 1979. “Utilitarian Logic in the Resource Mobilization Perspective.” In *The Dynamics of Social Movements*, edited by M. N. Zald and J. D. McCarthy, 8–44. Cambridge: Winthrop.

Freeman, J. 1975. *The Politics of Women’s Liberation: A Case Study of an Emerging Social Movement and Its Relation to the Policy Process*. New York: Longman, Inc.

Gambill, G. C. 2003. “FNC Triumphs in Baabda-Aley.” *Middle East Forum and United States Committee for a Free Lebanon* 5 (8–9).

Gamson, W. 1975. *The Strategy of Social Protest*. Homewood, IL: Dorsey.

Goffman, E. 1974. *Frame Analysis*. Boston: Northeastern University Press.

Hadad, G. Interview by this author. 2014. Hadath, September 17.

Hafez, M. M. 2003. *Why Muslims Rebel: Repression and Resistance in the Islamic World*. Boulder, CO: Lynne Rienner Publishers.

Hanna, E. Interview by this author. 2014. Rabieh, October 16.

Harb, T. Interview by this author. 2014. Beirut, October 30.

Harris, W. A. 1997. *Faces of Lebanon: Sects, Wars, and Global Extensions*. Princeton, NJ: Marcus Wiener Publishers.
Helou, J. P. 2015. "Policy Overcomes Confessional Hurdles: A Policy Strategy Tackles Challenges in the Segmented Society and State of Lebanon." *Athens Journal of Mediterranean Studies* 1 (4): 325–340.
Hirsch, E. L. 1986. "The Creation of Political Solidarity in Social Movement Organizations." *The Sociological Quarterly* 27 (3): 373–387.
———. 1990. "Sacrifice for the Cause: Group Processes, Recruitment, and Commitment in Student Social Movement." *American Sociological Review* 55: 243–254.
Hobeika, T. Interview by this author. 2014. Dbayeh, October 17.
Hottinger, A. 1961. "Zu'ama' and Parties in the Lebanese Crisis of 1958." *Middle East Journal* 15 (2): 127–140.
Johnson, M. 1986. *Class and Client in Beirut: The Sunni Muslim Community and the Lebanese State 1840–1985*. London: Ithaca Press.
Kanj, R. Interview by this author. 2014. Beirut, September 19.
Khalaf, S. 1968. "Primordial Ties and Politics in Lebanon." *Middle Eastern Studies* 4 (3): 243–269.
———. 2003. "On Roots and Roots: the Reassertion of Primordial Loyalties." In *Lebanon in Limbo: Postwar Society and State in an Uncertain Regional Environment*, edited by T. Hanf and N. Salam, Chap. 6. Baden-Baden: Nomos.
Kraidy, M. 1998. "Broadcasting Regulation and Civil Society in Postwar Lebanon." *Journal of Broadcasting & Electronic Media* 42: 387–401.
Maasri, Z. 2009. *Off the Wall*. London: I.B. Tauris.
McAdam, D. 1988. *Freedom Summer*. New York: Oxford University Press.
McCarthy, J. D., and M. N. Zald. 1973. *The Trend of Social Movements in America: Professionalization and Resource Mobilization*. Morristown, NJ: General Learning.
———. 1977. "Resource Mobilization and Social Movements: A Partial Theory." *American Journal of Sociology* 82: 1212–1241.
Melki, J. P. 2007. "Television News and the State in Lebanon." Ph.D. dissertation, University of Maryland.
Meyer, D. S. 2007. *The Politics of Protest*. New York: Oxford University Press.
Morris, A. 1981. "Black Southern Student Sit-in Movement: An Analysis of Internal Organization." *American Sociological Review* 46: 744–776.
Mouawad, R. 1996. "AlGeneral Aoun min Beytihi AlAali WalArzat AlKhams. 'General Aoun from His High House and the Five Cedars'." *Annahar*, April 21, 19419 ed.: 16.
Moukheiber, A. Interview by this author. 2014. Beirut, October 31.
Mrad, C. Interview by this author. 2014. Jbeil, November 12.
Munson, Z. 2010. "Mobilizing on Campus: Conservative Movements and Today's College Students." *Sociological Forum* 25 (4): 769–786.

Nasrallah, A. Interview by this author. 2014. Dbayeh, October 6.

Nemnom, E. Interview by this author. 2014. Beirut, September 9.

Oegema, D., and B. Klandermans. 1994. "Why Social Movement Sympathizers Don't Participate: Erosion and Nonconversion of Support." *American Sociological Review* 59 (5): 703–722.

Park, R. 1967. "Collective Behavior." In *Social Control and Collective Behavior*, edited by R. H. Turner. Chicago: University of Chicago Press.

Raffoul, P. Interview by this author. 2014. Beirut, October 2.

Salloukh, B. F., R. Barakat, J. S. Al-Habbal, L. W. Khattab, S. Mikaelian, and A. Nerguizian. 2015. *The Politics of Sectarianism in Postwar Lebanon*. London: Pluto Press.

Samizdat. 2004. "Weekly Political Publication." *Samizdat*, January.

———. 2004. "Weekly Political Publication." *Samizdat*, February.

———. 2004. "Weekly Political Publication." *Samizdat*, March.

Sarrouh, G. E. Interview by this author. 2014. Baabda, October 16.

Sassine, J. 1998. "Mou'akidan Khilafahu maa Arkan Altajamou' filQadaya AlDakhiliya Aoun Yashon Aanaf Maarikihi aala AlHariri. 'Confirming His Disagreement with the Pillars of the Gathering in Internal Affairs Aoun Launches Fiercest Battles Against Hariri'." *Annahar*, May 21, 20049 ed.

Sfeir, M. Interview by this author. 2014. Jounieh, September 30.

Smelser, N. 1962. *Theory of Collective Behavior*. New York: Free Press.

Snow, D. A., and R. D. Benford. 2000. "Framing Processes and Social Movements: An Overview and Assessment." *Annual Review of Sociology* 26: 611–639.

Snow, D. A., and S. A. Soule. 2010. *A Primer on Social Movements*. New York: W. W. Norton.

Soule, S. A. 1997. "The Student Divestment Movement in the United States and Tactical Diffusion: The Shantytown Protest." *Social Forces* 75: 855–882.

Syria Accountability and Lebanese Sovereignty Restoration Act of 2003. 2003. Public Law 108–175. 108th Congress, December 12.

Tarraf, R. Interview by this author. 2014. Hadath, September 11.

Taylor, V., and N. E. Whittier. 1992. "Collective Identities in Social Movement Communities: Lesbian Feminist Mobilization." In *Frontiers in Social Movement Theory*, edited by A. D. Morris and C. M. Mueller, 104–130. New Haven, CT: Yale University Press.

Wilson, J. Q. 1973. *Political Organizations*. New York: Basic Books.

Zhao, D. 1998. "Ecologies of Social Movements: Student Mobilization During the 1989 Prodemocracy Movement in Beijing." *American Journal of Sociology* 103 (6): 1493–1529.

Zuo, J., and R. D. Benford. 1995. "Mobilization Processes and the 1989 Chinese Democracy Movement." *Sociological Quarterly* 36 (1): 131–156.

CHAPTER 5

Risks of Party Transition and Sectarian Politics (2005–2015)

This chapter reveals the circumstances surrounding the Free Patriotic Movement's institutional transformation and the implications this had for the movement itself and Lebanese politics in general. In so doing, it discusses in some detail the role of political opportunities and the agency of leadership in contributing to the institutional transformation of the FPM. It also sheds light on the implications of this transformation; in more general terms, what debates, disagreements and political action did the transformation help bring about?

In complex political systems such as that of Lebanon, where the political elite have fragmented institutions, employed sectarian strategies and adopted clientelistic practices to mobilize their supporters, the decision to transform a political movement into a party and then take up more conventional forms of politics is dependent upon a decision made by the party leadership, in combination with sectarian politics and elite strategies of mobilizing supporters. When Michel Aoun took the decision to transform the Free Patriotic Movement into a political party following the withdrawal of Syrian troops from Lebanon in 2005, the FPM's need to participate in collective activity was not completely abandoned. Instead, the FPM, which had adopted a secular discourse throughout the period 1990–2005, found itself adopting sectarian strategies and discourses to mobilize its predominantly Christian support base in the post-2005 period and to compete with other political parties, such as the Kataeb and the Lebanese Forces (LF), whose political strategies were sectarian in nature.

J. P. Helou, *Activism, Change and Sectarianism in the Free Patriotic Movement in Lebanon*, Reform and Transition in the Mediterranean,
https://doi.org/10.1007/978-3-030-25704-0_5

This chapter is divided into three: events leading to the transformation, its consequences and to what extent it was successful. The first part reveals the various national and international political opportunities relevant to Lebanon that cumulatively resulted in more openness in the Lebanese political system, which, in turn, allowed for the FPM's participation in parliamentary elections in 2005. The second part explains that while the FPM was able to participate in conventional politics, such as in Parliament and inside the Council of Ministers as of 2005, it was the decision of Aoun that helped transform the movement into a political party in 2005. In addition, the decision to participate in collective activities, such as demonstrations and protests, became more influenced by Lebanon's sectarian politics and the FPM's strategies of mobilization in the post-2005 period, thus revealing that its participation in conventional politics did not completely abolish the need to protest. The final part analyzes how the FPM managed its growing membership, assigned individuals to party roles, held elections to ensure continuity of key party offices, and attempted to attain representation of its membership base. The successes and shortcomings of the FPM in carrying out these aspects of its institutional transformation are examined here.

Part I: Opportunities Making the FPM's Institutional Transformation Possible

As will be illustrated in this section, the cumulative effect of a number of national and international political opportunities led to the withdrawal of Syrian troops from Lebanon in 2005. Consequently, the FPM found itself free to participate in parliamentary elections and ask for representation inside the Council of Ministers. These political opportunities alone did not determine its institutional transformation, nor fully explain when the FPM, as a political party that engaged in conventional politics, adopted collective activity. Yet, a discussion of the cumulative effects of these political opportunities remains important because, without the withdrawal of Syrian troops from Lebanon, the movement could not have become a formal political player; that is to say, a movement with representatives in Parliament and inside the Council of Ministers.

Following his expatriation to France, Michel Aoun came to understand the importance of the presence of national and international determination for the liberation of Lebanon and labored to influence on both fronts. He informed a small group of supporters in a private meeting in Marseille,

France in September 1991: "liberating Lebanon cannot occur except when Lebanese determination and international determination meet. The Lebanese alone are not going to be able to oust Syria, and states cannot do anything if the Lebanese don't ask for it" (S. Abi Ramia, interview November 21, 2014). This national liberation determination, epitomized by FPM activism, intersected with the international will to liberate Lebanon following a series of political shifts that culminated in increased political openness in its political system, resulting in a political setting which was conducive to the establishment of political parties; in turn, this contributed to the institutional transformation of the FPM from a social movement into a political party. However, the main political opportunities that led to this increased openness began chronologically with the liberation of South Lebanon, the formation of the Lebanese opposition gathering of Qornet Chehwan and the US Congress's enactment of the Syria Accountability Act, and ended with the withdrawal of Syrian troops from Lebanon in April 2005.

Although the liberation of South Lebanon in 2000 witnessed a unilateral Israeli withdrawal that had clear ramifications for the fate of the Arab–Israeli peace talks, the political consequences of the Israeli withdrawal helped to debunk the official pretext for Syria's deployment of troops on Lebanese soil. Syria, whose main security concern was to fend off any potential attack from Israel, had lost its legitimacy to deploy its troops in Lebanon (Elhusseini 2012, p. 189). With the implementation of United Nations Security Council Resolution 425, which restored Lebanese sovereignty over the territory of South Lebanon that had been occupied by the Israeli forces (UNSCR 425 1978), the presence of Syrian troops in Lebanon no longer served the purpose of assisting the Lebanese army against a potential threat from Israel. As a result, the legitimacy of the Syrian presence in Lebanon, often defended on the basis of being necessary, temporary and legitimate, became a topic of intense political debate, especially among the ranks of Lebanese opposition groups and some politicians siding with them (Elhusseini 2012, p. 189).

This political debate pertaining to the status of the presence of Syrian forces deployed on Lebanese soil became the main focus of Qornet Chehwan, a political gathering encompassing the FPM, the progressive socialist party headed by Druze-leader Walid Jumblatt, and a number of political parties and independent political figures from the Christian community, in addition to a bishop representing the Christian-Maronite church in Lebanon (N. Abi Antoun, interview September 23, 2014).

Naim Aoun, a leading FPM activist, described in some detail the changing political conditions around the time of the formation of the Qornet Chehwan gathering in 2000:

> In 2000, the political game began changing. From 1990 to 2000, the Pax Syriana remained the same; the American, Syrian and Saudi agreement [personal analysis of an unwritten understanding] to dominate Lebanon remained the same. When Rafik Hariri [the Lebanese Prime Minister] was replaced by Salim El-Hoss in 1998, the political grounds began shaking. The region began changing. The issues began shaking. Walid Jumblatt took a position against the Syrians... Hafez Assad [Syrian President] passed away and the Qornet Chehwan gathering formed. So things began changing. (Interview September 18, 2014)

Some of the FPM activists interviewed viewed the liberation of South Lebanon from the Israeli army as an important political development that placed pressure on Syria to withdraw its troops from Lebanon. The FPM had seized the political opportunity of this increased openness in the Lebanese political order to voice its ideas and concerns. Therefore, the formation of the Qornet Chehwan gathering, accompanied by popular condemnation of the 2000 round of yet another rigged parliamentary election and the Maronite church's vehement critique of the Syrian military presence in Lebanon (Elhusseini 2012, pp. 189–192), all managed to put pressure on Syria by publicly discussing the issue of the legitimacy of the Syrian military presence in Lebanon. For that reason, the establishment of the gathering turned a new page in Lebanese politics by instituting a forum in Lebanon that launched fiery diatribes concerning Syria's intervention in Lebanese political affairs. The availability of more than one influential political party or personality in the ranks of the gathering served to reinforce the FPM's goal of freedom, sovereignty and independence, which had been voiced by the movement since 1990.

Following the terrorist attacks on the World Trade Center on September 11, 2001, the USA launched a global war on terror that had negative consequences for some Middle Eastern states. FPM activists viewed the political opportunity of the USA's shift after the September 11 events as indicating the right moment for action. Naim Aoun commented:

> We could say external factors to the game and internal factors influenced the situation in Lebanon. The FPM also began gaining ground... We were involved in the Syrian accountability act. September 11, 2001 also helped

us gain ground. UN Security Council Resolution 1559 was what we were pressing for. The event helped change things on the internal scene. The first half an hour, when the Americans declared September 11 to be the act of terrorists, we felt we were entering a new global political order. The USA entered a new strategy on the global level. (Interview September 18, 2014)

The resulting reorientation of the US political stance was recognized by FPM activists as a political opportunity mainly because it helped to increase pressure on Syria, which, in turn, began to hold on to its geopolitical interests in Lebanon.

The manner in which the September 11 events affected the internal scene in Lebanon first appeared in the form of a political rift between the USA and Syria when the former decided to wage its 2003 war on Iraq, which was believed to be in possession of weapons of mass destruction. Disagreement between the USA and Syria over security cooperation in Iraq in the period following the US-led war exacerbated political tensions between the two countries. Syria must have feared a US military presence in neighboring Iraq and thus refused to cooperate with the USA on security issues. Illustrating this point, Simon Abi Ramia, an FPM activist, stated: "Of course, let us not forget the existing situation of the Neo Conservatives in America who wanted to bring democracy to the Middle East. The domino effect view—that after Iraq came Saudi Arabia and Syria and so on—created fear in these countries of the extermination of their regimes. The Americans were heading in this direction" (interview November 21, 2014).

As a result, the USA stepped up measures against Syria by enacting the Syria Accountability Act 2003, which called on Syria to respect the sovereignty of Lebanon. Therefore, what started off as a political rift between the USA and Syria ended up delivering new-found US support for Lebanese sovereignty and independence without Syrian interference in Lebanese affairs.

During this period, the lobbying efforts of Michel Aoun and the FPM in the US Congress for the freedom, sovereignty and independence of Lebanon finally paid off due to the clear shift in American foreign policy toward Syria. On December 12, 2003, the US Congress enacted the Syria Accountability and Lebanese Sovereignty Restoration Act of 2003, which stressed the sovereignty, territorial integrity and political independence of Lebanon, in addition to calling on Syria to halt its support of non-state actors, such as Hezbollah, Hamas and other Palestinian groups (Syria Accountability Act 2003). In the congressional debate leading to the enactment of this law, Aoun was invited to speak in Congress. Elhusseini (2012, p. 191) notes that in his testimony to Congress Aoun drew a parallel between the USA's fight against terrorism and Lebanon's struggle with Syria, which he viewed as "a fight for freedom against terrorism and oppression." Although the Syria Accountability Act alone did not represent a seismic shock to the position of Damascus in Lebanon, it nevertheless signaled the US inclination to threaten Syria's geopolitical standing in the Middle East. Yet, many of the interviewed FPM activists considered the congressional act as a positive step toward international recognition of Lebanon's freedom, sovereignty and independence, which was in accord with the FPM's founding principles.

With these international pressures mounting on Syria, the Syria Accountability Act being a case in point, Damascus continued to meddle freehand in the political affairs of Lebanon. In 2004, its overt preference for and direct involvement in the extension of the term of office of Lebanese President Emile Lahoud, who was largely perceived as unpopular in the eyes of the West, won Damascus more enemies than friends (S. Abi Ramia, interview November 21, 2014). As a result, the UN Security Council convened on September 2, 2004 and issued UNSCR 1559, which called for free presidential elections in Lebanon, the withdrawal of all foreign troops, and the disbanding of Lebanese and non-Lebanese militias on Lebanese soil (UNSCR 1559, 2004). Ignoring mounting international pressure, Damascus intervened in Lebanese political affairs to influence the election of Omar Karami, a Sunni Muslim notable from Northern Lebanon and ally of Syria, to the premiership in Lebanon, further sidelining Saudi-backed Rafik Hariri, who also enjoyed good relations with the USA and France. As Rola Elhusseini noted: "Syria used Karami as a counterweight to Hariri's influence and manifested a public interest in Karami every time that it wished to send a cautionary message to Hariri" (2012, p. 98).

On February 14, 2005, Hariri was assassinated in a bomb attack that targeted his motorcade in Beirut, leading to a wave of international condemnation (ibid., p. 96). All fingers of blame pointed at Syria, since it had more than 20,000 troops garrisoned on Lebanese soil overseeing the security affairs of Lebanon. This political formulation of blame, regardless of who actually perpetrated the crime, led to a wave of international support for a swift Syrian withdrawal from Lebanon (ibid.).

On March 14, 2005, the Lebanese opposition, which included the FPM and other Christian parties, such as the LF, Kataeb and the National Liberal Party in the period 1990–2005, now expanded to include the Future Movement of the deceased Hariri to mobilize around one million individuals to Martyr Square in downtown Beirut to request the withdrawal of Syrian troops from Lebanon, which had long been an FPM goal (M. Chamoun, interview October 15, 2014). Coupled with international pressure on Syria to withdraw its military force from Lebanon, the mobilization for protests in Lebanon culminated in the withdrawal of Syrian troops from Lebanon by the end of April 2005, after 29 years of military presence on Lebanese soil (Elhusseini 2012, p. 193).

These rapid developments in Lebanese politics, topped off with the withdrawal of Syrian troops from the country in 2005, resulted in increased political openness that rendered previously banned forms of collective activity permissible in the new political environment. With the Syrian troops now outside Lebanon, national security institutions, such as the Lebanese army, Internal Security Forces, General Security Directorate and State Security Directorate, who were responsible for the detainment of FPM activists throughout the period 1990–2005, relaxed their grip on protests and allowed political movements to express their opinions freely. Therefore, FPM activism could take place freely and uninterruptedly, since the movement was now considered a formal political contender in Lebanon.

As a consequence of this new political setting, the FPM no longer faced the kind of challenges that used to impede FPM activism in the period 1990–2005. This had two clear implications for the movement. First, it no longer faced any difficulty in mobilizing individuals to activism. According to the majority of interviewed FPM activists, they were able to call for collective activity post-2005 without having to face the many challenges they used to encounter throughout the period 1990–2005. Secondly, the political openness generated by the withdrawal of Syrian troops from Lebanon culminated in the return of Michel Aoun from his 15-year exile in France on May 7, 2005.

Therefore, the withdrawal of Syrian troops from Lebanon provided a political environment that allowed for the participation of previously banned or excluded movements in the political process; that is to say, running for parliamentary elections and requesting representation inside the Council of Ministers. Yet, this does not mean that with the withdrawal of Syrian troops a fully democratic environment existed in Lebanon.

Most of the sectarian strategies on which the political elite relied in the period 1990–2005, such as gerrymandering electoral constituencies to ensure sizable parliamentary blocks, had resulted in distorted electoral constituencies that continued to favor those members of the post-1990 political elite even after the withdrawal of Syrian troops from Lebanon. Even though the FPM gained the right to participate in parliamentary elections following the Syrian withdrawal, which was not an insignificant gain given the harsh political circumstances it had to bear throughout the period 1990–2005, it still had to deal with the sectarian strategies of Lebanon's post-war political elite. We shall now turn to an examination of how the agency of Michel Aoun helped transform the FPM into a political party, and then consider how the FPM began adopting sectarian strategies to better represent its Christian voter base.

Part II: Party Transformation, Electoral Participation and Sectarian Strategies

The transformation of the FPM from social movement to political party had been determined by Aoun's decision to do so, but the FPM's adoption of sectarian political strategies in the post-2005 period emanated from the movement's participation in conventional politics; that is, participation in parliamentary elections and in the Council of Ministers. The FPM's strategies in the post-2005 period contrasted sharply with its previous political positions chiefly because, during this period, it participated in parliamentary elections and found itself obliged to express the political outlook of its predominantly Christian voter base. By expressing the interests of these largely Christian voters, both in terms of appointments of civil servants and in attaining more infrastructure projects than had been the case previously, the FPM compromised its standing as a secular movement and began adopting some sectarian strategies characteristic of its sectarian counterparts. Therefore, while Michel Aoun can be credited for the transformation of the FPM into a political party, the sectarian performance of the FPM in the post-2005 period is deeply rooted in an understanding of Lebanese politics that drew the movement away from its secular positions toward the adoption of more sectarian ones.

The FPM embarked on a process of institutional transformation based on the plans of Aoun who, upon his return to Lebanon, became the main decision-maker in almost all aspects of the movement. Illustrating this point, Simon Abi Ramia, an FPM activist, believes: "In 2005, General

Aoun could have said Lebanon is liberated and Syria is out. You have regained your freedom as Lebanese people. I am now going to leave you, because his message had been implemented. Instead he said 'I want to turn the movement into a party and begin changing and reforming.' We made the slogan of change and reform from this principle" (interview November 21, 2014). Therefore, it is clear that Aoun built on the openness in Lebanon's political order following the withdrawal of Syria to institute the FPM as a formal political party on September 18, 2005. This shows that the institutional transformation process the FPM underwent was not strictly due to the direct effect of the political opportunities prevailing in the political orbit of Lebanon, but was actually the result of the active role adopted by Aoun and the activists in deciding on and carrying out the institutional transformation of the FPM.

As early as 1989, activists who worked closely with Aoun spoke of his ambition to institute a party for his following in Lebanon, called the Assembly for Lebanon (P. Raffoul, interview October 2, 2014). However, Aoun's plans were interrupted by his ousting from the Baabda Palace on October 13, 1989, and his subsequent expatriation to France. During Aoun's years in exile, his movement in Lebanon gradually moved to adopting the formal movement name of the Free Patriotic Movement, for reasons already explained in the previous chapter.

According to the majority of activists who tabled the topic of the organization with Aoun during his years in exile, he consistently refused to structure the FPM in a manner that resembled the formal institutional set-up of a political party organization, lest it risk weakening the movement's activism if the Lebanese political elite ordered a crackdown on it. His predictions proved right when the Lebanese army did indeed crack down on a meeting of the FPM central command on August 7, 2001, which would have crippled the movement had it not been for the small, decentralized activist units, as explained in the previous chapter. Therefore, Aoun's decision to transform the FPM into a political party came only after he seized the political opportunity presented by the withdrawal of Syrian troops from Lebanon in 2005, which provided the freedom to convene and establish a political party.

Since Aoun was based in France during his exile, he enjoyed the assistance of a professional team of FPM activists who aided him in lobbying for the FPM cause abroad whenever conducive political opportunities presented themselves (S. Abi Ramia, interview November 21, 2014). This reality assisted Aoun in his political moves, especially when he decided to exploit opportunities to pursue discussions with other states. For example, several FPM activists discussed the importance of Aoun's rapprochement with the US administration because, after the events of September 11, 2001, it helped to advance the cause of Lebanese sovereignty in policy-making circles in Washington, as well as making Aoun's voice, as an exiled leader, heard more clearly. Therefore, the existence of an active FPM movement abroad, in countries such as France, Australia and the USA among others, helped Aoun seize political opportunities for the freedom and independence of Lebanon.

Following the assassination of former Lebanese Premier Rafik Hariri and the swift Syrian withdrawal that ensued, Aoun returned from his 15-year exile to engage in Lebanese politics and transform the FPM into a political party. In the summers of 2005 and 2009, Aoun ran parliamentary electoral lists that won him a block in Parliament. After spending a brief period without a presence in the Council of Ministers as of 2005, FPM members have participated in every government formed from 2008 till the present day, often receiving key ministerial portfolios, such as the Ministry of Energy, Communications and Foreign Affairs (P. ElKhoury, interview October 1, 2014). On September 18, 2005, the FPM was declared a political party with an organizational structure (Germanos 2013). However, Aoun's decisive role in determining the fate of the new-found political party and his clear involvement in national Lebanese politics transferred the main decision-making tasks from individual activists to himself.

On the other hand, the majority of the FPM activists interviewed for this book began to consider seriously the prospect of dropping social movement activity, such as pamphlet distribution, demonstrations, protests and so on, because they regarded those expressions as futile in the post-2005 phase, especially after the FPM gained a parliamentary block and the ability to influence politics from within state institutions. The Syrian withdrawal from Lebanon in April 2005 had stripped the movement of its main goal, which was liberating Lebanon from foreign occupation. While FPM activists unanimously agreed that they still had to achieve the goal of ensuring a corruption-free political order, they believed that the goal of liberating Lebanon mobilized people onto the streets more effectively than the goal of combating corruption. Walid Achkar, an FPM activist, illustrates this point: "After 2005, we lost the slogan of freedom, sovereignty, and independence. The Syrians withdrew from Lebanon. This slogan used to make us win a lot. Every time we proposed this slogan, people used to follow us. After 2005, the slogan we adopted was change and reform. It is not as attractive as freedom, sovereignty and independence. It made us lose the excitement we created to take people to the streets" (interview October 15, 2014). Therefore, in the period immediately after the Syrian withdrawal from Lebanon, FPM activists saw no real reason to carry on with their activism. For this reason, Aoun's decision to transform the FPM from a social movement to a political party helped to organize these activists into a new framework, one in which the central command of the FPM could more easily communicate with its members.

However, after the withdrawal of Syrian troops from Lebanon, the FPM's strategies and its decision to participate in activism became heavily influenced by sectarian calculations. Out of the 21 Members of Parliament the FPM was able to gain in the 2005 parliamentary elections, one was Sunni, two were Shia and eighteen were Christian (representing various denominations, such as Maronites, Greek Catholics, Greek Orthodox and Armenians). Although the FPM's parliamentary bloc was not composed of an exclusively Christian membership, it was predominantly Christian voters in the electoral districts of Kiserwan, Matn, Jbeil and Zahley who helped promote FPM candidates to Parliament in the 2005 elections, since Lebanon still relied on a majoritarian or winner-takes-all electoral system. As a result of this political reality, Aoun and the FPM became obliged to serve the interests of their electoral constituencies, even though the interests of those constituencies had to be articulated in sectarian terms.

In order to advance the interests of its predominantly Christian voter base, the FPM sought to increase its representation in conventional politics, specifically in Parliament and by requesting portfolios in the Council of Ministers. Since it so happens that the parliamentary elections of 2005 and 2009 revealed Aoun and the FPM's popularity among Christian voters, with 70 and 50% of the Christian voter base, respectively (Salloukh et al. 2015, p. 150), the FPM began portraying any political attempt to underrepresent it in the Council of Ministers as a devious plot to marginalize Christians. It gradually shifted away from its previously secular discourse toward the adoption of a more sectarian discourse by equating Aoun and the FPM with Christians in Lebanon.

This binary distinction can best be illustrated by referring to an example of how media stations framed their news. OTV, which is a television station officially launched in 2008 and affiliated with the FPM, offered such a binary sectarian description in one of its news bulletins in 2009. The bulletin described the process of cabinet formation in sectarian terms by stating: "The aim of Hariri's team is to select Christian ministers [without consulting with Christian leaders], crucify their leader, and declare a unity without them. Definitely, this shall not be replicated. And, definitely, Hariri shall not get what he seeks twice. The question, however, remains: Why this Hariri horror from [sic] Christian participation in [building] this nation? Why this horror from the participation of Michel Aoun in the government?" (Salloukh et al. 2015, pp. 150–151).

In advancing such an interpretation of events, the language used in this news bulletin attempted to portray Aoun as the leader of Christians in Lebanon and thus deserving of adequate representation in the Council of Ministers, namely by assuming key ministerial portfolios. On the other hand, by framing the Hariri team's unresponsiveness to the demands of the FPM in cabinet portfolios as an attempt to "crucify" Aoun, the channel was clearly describing this political phenomenon in sectarian terms to address, and perhaps help mobilize, the FPM's support base, which was composed predominantly of Christians. This mode of media discourse, according to Salloukh et al. (2015, pp. 150–151), helped consolidate sectarian modes of subjectification at the individual level and mobilization at the communal level. It both reflected and fueled social rivalries between Lebanon's sects.

In fact, this discourse helped the FPM mobilize its supporters to engage in demonstrations in the post-2005 period. By equating Aoun with Christians, the FPM's discussion of nominating a "representative candidate" to assume the role of the President of the Lebanese Republic meant that they supported no other candidate than Michel Aoun, who earned more than 50% of the Christian vote in the 2009 parliamentary elections, whereas the remaining percentage was spread across a number of parties. Therefore, on the 25th anniversary of the memorial of October 13, which marked the ousting of Aoun from the Baabda Palace in 1990, Aoun and the FPM were able to mobilize thousands of supporters to Baabda, which was very symbolic given the proximity to the palace that conjured up memories for many activists. Therefore, this sectarian discourse provided a useful tool for Aoun and FPM activists to demonstrate the challenges they faced to their supporters and thus helped to promote the mobilization of those supporters; needless to say, this occurred on several occasions in the post-2005 period and resulted in political rallies organized by the FPM.

In truth, the FPM was not the only political party engaged in this framing tactic in the post-2005 period. The Sunni Future movement of

Hariri, the Shia parties of Hezbollah and Amal and a number of Christian parties, such as Kataeb and the LF, each of which used its own media outlets (television, radio or websites), resorted to a degree of sectarian discourse (Salloukh et al. 2015). Since the FPM aimed to consolidate its position in conventional politics, it now had to face this sectarian discourse by revealing itself as a defender of the rights of its predominantly Christian voter base. Perhaps the vast resources the FPM's political opponents commanded in the post-2005 period helped them effectively demonize the political position of Aoun and the FPM in post-2005 Lebanon, which may explain the decrease of Christian support from 70 to 50% between the 2005 and 2009 Parliamentary electoral rounds. However, the FPM had been working on mobilizing resources since the 2009 round of parliamentary elections. Since Lebanon suspended parliamentary elections between 2009 and 2018, due to its delicate political circumstances and as a result of the war in neighboring Syria, the results of the 2018 parliamentary elections, which will be discussed in some detail in the next chapter, will illustrate the effectiveness of the FPM's mobilization.

Perhaps another reason for the FPM's adoption of sectarian discourse in the post-2005 period is because the Lebanese political system delineated politics with sectarian boundaries. In other words, because the FPM ran for parliamentary elections in 2005 and gained a parliamentary block of 21 Members of Parliament who represented constituencies of predominantly Christian voters, the movement was obliged to represent the interests of its mainly Christian support base. This meant that the FPM now demanded ministerial portfolios, appointments of public servants and infrastructure projects that favored its constituencies. Of course, development projects that benefited all the Lebanese people nationally, such as the FPM-backed plan to improve the provision of electricity, were also up for consideration. However, advancing the interests of its predominantly Christian constituencies required the FPM to adopt a sectarian discourse for sectarian modes of subjectification at the individual level and mobilization at the communal level, as described by Salloukh et al. (2015, p. 150).

The FPM also had to distribute some social welfare goods in the post-2005 period in order to service its support base. This issue was initially a topic of grave concern within the movement because, prior to 2005, it had warned against those politicians who engaged in clientelistic practices to gain the political support of voters during elections. However, after 2005, supporters of the FPM expected their movement to dispense social services, since it had become involved in government. This was illustrated in the words of Simon Abi Ramia, FPM activist and Member of Parliament as of 2009:

> The citizen that looked upon you as his hope to liberate Lebanon and restore his freedom is today the same person that wants you to employ his son, pave the street beside his house, and provide him $100 to pay a hospital bill… The most dangerous thing is when the citizen regards the FPM like all other parties because competition turns to who does more services. It would make us forget our ambitions of building a nation where every person would receive their rights equally… Because the state is in its present shape, we are obliged to adapt to the conditions. When someone has a problem with a police station and the station is at fault, I'm definitely going to have to contact the police station, judge and general prosecutor to help him. We are being drawn into the system without being supporters of this system. We need to find a balance between both. (Interview November 21, 2014)

This grim reality of politics highlights the extent to which the patron–client politics of social services has become the norm in Lebanon.

Citizens have become accustomed to receiving services from their politicians as opposed to state institutions, which they probably consider inefficient. Therefore, this awkward reality constitutes a challenge for the FPM that had, as a movement, rejected this form of politics. To survive as a party, the FPM had to tap into its existing resources and connections to service its supporters, while simultaneously educating the citizenship on the importance of parliamentary policy proposals to receive their rights without the intercession of influential politicians.

The FPM cannot reform the political system, which depends on an extensive patron–client network of social services, by immediately relying on sweeping policy proposals without dispensing some services to its support base, because it would run the risk of losing supporters. Speaking of the importance of adopting a gradual approach to reforming society while simultaneously providing services, Antoine Moukheiber, an FPM activist, stated:

> Our idea was that the state has to service the citizen, and not the MP, Minister, or Chief… But in order to reach this phase, you have to go through a transitional phase. We are not adopting this transitional phase. You reached a place where you had ten ministers [FPM's number of Ministers in the Cabinet headed by PM Najib Mikati]. You are at a stage where you are

> not ready to do a service. It affected you negatively because you did not educate the Lebanese citizens and you were not able to develop the state. If you go to the electricity company and request a service, it would take you forever. The reason is that the employee is used to receiving 20,000 liras [bribe] in return for the service he's going to carry out. So we have to intercede on behalf of the citizen to reach a stage whereby the citizen has all his rights, like in France, USA, or anywhere else… In my village, someone passed away. His brother sent the obituary to the MPs of Jbeil. It so happened that they couldn't attend. He tells me I'm no longer going to vote for the FPM. This is the way the citizen thinks. (Interview October 31, 2014)

Both Antoine Moukheiber and Simon Abi Ramia discuss the importance of striking a balance between the goals of the FPM in the policy proposal field and serving the people.

In fact, the reason the FPM began to consider the adoption of strategies of social welfare distribution to its predominantly Christian constituencies is because it was facing competition from other Christian parties as well. Melani Cammett (2014) finds that the Kataeb, LF and FPM all engaged in the strategy of distributing social welfare to mainly Christian constituencies. She shows that the Kataeb and the LF had extensive social welfare programs during the Lebanese Civil War, which were dismantled in 1994. However, with the withdrawal of Syria from Lebanon in 2005, these parties took to reinstituting their social welfare programs. Since these parties, along with the FPM, adopted an intra-state strategy, implying that they sought to gain power through constitutional processes such as elections, they now were obliged to dispense some social welfare benefits to their supporters, in addition to non-supporters from within mainly Christian constituencies, to help sway some non-partisan voters during electoral rounds.

While the strategy to distribute social welfare is not a new phenomenon in Lebanese politics, especially when considering the extensive patron—client relations that characterized Lebanese politics throughout a considerable part of the twentieth century, the FPM's adoption of such strategies, given its diatribe against the clientelistic practices of Lebanese political patrons in the period 1990–2005, appears somewhat contradictory, yet simultaneously understandable, because the FPM as a party post-2005 was interested in revealing its popularity in the parliamentary electoral rounds. Perhaps the FPM was late in considering the development of a social welfare program by 2008 because of the high level of representation of middle-class professionals in its ranks and, as a consequence, possessed the least developed program of all the Christian parties (Cammett 2014, p. 178). However, by 2008, the FPM had begun providing some healthcare and social assistance to supporters and non-partisans, who were mainly Christians.

For example, the FPM established the 8 Oranges program, which is a private mutual fund or rewards program. It provides its card-holders with discounts at gas stations, supermarkets, pharmacies and commercial venues that have agreed to participate in this arrangement (Cammett 2014, p. 179). It also provides members with the option of buying a personal accident insurance policy and receiving health and dental insurance from a British company, Cumberland Insurance and Reinsurance, which sponsors the program (ibid.). In addition, subscribers can benefit from reduced fees at clinics that have established contracts with the program. By paying an annual fee of $11, subscribers gain access to discounted goods and services at participating establishments, while the party receives 25% of the company's profits (ibid.).

Although the 8 Oranges program provides all its subscribers with rewards, FPM members benefit the most from it. Participation in 8 Oranges is synonymous with a declaration of support for the party given the political symbolism of the program's logos and orange-colored products (Cammett 2014, p. 179). Because the color orange is now clearly linked to the FPM, the program's orange symbols express one's political stance or indicate a political statement supportive of the FPM that is largely understood in Lebanese social and political life (ibid.). Moreover, the 8 Oranges program recruits its staff from the FPM membership, which also helps provide jobs for party members (ibid.).

Like other political parties in Lebanon, the FPM has come to rely on personal connections to broker access to healthcare and other social services. Occasionally, FPM officials and Members of Parliament contact the Ministry of Public Health to ensure the public coverage of hospital bills for supporters (Cammett 2014, p. 180). FPM members working in the medical and pharmaceutical fields volunteer their time and offer discounted services (ibid.). The FPM's connections in professional syndicates, particularly in the Syndicate of Pharmacists, allow the party to dispense subsidized medication to its supporters (ibid.). Cammett (2014, p. 180) finds that some clinics run by FPM members operate on an informal and voluntary basis to provide low-cost services on behalf of the party.

She finds that two of these facilities are located in Kiserwan and Batroun, both predominantly Christian areas.

Therefore it has been shown that the FPM adopted some clientelistic services for distributing social welfare in order to compete with other political parties, particularly the Kataeb and the LF, in parliamentary electoral rounds. As Cammett's (2014, p. 181) research shows, the FPM prioritized group members in its distribution of social welfare, but also provided some assistance to individuals who were not FPM supporters. Cammett cites one of her interviewees who claimed that the FPM's responsiveness to her requests for medical assistance had compelled her to switch her allegiance to the party (ibid.).

Cammett (2014, p. 182) argues that although not all Christian parties are viewed as equally sectarian in their ideology (perhaps implying that the FPM is less so), they favor Christians in provisioning benefits and brokering access to third-party services. She finds that these parties generously reward loyalists, as opposed to other group members, in order to incentivize individuals to remain committed to their political activity (ibid.). She also believes that due to the imperatives of the Lebanese power-sharing system and the fierce competition between the major Christian parties, even the FPM, which portrays itself as non-sectarian, is obliged to present itself as the true representative of Christians (ibid.). As a result, the FPM, like its counterparts, is bound to distribute social services to its supporters and some non-partisans to attempt to earn better representation in parliamentary elections.

While Aoun's decision to transform the FPM into a political party is the main reason for its institutional transformation, its adoption of sectarian discourse and strategies of mobilization is rooted in the reality of Lebanese politics. Since the FPM operated as a social movement from 1990 to 2005, it enjoyed a margin to formulate secular ideas because it was not held accountable by an electoral voter base. This means that the movement was conscious of its predominantly Christian support base, but never felt obliged to give into sectarian modes of subjectification, nor to adopt sectarian modes of mobilization of supporters, since the cause of liberating Lebanon from occupation by the Syrian troops helped mobilize the movement's supporters.

On the other hand, upon the return of Aoun from exile, the FPM participated in formal office by running for the 2005 round of parliamentary elections. In this particular election, Aoun and the FPM earned 70% of the Christian voter base and thus had to represent the constituencies that elected them. Since the constituencies that elected FPM candidates comprised predominantly Christian voters, Aoun and the FPM were compelled to express their political demands in a more sectarian discourse. Of course, in the wake of Hariri's assassination in 2005, sectarian discourse became more pronounced in Lebanon. Therefore, the FPM alone could not have been fully responsible for its own adoption of sectarian strategies and discourse, because those strategies were adopted by the movement based on its reaction to the prevailing modes of politics in post-2005 Lebanon; that is to say, other parties were adopting such sectarian practices to compete with the FPM.

However, the fact that the FPM was embracing this kind of discourse seemed contradictory in comparison to its previous positions, but appeared natural when considering that its competitors, such as the Kataeb and the LF, adopted sectarian strategies in terms of clientelist practices and discourse, which, in turn, helped mobilize supporters from the Christian community. This means that the FPM maintained its majority support among the Christian voter base in Lebanon by resorting to sectarian discourse, which helped shape sectarian subjects in post-2005 Lebanon, and by adopting some clientelistic strategies, which helped the movement compete with its counterparts who were vying for the support of the same electoral constituencies that voted for the FPM. This is not to say that the FPM had no proposals that aimed to serve the interests of the Lebanese people nationally, regardless of their sectarian affiliation, but seeks to show that the FPM became more realistic in recognizing its support base and addressing their concerns. Therefore, even though the FPM shifted away from its previously secular positions toward the adoption of some sectarian strategies and clientelistic practices, it still was able to address political topics and infrastructure development projects that concerned the majority of the Lebanese people, such as reforming the electoral laws and advancing plans to restore Lebanon's worn-out electric power plants. The focus of this chapter now turns to an examination of the impact of the institutional transformation of the FPM from a social movement into a political party.

Part III: Impact of Institutional Transformation

The predicament of the FPM's institutional transformation process lay not only in attempting to structure the best party organization, but also in moving the FPM from an already existing social movement, with its membership, political mindset and movement structures of small, decentralized groups, to a political party that was expected to welcome new individuals to its ranks. Whereas the FPM had around 3000 activists in its ranks from 1990 to 2005, it registered more than 60,000 members upon its inception as a political party (L. Chakour, interview September 29, 2014). With the influx of such a large number of individuals, the immediate challenge for the FPM in the institutional transformation phase became the management of its membership, assigning individuals to party roles, holding elections to ensure continuity of key party offices and attempting to attain the representation of its membership base. The task of balancing representation between FPM activists who had contributed to the persistence of the movement throughout the period 1990–2005 and the newcomers—that is, movement sympathizers, businesspeople and political figures, who increased the representation of the FPM on a national level—proved to be a challenging issue for the FPM as a political party.

FPM Party Structure

In fact, the proposed FPM party set out an organizational arrangement that intended to involve all members on various levels of the party. On the membership level, it advanced a unique structure that categorized members as committed or supportive. Both committed and supportive members participate in nominating FPM candidates for the parliamentary, municipal and professional syndicate electoral races, while supportive members do not participate in internal party elections or private party activities (Saoud, February 7, 2015). This arrangement allows committed members to play a role in fashioning internal party politics, while providing supportive members a say in the FPM's national preferences and nominating candidates to parliamentary, municipal and syndicate electoral races, which increases the chances of victory for the FPM in all these arenas.

In order to provide better representation for individuals on FPM local and provincial committees, the party adopted a majoritarian electoral system in villages where the FPM presence is small, and a proportional electoral system in villages where the FPM enjoys a wider presence. For instance, local committees in villages or towns that contain fewer than 50 FPM members would run elections based on the majoritarian electoral system. Those areas that contain more than 50 members would adopt the proportional electoral system, with closed electoral slates for local committee elections. Mansour Fadel, an FPM activist in charge of the movement's elections dossier, stated:

> We are going to have a combined proportional and majoritarian electoral system. Those villages that cannot stand proportional representation will have a majoritarian system. In a village that has 10 FPM members, elections cannot be held on the basis of proportional representation. If the FPM membership increases, they could switch to a proportional system… In the village that contains 50 to 100 activists, closed lists run against each other on the basis of proportional representation. The list that gains the higher percentage of votes wins and takes the positions of coordinator, treasurer and secretary. Candidates from the losing list are also represented on the village committee based on the percentage of votes they gained. (Interview November 20, 2014)

FPM local committees adopting any of the majoritarian or proportional electoral systems would also elect a president, secretary and treasurer to the committee.

The FPM has structured its organization to ensure a more equitable representation of party members in the provincial districts. In the case of provincial committees, the proportional electoral system also applies. In parallel with the provincial committee, the FPM hosts a provincial council comprising a coordinator, an officer for provincial municipal affairs, an officer for provincial public relations, current and former party Members of Parliament and Ministers, FPM heads of professional syndicates, FPM heads of municipal councils and others (Saoud, February 28, 2015). This widespread presence of political officials in the provincial council helps render this organizational body an important vehicle for political mobilization, because the members comprising this council are able to mobilize supporters in villages, towns and cities, and also to gain access to the resources of municipalities and the political system.

In addition, the FPM organizational structure incorporates a national assembly and an executive council that comprises 14 central committees. The party also includes an advisory council, political council and the general secretariat. The president's office contains a president and a vice-president for political affairs, in addition to a vice-president for administrative affairs (Saoud, February 28, 2015). The president is elected by the general assembly; that is, all the members of the FPM.

Based on interviews with FPM activists, it can be discerned that the main disagreement within the party was rarely over its internal organizational structure, but usually centered on the importance of conducting internal party elections and establishing clear criteria for political ascendancy within the party. These issues may seem rudimentary when instituting any other political party in ordinary circumstances, but posed certain complications in the case of the FPM, since it had been an existing social movement with movement structures, albeit informal in nature. For this reason, the issues pertaining to the institutional transformation process between FPM activists require close attention, rather than dwelling on the shape and form of the party. Therefore, the next section analyzes the relative successes and shortcomings of the institutional transformation process.

Issues with the FPM's Institutional Transformation

The crisis the FPM suffered during its transformation phase from a social movement to a political party emanated from the detrimental competition between FPM activists, members of the FPM abroad and newcomers to the FPM, such as businesspeople, who were vying to establish themselves within the party and the political system. Since Aoun enjoyed the support of a predominantly Christian following, his presence in Lebanon had, in the words of Naaman Abi Antoun, an FPM activist, turned his home in Rabieh into "a power point of attraction for many" (interview, Beirut, September 23, 2014). According to a number of FPM activists, this power point of attraction meant that with his return from France following the withdrawal of Syrian troops from Lebanon, Aoun became an important player whom political hopefuls had to embrace to make their way into Parliament, ministerial positions and state offices, let alone the FPM. These activists believed that the nature of the political order in Lebanon, which required the representation of political families to ensure the victory of an electoral slate and resources to spend on electoral campaigns, probably made Aoun more conscious of the importance of welcoming capable businesspeople into the ranks of the FPM party, instead of only assigning those FPM activists who engaged in the movement's collective activity throughout the period 1990–2005 to positions within the party and inside state institutions.

As a result of this new-found reality within the FPM, a major point of debate in the post-2005 phase centered on how large a role newcomers joining the FPM should play vis-à-vis older activists who had greatly contributed to the movement's cause. This debate may be illustrated in the words of Roland ElKhoury, an FPM activist, who stated: "The General believes he needs these people. He wants to expand the membership of the FPM. I agree with the General on this point. However, you get these people but don't provide them first-row seats. Elias Bou Saab and Fadi Aboud [both ministers representing the FPM in the Council of Ministers] were not with us… Emile Rahmeh [MP who ran on an FPM-backed electoral slate] was against us. Capitalists with the FPM were not with us" (interview September 26, 2014). Elias Bou Saab, Fadi Aboud and Emile Rahmeh epitomize examples of individuals who allied themselves with the FPM after 2005 and, by virtue of that relationship, represented the FPM inside the Council of Ministers or Parliament.

Although the FPM's membership was composed of mainly middle-class professionals, this composition was fluid and subject to change after the withdrawal of Syrian troops from Lebanon in 2005. Based on interviews with FPM activists, one can gather that some businesspeople were sympathetic to the cause of the FPM, even offering some financial assistance to support the movement's activism in the period 1990–2005, but preferred to remain anonymous in order to preserve their business interests from the consequences associated with the support of the FPM; that is, from retaliation by the political elite.

Yet, according to some activists, both those elites who were sympathetic and not sympathetic to the cause of the FPM in the period 1990–2005 were welcomed into its ranks. Perhaps after describing in some detail the strategies the FPM adopted in post-2005 Lebanon, particularly with regard to its distribution of social services (Cammett 2014, pp. 178–182), it becomes clear why the role of businesspeople in the FPM was much needed. However, for veteran FPM activists who bore with the taxing repercussions of organizing collective activity in the period 1990–2005, the entry of newcomers in the ranks of the FPM posed a challenge to their position within the party.

However, by calling for better representation of veteran FPM activists inside the party and in positions in state bureaucracies, veteran FPM activists did not categorically reject the active participation of newcomers in their party, but believed that political ascendancy within its ranks should be commensurate with a person's years of active involvement in FPM activity. Roland ElKhoury stated: "Of course, we want integration. But we want fair play or fair competition" (interview September 26, 2014). Since political ascendancy inside the party was not rooted in clearly established criteria, FPM activists felt that members of their political party were grossly under-represented in areas where their movement could have attained a higher level of representation. For instance, in the Change and Reform bloc, the parliamentary bloc of the FPM headed by Aoun, a number of the FPM activists interviewed for this book believed that their party members were entitled to more than their current representation of 30% of MPs, even if this increase of representation came at the expense of decreasing the representation of independent candidates who were simply FPM political allies.

The lack of a viable party mechanism to ensure the right person-to-position match within the party and to manage the relationship between FPM activists in Lebanon and those returning from abroad on the one hand, and between old FPM activists and newcomers on the other, contributed to activists' growing dissatisfaction with the institutional transformation process. This dissatisfaction led them to cast doubt on the intentions of newcomers to the FPM and even those FPM members returning from abroad. This was illustrated in the words of George Choucair, an FPM activist, who stated: "We were upset because we did not share the space. We were replaced… They came to form a party and handed responsibilities to people that returned from abroad. Some of them were not competent. We did not even know these people. It was as if they lived in Texas, and wanted to apply Western models in Lebanon at a time where Lebanon had evolved in a different fashion" (interview October 16, 2014). If no mechanism for the fair distribution of positions between old and new members and FPM activists inside Lebanon versus those living abroad is devised, this issue may very well continue to fan the flames of internal party conflict for many years to come.

When the operations of the FPM in small, decentralized units formed by activists were analyzed in the previous chapter, it became clear that the activists seemed to agree on their leadership by a process of natural selection. Those activists who had more experience in collective activity displayed a willingness to make sacrifices for the FPM's cause (often by facing detainment and prison sentences), and invested enormous resources and effort in the organization of FPM activity to become the de facto leaders of their activist groups. These dedicated FPM activists constituted dozens of individuals from a sample of hundreds of active movement members. However, this natural selection process that applied in the case of a social movement, which was roughly 3000 activists in size, could not be implemented in the case of a political party that encompassed more than 60,000 registered members in the post-2005 period (L. Chakour, interview September 29, 2014). The FPM party was in dire need of some kind of conflict resolution mechanism—namely, internal party elections—to determine the right person-to-position match based on the vote of party members.

Yet, what exacerbated the situation during the institutional transformation of the FPM was the reliance on the assignment of individuals to party positions and the consistent failure to hold periodic party elections for local committees, provincial committees and the presidency of the party, because this reality risked concentrating authority in the hands of a select few, which also risked rendering the resulting party leadership less democratic and less representative of party members. The centralization of authority in the hands of a select few within the FPM could not only have rendered the movement less democratic, but could also have led to failures on the management level of the political party. Liwa Chakour, an FPM activist, addressed this point by stating: "Can Liwa Chakour deal with all the 63,000 applications of membership of the FPM? Here is the mistake we fell into… One person can't assign the Mayor, the municipal candidates, local committees within the FPM, FPM coordinators, nominees to the syndicates, nominees to the parliamentary elections, ministers, and the Vice Prime Minister… The solution would be to institutionalize the FPM. Every time we postponed the elections [internal FPM party elections] for a different reason" (interview September 29, 2014). Therefore, by promoting a proper institutional party form, with periodic elections on all levels to replace assignments within the party, FPM activists hoped to put together a framework that could ensure the establishment of their party in accordance with clear criteria.

The concentration of authority in the hands of a few within the FPM also made party members more accountable to, and concerned with, fulfilling the interests of those influential individuals, rather than the demands of the FPM constituency, which, in turn, risked widening the gap between the party and its membership. Georges Sarrouh, an FPM activist, commented: "People shouldn't be with the General to be assigned. They should be next to the people to be elected. Before, we used to be closer to the people. We used to recruit new people that way" (interview October 16, 2014). Therefore, to overcome the difficulties embedded in the institutional transformation process, the FPM party should devise a system of checks and balances alongside representative measures to truly reflect the demands and interests of its members. If the FPM fails to hold periodic elections to represent the interests of its membership base, the party runs the risk of widening the gap between its leadership and its members, which may result in political disinterest and disconnectedness on behalf of rank-and-file party membership.

Because the FPM had been an active social movement in Lebanese politics throughout the period 1990–2005, its post-2005 institutional transformation involved some vicissitudes related to the reshuffling of an already existing phenomenon into a political party where new members and veterans compete on an equal footing. Antoine Nasrallah, lawyer and FPM activist, discerned this difficulty when mentioning that "the toughest thing about the FPM is that you are creating a party for an existing phenomenon. We are not creating a party for a phenomenon that we want to create. So we are placing people within organizational structures" (interview October 6, 2014). This placement of individuals to fill positions within a party that used to operate as a social movement had certain consequences for the FPM at large. First, the nature of movement operations provided activists with a sense of leadership because of their perceived ability to make decisions and execute them. To a large extent, the way the FPM as a social movement carried out collective activity from 1990 to 2005, in small, loosely connected and decentralized units, provided activists with a wide margin to determine the time and place of their peaceful collective activity. Therefore, the sudden shift to a party discipline with clear, hierarchical roles appeared quite hard to stomach for many FPM activists.

Second, the random political appointments that took place within the FPM, especially without clear criteria or competitive elections to fill those positions, further disgruntled long-time activists. This was illustrated in the words of Georges Sarrouh, who stated that "assignments occurred on both the executive and representative levels. I understand that one could assign a finance director or secretary, but I couldn't assign a provincial or local representative. What if that person does not represent the province?... We had to apply the structure and laws... Georges Sarrouh would have been outside the structure because nobody voted for him" (interview October 16, 2014). Therefore, the establishment of clear and transparent mechanisms for party assignments within the FPM was vital to ensure the success of the movement's transformation into a political party by voting into office those individuals who best represented the FPM membership.

Even the selection of candidates to represent the FPM in parliamentary elections, despite being carried out by Aoun himself, followed no clear criteria and disgruntled long-time activists. Illustrating this point is Mansour Fadel, an FPM activist in charge of the elections dossier in the FPM, who stated:

> In 2005, with the return of General Aoun, he wanted to run elections quickly. He imposed some candidates on us. In 2005, there was a crisis between the people over here and those who left with the General. These people included Shamel Mouzaya, Nabil Nicolas, and Ibrahim Kanaan [who became FPM MPs in 2005]. There were two teams on the ground in 2005. There was the team that had carried out the struggle on the ground and those who returned from abroad. We considered that they were coming to take over our roles. They considered we did not want them. So the crises between the old and the new members began. (Interview November 20, 2014)

Therefore, as mentioned previously, the main source of disagreement within the FPM revolved around the roles FPM veterans considered they deserved to assume, as opposed to those taken up by new members. The fact that there existed weak criteria for the selection of candidates from among these groups—that is, old and new members—continued to fan the flames of internal party conflict.

During this author's interviews with FPM activists in 2014, the proposal to hold an opinion poll to discover the FPM's most favored candidates within every electoral constituency for parliamentary elections seemed to be the most reasonable solution to resolve the disagreements between old and new members. Pierre Raffoul, General Coordinator of the FPM, stated "Let's say there are 8 seats in elections and I received 5 candidates. To run 5 MPs, I would refer them to an opinion poll in the Matn district. Those that receive the 5 highest votes will run with the FPM… I want to win as a party. I want to have a big block. For the remaining three, I will deal with the other parties [share allocated for FPM allies]" (interview October 2, 2014). This proposed system was employed within the FPM to nominate the party's candidates for the parliamentary elections of 2018. Yet, this system continues to display some shortcomings, which will be discussed in the next chapter.

Another view voiced by some FPM activists is that the appointment of individuals to positions within the FPM occurred not strictly because FPM leadership failed to organize party elections, but because early electoral attempts within the party culminated in disagreement among FPM members. The reason for party members' rejection of the FPM's electoral results for local and provincial representatives on October 25, 2007, stemmed from their poor understanding of the strict discipline characterizing party politics, especially because they were used to operating according to the loose rules and regulations that had prevailed within the FPM as a social movement.

During this FPM electoral race for local committees, FPM members elected many individuals to represent them on local FPM committees in towns and villages through consensus. Major disagreements emerged when FPM members convened to decide on who should head these local committees. Pierre Raffoul, General Coordinator of the FPM, stated: "more than 95% of our lists won by consensus. This occurred in 95% of the 410 committees. We only had 19 centers that ran elections. But later, they did not agree with one another. The entire structure fell down. Some people left, while others stayed" (interview October 2, 2014).

Yet, instead of simply attempting to intervene to resolve matters or establish criteria for the selection of committee heads, the FPM averted another conflict by calling off the election. The FPM feared that disagreement in FPM local committees may have a negative impact on the movement's ability to run for and score victories in the Lebanese parliamentary elections, which were fast approaching in 2009. Pierre Raffoul commented: "We were close to the 2009 elections so we did not mention it" (interview October 2, 2014). Therefore, the mentality and attitude of FPM members toward political party discipline contributed to its weak institutional form as a political party.

Once again, the FPM repeated the mistake of avoiding electoral competition between Gebran Bassil (son-in-law of Michel Aoun) and Alain Aoun (nephew of Michel Aoun) in the electoral race for the FPM presidency, which was scheduled to take place in the summer of 2015. With key party figures supporting both candidates, the chances of either candidate attaining an overwhelming victory were slim. Internal party mediation attempts successfully averted an electoral showdown that might have led to increased division within the party, and would have highlighted the inability of Michel Aoun to resolve conflict within the FPM (Saoud, August 21, 2015). As a result of this mediation attempt, Alain Aoun withdrew from the electoral race, rendering Gebran Bassil President of the FPM by default (ibid.).

This mediation attempt risked debilitating the party structures and founding principles of the FPM by preventing its members from taking part in its political decisions. Though the settlement of the electoral race for the office of FPM presidency in the summer of 2015 might have resulted in reduced electoral tensions within the FPM, its political ramifications reverberated across the party, because its members were robbed of the first democratic opportunity to elect their party president. Regardless of the outcome, elections had to take place in order to ensure a transition into democratic party politics from social movement activity, in which several individuals emerged as leaders in the collective activity of the movement.

If FPM members had experienced any disconnectedness due to their inability to actively participate in the political affairs of their party, this mediation effort prevented members from fully expressing their political preferences in determining its leadership (Saoud, August 21, 2015). This attempt also supplanted party representation with a contorted system of political bargaining between the top echelons of the FPM to determine party leadership (ibid.), which might have dire consequences for the fate of the FPM if repeated. Preventing FPM members from actively engaging in the affairs of their party—namely, from electing party representatives—risks decreasing their commitment to its political activities.

On the other hand, the FPM had been quite vocal in opposing political feudalism or the promotion of individuals to political prominence on the basis of family connections. Although Alain Aoun and Gebran Bassil both had a long history with the FPM, their relationship to Michel Aoun risked turning the party into a family-run political structure, which might have deleterious effects, since political feudalism was precisely what the FPM was intent on combating as a social movement.

Whether running elections on the local, provincial or presidential level of the party, the FPM can only represent the interests and reflect the political inclinations of its members by conducting transparent rounds of internal party elections. The internal party elections that occurred in early 2016 marked the first serious attempt on behalf of the leadership to contribute to the institutional transformation of the former social movement into a political party. This offers a glimmer of hope in the long phase of the FPM's shaky institutional transformation process, but should be followed with regular rounds of such elections to ensure this becomes periodic practice within the party. Since the principles of the movement were founded on combating political feudalism, corruption and inequality, as well as supporting the freedom, sovereignty and independence of Lebanon, any unrepresentative measures taken by the party leadership, such as the appointment of individuals to party positions, risk shattering the founding principles of the party. Therefore, the FPM faces the challenge of organizing its internal party structures to ensure a successful party form that relies mainly on the representation of its membership base. In order to remain faithful to its principles and institutionalize them into the new-found party form, the FPM should stress the importance of conducting periodic and representative rounds of elections that absorb members into decision-making roles.

Conclusion

A series of political opportunities led to openness in the political context of Lebanon, which provided a conducive environment for the institutional transformation of the FPM into a political party. The liberation of South Lebanon, the formation of the political gathering of Qornet Chehwan, the enactment of the Syria Accountability Act by the US Congress and the issuing of UN Security Council Resolution 1559 were the political opportunities that helped exert pressure on Syria, which withdrew its troops from Lebanon following the assassination of former Lebanese Prime Minister Rafik Hariri in 2005. The withdrawal of Syrian troops led to the return of Michel Aoun to Lebanon on May 7, 2005. Perhaps these opportunities alone did not lead to the transformation of the FPM into a political party, but they paved the way for the return of Aoun, who subsequently declared the FPM a political party.

This declaration took place on September 18, 2005, and Aoun immediately assumed the central leadership role of the former social movement, which many FPM activists simply considered a natural phenomenon given their support for him. However, the performance of the FPM in post-2005 Lebanese politics shifted away from the movement's previously secular positions toward the adoption of sectarian strategies of mobilization and sectarian discourse. The FPM's adoption of such sectarian modes of subjectification and mobilization emanated from two main factors: first, the post-2005 political setting in Lebanon, in which sectarian modes of mobilization became more pronounced, as demonstrated by Salloukh et al. (2015), and second, the competition the FPM faced from other Christian parties, particularly the Kataeb and the LF, who also vied to win the support of those electoral constituencies that elected the FPM's MPs (Cammett 2014). With these political realities as a backdrop, the FPM, by virtue of participating in conventional politics—that is, Parliament and the Council of Ministers—found itself adopting sectarian strategies to reflect the interests of its predominantly Christian support base, whether by calling for increased representation in conventional politics, a larger share of appointments of public servants or infrastructural development projects.

However, a more problematic aspect of the institutional transformation process involved the transformation of an existing social movement into new political party structures on the one hand, and the management of a membership that now included veteran FPM activists who operated in Lebanon, members of the FPM who had returned from abroad and new FPM members who joined the movement in the post-2005 period on the other. During this transformation phase, the FPM switched from being a social movement with roughly 3000 activists to a party with more than 60,000 registered members (L. Chakour, interview September 29, 2014). The resolution of emerging conflict between old and new members, as well as those FPM members inside Lebanon versus those who returned from abroad, proved to be a tedious task. The issue fanning the flames of this conflict was the random assignment of individuals to political positions within the party.

The next chapter turns to an analysis of the FPM's performance in national politics. It explores the roles of Michel Aoun, Gebran Bassil and other political factors in contributing to the longevity of the FPM or otherwise compromising the party's vitality.

References

Abi Antoun, N. Interview by this author. 2014. Beirut, September 23.
Abi Ramia, S. Interview by this author. 2014. Beirut, November 21.
Achkar, W. Interview by this author. 2014. Jounieh, October 15.
Aoun, N. Interview by this author. 2014. Awkar, September 18.
Cammett, M. 2014. *Compassionate Communalism: Welfare and Sectarianism in Lebanon*. Ithaca: Cornell University Press.
Chakour, L. Interview by this author. 2014. Jbeil, September 29.
Choucair, G., Interview by this author. 2014. Beirut, October 16.
El-Husseini, R. 2012. *Pax Syriana Elite Politics in Post-war Lebanon*. New York: Syracuse University Press.
ElKhoury, P. Interview by this author. 2014. Dbayeh, October 1.
ElKhoury, R. Interview by this author. 2014. Jounieh, September 26.
Fadel, M. Interview by this author. 2014. Dekwaneh, November 20.
Germanos, C. 2013. "Hizbullah and the Free Patriotic Movement: The Politics of Perception and a Failed Search for a National Territory." *The Singapore Middle East Papers* 4: 1–69.

Moukheiber, A. Interview by this author. 2014. Beirut, October 31.

Nasrallah, A. Interview by this author. 2014. Dbayeh, October 6.

Raffoul, P. Interview by this author. 2014. Beirut, October 2.

Salloukh, B. F., R. Barakat, J. S. Al-Habbal, L. W. Khattab, S. Mikaelian, and A. Nerguizian. 2015. *The Politics of Sectarianism in Postwar Lebanon*. London: Pluto Press.

Saoud, G. 2015. "Akhiran Youmkin lilAouniyeen Tay Safhet AlKeel Wal Qal. 'At Last Aounists Can Turn the Page of Bickering'." *Al-Akhbar*, August 21.

———. 2015. "Masassat Attayyar Albourtouqali: Hal Yafaalounaha AlAouniyoun Akhiran. 'The Institutionalization of the Orange Movement: Will Aounists Finally Make It'." *Al-Akhbar*, February 7.

———. 2015. "Yabdu Anal Aouniyeen Tajaraaou Kas AlIntikhabat AlDakhilya. 'It Seems Like the Aounists Drank the Cup of Internal Elections'." *Al-Akhbar*, August 28.

Sarrouh, G. E. Interview by this author. 2014. Baabda, October 16.

Syria Accountability and Lebanese Sovereignty Restoration Act of 2003. 2003. Public Law 108–175. 108th Congress, December 12.

UNSCR 1559. 2004. United Nations S/Res/1559. Security Council (04-49892), September 2.

UNSCR 425. 1978. United Nations S/Res/425. Security Council, March 14.

CHAPTER 6

The General Turned President, the Son-in-Law Groomed as Leader and the Dream Lost in Translation

During the preparatory phases of this book, this author came across various requests to elucidate what will happen to the Free Patriotic Movement (FPM) in the future, especially following the death of its founder, President Michel Aoun. Many conversations concerning the fate of the FPM as a political party cast doubt on the ability of Aoun's successor, whether his son-in-lawGebran Bassil or another party member, to walk in the moccasins of the FPM founder. As such, there seems to be a common belief lurking in the minds of FPM sympathizers and foes alike that the post-Aoun phase will witness the waning of the FPM's popularity, which, in turn, could mean a shrinking of its representation in Parliament, its voter base and its ability to rally supporters.

While the social sciences remain limited in their ability to make predictions, this concluding chapter seeks to shed light on the future of the FPM as a potent political force in Lebanese politics. The analysis will focus on several projects in which the party is engaged. It will also discuss in some detail the role of Gebran Bassil in attracting much-needed resources that will help contribute to the political longevity of the FPM. Furthermore, it will critique the party for backtracking on its promises to introduce progressive reforms into the political system of Lebanon; by so doing, it seeks to assess whether this drawing back was intentionally provoked or externally imposed on the movement.

No matter how progressively minded the FPM appears, the party's fate greatly depends on its ability to garner widespread support among the

J. P. Helou, *Activism, Change and Sectarianism in the Free Patriotic Movement in Lebanon*, Reform and Transition in the Mediterranean,
https://doi.org/10.1007/978-3-030-25704-0_6

Christians of Lebanon, because any attempt to secure a base of support beyond the Christian community of Lebanon will be met by adamant opposition from the FPM's sectarian counterparts. The political longevity of the FPM can be achieved if Michel Aoun translates the party's goals and principles into actual political projects during his tenure as President of the Lebanese Republic, and if Gebran Bassil, as President of the FPM, consolidates the resource base of the party by inviting financially able persons to play an active role within it, leading members of the diaspora to join the FPM and contribute to Lebanese politics, and by responding to the economic concerns of the lower-middle class and/or underprivileged Christians. The FPM's fate also depends on streamlining the expectations of the party's support base with the new-found realities of Lebanese politics; both FPM activists and supporters will need to reassess the plausibility of achieving its goal of a non-sectarian political system (with a long-term time frame), identify contextual factors preventing the realization of various FPM goals and set out to fulfill those FPM goals that can be attained in the short term.

This chapter is sub-divided into three. The first part analyzes the political circumstances that contributed to the election of Michel Aoun to the Presidency of the Lebanese Republic. It also discusses how these conditions helped put an end to the political polarity that had prevailed in Lebanon since the assassination of Premier Rafik Hariri in 2005. The second part discusses in some detail the pivotal role played by Gebran Bassil in the FPM leadership and Lebanese politics. It focuses on the intensification of sectarian political identities following the adoption of the proportional electoral system in the parliamentary elections of 2018. It also analyzes several attempts by the FPM to introduce policy proposals, advance public infrastructure and invite members of the Lebanese diaspora back to their home country. The final part concludes by discussing why the FPM should redefine its goals and dream of a progressive, secular Lebanon in order to achieve the party's longevity.

Part I: The 2016 Lebanese Presidential Elections and the End of Bipolar Politics

This section demonstrates that the election of Aoun as President of the Lebanese Republic ushered in new practices in Lebanese politics on the national level and rejuvenated the FPM, whose members had long awaited the election of their leader to the Lebanese presidency, believing that he could effect much-needed change at the helm of the country. While this delivered positive results for the FPM, it also constrained Aoun, in that he was now expected to behave as an impartial arbiter in his position as President. The political alliances that he had to forge with several political groups, most notably the Sunni Future Movement of Saad Hariri, the Shia Hezbollah and the Christian Lebanese Forces (LF) party, meant that the President had to manage any future political collision between national political parties with more prudence than had been the case prior to his election.

Upon his return to Lebanon in May 2005, Aoun was met with much political ambivalence by the various members of the country's elite. This reception ranged from those who warmly welcomed the opposition leader (perhaps seeking a political alliance with him) and those who viewed his return as constituting a threat to their electoral voter base (Ilias 2010), since Aoun had been a long-time rival of Syria, whereas many of his counterparts had just shifted out of Syria's orbit. With parliamentary elections fast approaching in June 2005, Aoun formed his electoral lists hosting candidates who were opposed to Syria and some who were close allies of Syria, such as Elias Scaf of the Zahley district, Sleiman Frangiyeh of the Zgharta district and Michel ElMurr of the Matn district (ibid.).

Emerging from the 2005 electoral round with a parliamentary bloc of 22 MPs, the repatriated leader carved a presence on the Lebanese political landscape as the representative of a predominantly Christian constituency. Even though the FPM sought to present itself as a secular party with supporters from across Lebanon's multi-sectarian spectrum, the FPM's competition for votes in predominantly Christian electoral constituencies with the Christian parties of the LF and the Kataeb transformed the former into a champion of Christian causes, which was illustrated in the discourse adopted by FPM party members after 2005 (Cammet 2014; Salloukh et al. 2015).

While the FPM tilted toward sectarian modes of political subjectification, illustrated by its evolving sectarian mobilization and discourse, it transcended narrow sectarian rifts when forging national political alliances. Such behavior led it to sign a memorandum of understanding (MoU) with the Shia party Hezbollah on February 6, 2006 following violent protests by Sunni crowds enraged at a cartoon caricature of the Prophet Mohammad published in a Danish newspaper (CNN 2006; Yacoubian 2009). Today we know that the signing of the MoU may have occurred immediately after these protests to offset any potential sectarian reaction by members of the Christian community, whose streets and alleys were violated, since the Danish embassy was located in a Christian quarter of Beirut; in fact, the actual preparation for the alliance took months of deliberation prior to the signing ceremony (Z. Abs, interview October 31, 2014).

Another reason for the formation of a political alliance between the FPM and Hezbollah in 2006 lay in shifting political alliances among various Lebanese parties after the 2005 parliamentary elections. The FPM was a major participant in the protests on March 14, 2005, which brought one million people to downtown Beirut to call for the withdrawal of Syria from Lebanon (M. Chamoun, interview October 15, 2014). On the other hand, Hezbollah and its allies had gathered a large-scale protest in downtown Beirut on March 8, 2005 to thank Syria for its stabilizing role in Lebanon. However, the main pillars of the March 14 movement, such as the Sunni Future movement, the Druze Progressive Socialist Party and the Christian LF, were hardly enthused at the prospect of allying with the FPM in the parliamentary elections of 2005 (perhaps in an attempt to contain the size of the FPM's expected parliamentary bloc) and ended up running their own lists with the Shia heavyweights of Hezbollah and Amal (Ilias 2010).

This combined March 14–Hezbollah alliance, also known as the Quadruple Alliance, helped ensure a parliamentary majority for the March 14 movement in the 2005 round of parliamentary elections, since Hezbollah had a strong demographic presence in the electoral district of Baabda-Aley, which tipped the results in favor of March 14 according to the winner-takes-all electoral system (Ilias 2010). Quickly thereafter, a political rupture occurred in the Quadruple Alliance when fingers were pointed at Syria for its alleged role in the Hariri assassination. Hezbollah, which was later accused of participating in the plot to assassinate Hariri, drifted away from the March 14 movement.

With Hezbollah and Amal outside the Quadruple Alliance and Aoun's FPM existing as a sizable parliamentary bloc, these actors naturally gravitated toward one another, as illustrated in several electoral races for student governments on university campuses and in professional syndicates during the period from Summer 2005 to February 2006. This author closely observed political events at first hand during this period and noticed the formation of political alliances between the FPM, Hezbollah and Amal, even prior to the MoU of February 6, 2006.

Further cementing the relationship between the FPM and Hezbollah were the cordial inter-party relations during the July 2006 war launched by Israel against Lebanon in retaliation for Hezbollah's kidnapping of two Israeli soldiers along the United Nations-designated Blue Line in South Lebanon. The ensuing Israeli bombardment of infrastructure and houses in South Lebanon left thousands of Shia seeking refuge in Beirut and the predominantly Christian governorate of Mount Lebanon (Ilias 2010). These internally displaced Shia were warmly received by the Christian community of Mount Lebanon thanks to the support granted by Aoun and his FPM party. This FPM support involved the distribution of some aid and provision of accommodation, and ensured the frictionless Christian communal reception of displaced Shia, whose numbers temporarily increased the population density of Mount Lebanon (ibid.).

Following the 34-day war in 2006, Hezbollah must have perceived Aoun as a nationalist figure and a reliable ally within the Christian community, thus displaying an interest in maintaining a strong relationship with him. While this relationship should have expanded Aoun's cross-sectarian support and increased the FPM's gains in Lebanese politics, it actually encumbered Aoun and his movement with enormous political challenges as the ally of Hezbollah in an intensifying sectarian and bipolar political environment. This bipolar environment had regional supporters, with Iran and Syria backing the March 8 movement and Saudi Arabia sponsoring the March 14 movement, which brought home the Iran–Saudi regional confrontation by proxy.

Shortly after the July 2006 war, political disagreement regarding the establishment of an international tribunal to try Hariri's assassins turned fragile the already brittle relations between the March 14 and March 8 alliances which coexisted in the government headed by Fouad Seniora. By the end of 2006, five Shia cabinet ministers affiliated with Amal and Hezbollah resigned, in addition to the then Minister of Environment Yakoub Sarraf (a Christian ally of March 8; Al-Jazeera, November 13, 2006). The cabinet members who resigned called for the correction of the national unity government by representation of the FPM inside the Council of Ministers, but were implicitly aiming at the subversion of the international tribunal, which was perceived by March 8 as a plot to destabilize Lebanese politics by implicating Hezbollah and Syria in Hariri's assassination.

When Premier Seniora faced large-scale protests organized by the March 8 alliance and the FPM calling for his resignation, the Premier refused to budge. His obstinate stance was matched by Hezbollah's unflinching commitment to bringing down a government that no longer represented the leading parties of Lebanon's Shia and Christian communities. This political stalemate resulted in a two-year sit-in in downtown Beirut, which the predominantly Sunni Future movement regarded as the crown jewel of post-war reconstruction led by its martyr Rafik Hariri. Therefore, this extensive occupation of public spaces in downtown Beirut helped portray Hezbollah and the FPM as enemies of progress and modernity, disrespectful to Sunni politicians and martyrs (chiefly the Prime Minister) and intruders to the city, especially in the media outlets of the March 14 alliance. This prevailing political environment aggravated sectarian tensions in Lebanese politics.

While the March 8 alliance alongside the FPM commanded considerable support in Lebanon, arguably the popular majority, March 14 commanded international legitimacy and the support of the international community. The March 14 alliance and the Future movement, notably the backbone of this alliance, drew on several UN Security Council Resolutions, such as UNSCR 1595 that established the international tribunal (UNSCR 1595 2005), when facing off against political counterparts. They attempted to portray their actions as legitimate, endorsed by the UN and politically supported by the international community and the axis of moderation, including Saudi Arabia, which sharply contrasted with the actions of Hezbollah, which they pictured as a destabilizing force in Lebanese politics, a rogue element in international politics and a marionette of the axis of evil led by Iran and Syria.

This March 14 media campaign dovetailed with the US-led campaign to discredit Hezbollah, which, according to former US ambassador to Lebanon Jeffrey Feltman, led the USA to channel $500 million to sway Lebanese youth away from Hezbollah, but failed (Rida 2010; Hage Ali, December 8, 2010). On the other hand, Hezbollah, backed by Iran and the FPM, funneled funds for media campaigns, but these were no match to those garnered by March 14 and its American and Saudi sponsors.

The government headed by Seniora delivered a decisive blow to the political stalemate prevailing in Lebanon when it voted to dismantle Hezbollah's telecoms network on May 5, 2008. It could not have carried out such an action alone, but sought to undermine Hezbollah by spelling out its outlaw status, as the group was likely to reject the government's decision to dismantle its private landline network.

Shootings by random sources at labor strikes quickly unfolded into a large-scale raid on Beirut on May 7, 2008. Hezbollah, assisted by the Amal movement and the Syrian Socialist Nationalist Party, curbed the unorganized and ill-equipped fighters of the Future movement (Bakri and Cowell, May 21, 2008). This raid, which became known in Lebanese political discourse as the May 7 events, did not involve the FPM in its organization or execution. Yet, the FPM bore the brunt of its alliance with Hezbollah for providing the cross-sectarian political aegis the group needed to legitimize such extra-institutional behavior in Lebanese politics.

For several years after the May 7 events, the FPM had to respond to accusations of political blame, partly holding the movement responsible for Hezbollah's armed siege of Beirut. This issue, coupled with fierce media campaigns against the FPM, contributed to the movement's dwindling support, from 70% of Christian votes in the 2005 round of parliamentary elections to just 52% of Christian votes in the 2009 parliamentary elections (Salloukh et al. 2015, p. 150).

Following the May 7, 2008 infighting, Qatari mediation among the disputing Lebanese parties and their regional sponsors broke the deadlock when various Lebanese parties attended peace talks in Doha (BBC, May 21, 2008). Aoun went to this conference to express his political demands, which championed Christian political representation (Abdallah, May 22, 2008). For instance, the Doha Accords stressed the adoption of the 1960 electoral law with some gerrymandering of electoral constituencies (ibid.). Baabda and Aley would become two separate districts, the single electoral district of Beirut would be divided into three and the Christian districts of Northern Lebanon would be separated from Tripoli, whose large Sunni voter base used to determine all the candidates representing Christians in the North. Although this agreement still maintained the principle of the winner-takes-all electoral system, it helped Christian political parties to draw up electoral constituencies that ensured better representation than the pre-existing electoral law, which had been devised by Ghazi Kanaan (the Syrian intelligence chief based in Lebanon) to ensure the victory of Syria's allies in the Lebanese parliamentary elections of 2000.

As part of the Doha agreement, Lebanese politicians agreed to elect the politically neutral Lebanese army commander Michel Sleiman as President of the Lebanese Republic. The principle of the formation of national unity governments was reasserted and the FPM and March 8 gained the constitutional veto in the government formed after the presidential elections of 2008, which permitted them to block the required quorum and dissolve the government simply by declaring the resignation of more than one-third of cabinet ministers. The FPM and its allies later resorted to resignation from this bloc in the government formed and headed by Saad Hariri following the parliamentary elections of 2009, which also contributed to the aggravation of sectarian tensions in Lebanon, as this move was widely perceived as a Hezbollah-orchestrated plot to debunk Hariri. However, as of 2008, the FPM participated in the Council of Ministers and held key ministerial portfolios that allowed it to introduce reformist proposals.

Indeed, the FPM reaped favorable political results from its alliance with Hezbollah, but could not simultaneously pursue many options as the bipolarity prevailing in Lebanon restricted avenues for political maneuvering. For instance, lavish sums were spent in the 2009 round of parliamentary elections, estimated to be one of the most expensive elections in the tiny republic's history (costing a total sum of US$1 billion), by the March 14 and March 8 alliances to secure a parliamentary majority (Hage Ali, December 8, 2010). The FPM received a barrage of criticism on media stations sympathetic to the March 14 movement for backing Hezbollah. This situation was further consolidated during the presidency of Michel Suleiman, who eventually shed his cloak of impartiality by expressing support for the political stance of the March 14 movement; his fierce censure of Hezbollah's intervention in the Syrian conflict after 2011 also encumbered the FPM politically.

Seeing that both the March 14 and March 8 leaderships were heavily imbued in domestic sectarian terms with regional sponsors, Sunni in the former and Shia in the latter, Aoun found himself asserting leadership in defense of his predominantly Christian voter base. Although he and some FPM members remained conscious of their former secular ideas, they attributed their sectarian positions to the prevailing sectarian system that necessitated such reactions or else risked losing support at the polls.

Aoun found himself redefining his political outlook as a Christian leader within Lebanon and within the East (Qazi, October 31, 2013). As such, he capitalized on his improving relations with Syria following its withdrawal from Lebanon and made several visits to the Syrian city of Brad, which is the burial site of St. Maron (monk and founding father of the Maronite sect of Lebanon; France24, December 4, 2008; Haddad, February 13, 2010). His new outlook allowed him to relabel himself as a Christian Orientalist, which was a title that could provide him with the authority to speak on behalf of Christian minorities in the Middle East, because Lebanon's political system only promotes a Christian Maronite to the Presidency of the Republic, allocates Christians 50% of parliamentary seats and ministerial portfolios and accords Christians considerable representation in state offices.

Aoun must have been concerned at the plight of Christian communities in some Middle Eastern countries affected by the 2011 Arab Spring protests. The resulting security vacuum in some of the countries hosting Arab Spring protests quickly spiraled into the kind of chaos conducive for the rise of extremist Islamist groups, Syria being a case in point. Alternatively, countries such as Egypt, which were influenced by Arab Spring protests and yet still managed to make a transition to some semblance of representative politics, albeit short-lived, were also home to Islamist parties. Both these outcomes were obstructive to the continued coexistence of Christian minorities, as they compromised national citizenship by suggesting an exclusionary ideological outlook, to say nothing of failing to prevent the persecution of Christians.

Therefore, this regional political environment hosting overt sectarian practices percolated into Lebanese politics, obliging domestic political actors to pinpoint friends and foes in the region. While Lebanese politicians considered multiple factors when forging internal and external relations, their discourse underwent drastic change with the shifting sands of regional alliances; that is to say, the Iran–Saudi confrontation weighed in heavily on Lebanese politics. To paraphrase Farid El-Khazen (2003), who described the Syrian suzerainty of Lebanon as "authoritarianism by diffusion," the repercussions of this intensifying bipolar regional struggle between Iran and Saudi Arabia, cloaked in a sectarian hue, could be dubbed sectarianism by diffusion.

With these internal and external political conditions as a backdrop, Aoun changed his discourse and outlook much as other political parties, such as the Sunni Future movement, the Shia Hezbollah and Amal, the Druze Progressive Socialist Party and the Christian LF, realigned their positions in light of major developments. These major developments included the withdrawal of Syrian troops from Lebanon in 2005, the July 2006 war against Israel, the establishment of an international tribunal investigating the assassination of Rafic Hariri (insinuating the implication of Syria and Hezbollah), the Arab Spring events and the proliferation of terrorist cells in Lebanon linked to Islamic State or ISIS. This brewing political environment and the repercussions it may have delivered to the Lebanese arena required Lebanese parties to adopt clear positions on the salient issues of the day.

After 2005, Aoun and the FPM became political players who ran in electoral races, campaigned for the minds and hearts of supporters, attempted to present their supporters with services and electoral promises, put forth a political platform and, most importantly, dealt with the conflagrations of a regional political order that did not encourage bystanders. Perhaps the policy options they adopted could constitute the topic of future research. For now, it is important to mention that Aoun, like his counterparts, made key political decisions during the period 2005–2014 that may have contributed to the consolidation of bipolarity in Lebanese politics. But if the domestic and regional political milieu deeply splintered Lebanese politics, how was Aoun able to override this bipolar political order to receive the votes of the political elite to win the race for the Presidency of the Lebanese Republic?

President Michel Sleiman's term expired on May 2014 without a successor to occupy the presidential office. For the next 30 months, various attempts to elect a President were proposed; meetings between Saad Hariri (head of the Sunni Future movement) and Michel Aoun occurred, but were of no avail since, according to Lebanese political jargon, the genie can only leave the bottle if Saudi Arabia supports the election of the prospective Lebanese President. The size of the FPM's parliamentary bloc and its cordial relations with Hezbollah made Saad Hariri and Saudi Arabia think twice about supporting Aoun for the presidency, for fear of allowing Iran to score a political victory in an Arab country.

However, instead of supporting another March 14 candidate, Saad Hariri nominated Sleiman Frangiyeh, who was an even closer ally of Syria, a personal friend of Syrian President Bashar Al-Assad and a political ally of Hezbollah, as well as a political ally of the FPM parliamentary bloc. Hariri must have thought that by supporting Frangiyeh, he could either drive a wedge through the March 8 alliance or oblige Hezbollah to abandon Aoun in favor of Frangiyeh. In turn, Hezbollah refused to budge and continued to support Aoun for the presidency (Perry, October 30, 2016).

As Frangiyeh contested the presidential race, the FPM sought to further consolidate its position within the Christian community of Lebanon. Detailed discussions led by the FPM MP Ibrahim Kanaan and the LF member in charge of media and communications Melhem Riyashi, culminated in a Declaration of Intent between these political groups (*Annahar*, January 18, 2016). Both groups had a vested interest in preventing Frangiyeh from becoming president (for different reasons). As a result of this understanding, the FPM fully endorsed the principles set forth in the Taif Accords, which had long constituted a target of FPM criticism. Both parties agreed to turn the page on rivalries pre-dating the Lebanese Civil

War, coordinate closely with one another and support Aoun's candidacy for the presidency (ibid.).

With the support of Hezbollah and now the LF as a backdrop, Hariri's Future movement was left with little choice but to vote for Aoun. We now know that mediators from both the Future movement and the FPM worked diligently to bridge the gaps between the former political rivals, which resulted in support for Aoun's candidacy. Hariri's worsening private fortune in Saudi Arabia as well as signs of Saudi acquiescence also contributed to the election of Aoun on October 31, 2016 (Perry, October 30, 2016).

The shifting alliances prior to the election of Aoun reshuffled the decks by confirming the end of the March 14 and March 8 bipolarity prevailing in Lebanese politics as of 2005. Several of Aoun's political opponents, such as the Future movement and the LF, were now willing to work closely with the FPM on many dossiers, whereas some of Aoun's former political allies, for example Amal, had supported Frangiyeh during the presidential race and now enjoyed lukewarm political relations with Aoun.

Most Lebanese parties seem to recognize their counterparts' right to represent their sectarian communities in government and in posts across state bureaucracies following the presidential elections of 2016. While this has generated a period of relative stability in Lebanese politics, it has reasserted sectarianism as a political order, instead of tabling the topic of the abrogation of sectarian representation for discussion. Sectarianism and its modes of political subjectification and mobilization are not expected to wane any time soon. Therefore, Aoun's election heralds the return of Christian politicians to power, especially the presidency of the republic, for the first time in post-war Lebanon, since Hrawi, Lahoud and Sleiman all lacked a parliamentary bloc before their election to the presidency.

Yet, Aoun will face a number of political and economic challenges during his tenure as President. These challenges are rooted in the worsening economic conditions prevailing in Lebanon, the Lebanese people's perception of rampant corruption in government and the resistance to reform by multiple business, sectarian and political actors (Mahdi and Garrote Sanchez 2019). Therefore, Aoun's original goal of wiping out corruption from state institutions, protecting Lebanese sovereignty and precluding foreign intervention in Lebanese affairs becomes harder to implement in a politically fragmented scene hosting political parties allied with opposing regional poles (Syria and Iran versus Saudi Arabia and occasionally

Qatar), not to mention the intersection between several local and regional dossiers, the Syrian conflict being a case in point.

This chronological sequencing of events reveals that the FPM tilted toward the adoption of sectarian discourse and mobilization in reaction to externally imposed political factors. While this change in performance must have been taken by party leadership, it was fierce electoral races, media campaigns and the support of external powers that contributed to the formation of the powerful bipolarity in Lebanese politics epitomized by the March 14 and March 8 alliances. In the same spirit, Abbas Assi (2016) argues that intra-sectarian disagreements, inter-sectarian disagreements and external challenges weighed in heavily on Christians in the post-2005 period and prevented them from ensuring political gains in the consociational political system of Lebanon. Perhaps these factors also contributed to the continuing postponement of internal FPM party elections, the application of reforms and the establishment of adequate party organizational structures, as Aoun had been engrossed in national affairs.

The next section will turn to the role of Gebran Bassil in FPM party affairs and national politics and evaluate his successes and shortcomings.

Part II: Gebran Bassil and Political Campaigns

Upon the return of Michel Aoun to Lebanon in 2005, no signs of grooming his son-in-law Gebran Bassil as leader of the FPM loomed on the political horizon. Bassil competed for the parliamentary seat of his northern district of Batroun and lost in both the 2005 and 2009 parliamentary electoral rounds due to the size of the electoral constituency and the winner-takes-all electoral law. His first occupation of formal office came with his appointment as Minister of Telecoms in the government formed after the presidential elections of 2008. His consolidation of power within the FPM was made possible by his positive performance in national politics and by ruling out potential contenders in the party.

This section demonstrates that Bassil carries the keys to party success due to his active political campaigns in a number of ministerial portfolios, while simultaneously exhibiting party shortcomings due to his confrontational style with several political heavyweights in Lebanon. He continues to make headlines in evening news bulletins and on talk shows due to his controversial character when dealing with party cohorts, other party leaders and the international community; this man displays features of a confrontational politician, unyielding decision-maker and diplomatic Foreign Minister, depending on the context in which he operates.

Bassil scored successes as Minister of Telecoms, Energy and Foreign Affairs (portfolios he assumed consecutively as of 2008), especially when contrasted with the achievements of many other politicians assuming ministerial portfolios. Although many issues in these portfolios remain unresolved, Bassil introduced planning, reform programs and policy-making as integral aspects of ministerial work, which sharply contrasted with the ad hoc and random nature of decision-making in many post-war governments that went unmonitored and unpunished. Bassil decreased the indirect taxes paid by cell-phone users on a monthly basis (almost halving the fixed costs of cell-phone bills) during his tenure as Minister of Telecoms, which was warmly received by large segments of the Lebanese population. His plan to revitalize Lebanon's cadaverous power grid received unanimous support in the Council of Ministers in 2010, which, despite all critique against it, continues to form the basis for the revised plan introduced by other FPM members serving as Minister of Energy and endorsed by the Council of Ministers on April 8, 2019 (*Asharq Al-awsat*, April 8, 2019).

Even after his consecutive appointments as Minister of Foreign Affairs in governments formed from 2014 until now, Bassil continues to support the efforts of FPM members occupying the post of Minister of Energy. This effort helped mediate an agreement among the various members of the Lebanese political elite to grant licenses to international oil and gas companies to begin drilling in Lebanese waters (Habib and Kanaan, April 3, 2019). Bassil, as Minister of Foreign Affairs, also manages marine border disputes with Israel via American mediation to assert Lebanon's rights in fossil fuel explorations in South Lebanon (Rida, March 24, 2019).

FPM ministers are working diligently to introduce some regulation to a highly deregulated and chaotic energy sector that relies heavily on private electricity providers to service the Lebanese people during power shortages. These private electricity providers, operating through their ownership of generators across thousands of Lebanese towns and villages, enjoyed the privilege of setting prices for years following the end of the Lebanese Civil War in 1990, and contributed to extensive hybridity in the governance of the electricity sector in the country (Stel and Naudé 2016). Therefore, the imposition of an electricity meter for private electricity consumers in 2018 (price per kilowatt consumed) has already brought down prices to an all-time low; it promises huge annual national savings (estimates reach $500 million), which can then be spent as disposable income by consumers (Abou Rizk, August 30, 2018; Ministry of Economy and Trade 2018).

Although no clear information exists explicitly connecting Bassil's foreign meetings, the content of those talks or their outcomes to the election of Aoun as President, Bassil's role in the ministerial portfolio of foreign affairs as of 2014 broadly identified where the FPM stood on several issues pertaining to regional power balances, which must have contributed positively to Aoun's election. For instance, Bassil voiced opposition to foreign intervention in the Syrian Civil War and cited the Syrian people's right to determine their own fate, which was likely to be warmly received by the Syrian regime as an implicit sign of support. He obviated the need to consistently criticize Hezbollah for its intervention in the Syrian war by stressing the importance of a withdrawal of all foreign fighters from Syria, which was a face-saving move in relation to the FPM's inter-party Lebanese alliances and to regional states opposed to Hezbollah.

The Foreign Minister also stressed the need to maintain cordial relations with the states of the Arabian Gulf, such as Saudi Arabia, the United Arab Emirates, Qatar and others, which placated members of the March 14 alliance sympathetic to Saudi Arabia. While this move aimed to stabilize Lebanese politics locally, it also sought to preserve the security of thousands in the Lebanese diaspora communities in Gulf countries.

Leading Lebanon's foreign diplomatic missions in an intensely polarized regional environment is no easy matter, because the Foreign Minister is required to maintain a stable balance between his internal party alliances as the head of the FPM and preserving the government's policy of self-abstinence in several regional dossiers. This scenario limits the policy options that can be pursued by any diplomat, no matter how skillful, because expressing support for or criticism of the policies adopted by regional states compromises Lebanon's neutrality in foreign affairs. While various political parties in Lebanon clearly express a preference for certain regional powers—Iran and Saudi Arabia by Hezbollah and the Future movement, respectively—the government's maintenance of a neutral Lebanese foreign policy is crucial to prevent the seeping effect of regional disputes onto the Lebanese political arena.

However, Bassil braced his position as Foreign Minister with the overwhelming support of multiple sectarian communities in Lebanon when he moved quickly to free Premier Saad Hariri, who was suspected of being held hostage in Saudi Arabia on November 4, 2017 (Helou, December 11, 2017). This strategic blunder of seizing a sitting Prime Minister was perpetrated by Saudi Arabia as part of a campaign by Crown Prince Mohammad Bin Salman to hold accountable dozens of members of the royal family and Saudi businesspeople. Since Hariri held duel Saudi–Lebanese citizenship, the Saudi authorities must have obliged him to declare his resignation in a well-orchestrated move on a Saudi-controlled television channel in order to seize him as a Saudi citizen.

President Aoun dismissed Hariri's resignation as unjustifiable in form and content, and demanded that the Premier return to Lebanon and submit his resignation letter in person to the President, which was a move to buy Hariri time and legitimacy as a Prime Minister held in captivity (Al-Jazeera, November 15, 2017). Aoun dispatched Bassil, who flew to France, Germany, Russia and other states to highlight the violation of the Treaty of Rome, which accords a Prime Minister diplomatic immunity and thus prevents holding in captivity a sitting Prime Minister (Helou, December 11, 2017). As a consequence of this diplomatic initiative, France became more aware of Premier Hariri's condition in Saudi Arabia and exerted its weight in brokering his release. Therefore, Bassil's role in freeing Hariri won the FPM and President Aoun the sympathy of Future movement supporters and the trust of the liberated Hariri, who now drew closer to the FPM.

Bassil's initiatives in the Foreign Ministry constitute a main pillar of support for Aoun's policies and presidency, since the Foreign Minister works with an extensive team of advisers, staff and established figures who facilitate communication with the external world. For instance, the appointment of Gabi Issa, who was the former FPM representative in the USA who facilitated Aoun's appearance in Congress in 1998, as Lebanese Ambassador to the USA strengthens Aoun and the FPM's access to congressional figures. Former FPM MP Amal Abou Zeid reportedly enjoys privileged relations with politicians in Moscow and continues to serve as an important intermediary for Aoun with Russia. Current FPM MP and presidential adviser Elias Bou Saab enjoys solid relations with the United Arab Emirates. With such influential figures working alongside the FPM and Aoun, the foreign policy designed by the Lebanese government stands a higher chance of being warmly received in foreign capitals, or at least tabled for discussion as an item on the policy agenda.

Perhaps one of the most important achievements of Bassil's tenure in the Ministry of Foreign Affairs is reaching out to members within Lebanese diaspora communities, which, in turn, should influence them to consider establishing a relationship with their home country (G. Bassil, interview 2016). This was illustrated in his insistence on hosting voting centers at the Lebanese embassies in the Gulf Cooperation Council region, Europe, Africa, Australia and North and South America during the parliamentary elections of 2018, which marked the first time members of the Lebanese diaspora were able to vote in their home country's parliamentary elections (Ajroudi and Chughtai, May 2, 2018). Bassil traveled across the globe to meet members of the Lebanese diaspora communities, sometimes visiting countries such as Jamaica whose Lebanese community had never received government officials from their home country. Although it is too early to tell if members of Lebanese diaspora communities will adopt a more proactive approach toward Lebanon as a result of these visits, such initiatives transformed government policy from its previous state of passivity toward a proactive approach that seeks to integrate members of Lebanese diaspora communities into Lebanese politics.

Bassil's role in hosting the Lebanese Diaspora Energy (LDE) conferences in several countries, such as the USA, France, Canada, the Ivory Coast and in Beirut, seeks to combine Lebanese talent in a conference that provides tremendous networking opportunities. This initiative promises great returns for Lebanon if members of the Lebanese diaspora decide to invest in their home country (LDE 2019). These meetings also constitute an important political-economic bridge between Lebanon and the world, since members of Lebanese diaspora communities could now represent the interests of their home country abroad.

While various FPM members occupied ministerial portfolios, Bassil's ability to manage multiple dossiers must have impressed Aoun, whose trust helped Bassil consolidate his position within the FPM. Truth be told, Bassil is far from achieving ultimate success in many of the portfolios the FPM manages due to political obstructions from other political parties, the fragmented institutional structure of the Lebanese state, a high level of corruption in Lebanese politics and the complex regional environment in which Lebanon is subsumed (see Leenders 2012; Salloukh et al. 2015). Yet, his relentless efforts to advance reforms in the dossiers the FPM occupies marks him out as an active politician.

However, the most ominous threat to the founding principles of the FPM remains the sectarian discourse and practices adopted by FPM politicians following 2005, which seem to be intensifying in reaction to prevailing political practices in Lebanon and the region. The principle of proportional elections, which was introduced in the 2018 parliamentary elections for the first time in Lebanon's history, should have showcased the FPM's popularity in multiple sectarian communities, but ended up revealing its popularity among Christian voters. Rather than providing an avenue for political expression outside the confines of this sectarian system, Lebanon's adoption of an electoral law based on proportionality led to a 49.7% national voter turnout, which dropped from the 55% turnout of the 2009 elections conducted on the basis of the majoritarian electoral system (Mourad and Garrote Sanchez 2019). But perhaps voters felt disinclined to vote due to their lack of awareness of proportionality, their understanding that the same sectarian elite (who designed and approved the law) had a higher chance of success than newcomers and an overwhelming feeling of hopelessness sweeping the country as a result of economic hardships.

The committee tasked with designing a new electoral law for the 2018 parliamentary elections comprised representatives from the FPM, Future movement, Hezbollah, Amal and the LF, whose main objective was to maximize their representation in Parliament. As such, Lebanon's electoral districts continued to witness distortions with regard to the deputy-to-voter ratio, but were overshadowed by the reality of pre-printed party lists with a single preferential vote. The list earning the highest percentage of overall votes would promote to Parliament its candidates who scored the highest number of preferential votes, whereas the list receiving a lower percentage of votes might have to promote those candidates on its list receiving fewer preferential votes, especially if a sectarian mismatch between top-ranking candidates and the remaining unfilled seats existed.

In other words, this electoral law incentivized candidates to forge alliances with, or join the ranks of, political parties that, in turn, had to receive a certain threshold to determine how many candidates they could secure in Parliament from a specific district; yet, those parties could not fully determine who the victorious candidates would be. Those lists that fail to secure the voter threshold are discounted from the race and their votes are wasted. Thus, one of the flaws of this law is that it encourages inter-party competition among candidates running on the same parliamentary electoral slate.

Although exact figures on vote buying and election spending are hard to document accurately in Lebanon, it is common to hear analysts discuss how much a parliamentary candidate must have spent during his electoral campaign; some of those costs sway voters to transfer their preferential votes to a specific candidate (see Mourad and Garrote Sanchez 2019). As a consequence of such practices, political parties have increasingly turned to the practice of staffing their lists with well-to-do businesspeople who can afford expensive electoral campaigns. For instance, the sudden nomination of Sarkis Sarkis (a millionaire from the Matn district) to the FPM parliamentary slate raised suspicions regarding his role in electoral spending, since Sarkis had not been with the FPM prior to his nomination by the party.

The most egregious impact of this electoral law is the adoption of proportional voting in large constituencies, in order to secure a solid position for the political party, and preferential voting in smaller constituencies to secure the narrow parochial interests of candidates within their communities (Elghossain 2017). For example, the electoral district of Kiserwan–Jbeil hosted various lists competing for eight parliamentary seats on the same slate in proportional elections; however, voters in Kiserwan could cast a single preferential vote for a candidate among five nominees, and voters in Jbeil could cast a single preferential vote for a single candidate among the remaining three nominees out of the initial slate of eight candidates. Such behavior contributed to the consolidation of sectarian mobilization in local communities, especially in electoral districts where sectarian minorities could ensure the promotion of their preferred candidate to Parliament. This was illustrated in the election of a Maronite MP from the LF in the Der-el-Ahmar district, where Hezbollah previously secured all parliamentary seats under the majoritarian electoral law.

Considering that this electoral law introduced the principle of proportionality in the 2018 parliamentary elections, it could have provided the avenue for the Lebanese people to escape the confines of this pervasive sectarian system, but it failed to do so since the strategy of political subjectification, adopted by Lebanese parties, ensured the loyalty of their voters. Therefore, various political parties vied for a dominant position within their sectarian communities. Hezbollah and Amal sought to secure all the seats allocated for Shia members in Parliament; the Future movement sought to emerge as the leading party within the Sunni community; the Druze-based Progressive Socialist Party aimed to secure the majority of Druze seats; and Christian parties, such as the FPM and the LF, competed to assert their popularity among Christian voters. As such, a majority of Lebanese voters rushed to the polls in support of their sectarian political parties, since only a single MP emerged from the newly established and non-sectarian party Seven.

The main question that should be posed here is whether Bassil and the FPM party can be faulted for participating in the intensification of this sectarian representation of Lebanese Christians, or whether they were responding to the existing rules of engagement, which is a topic that could form the basis of future research. Suffice it to say that at the time of their formal entry into conventional politics—that is, the parliamentary elections of 2005—Lebanon hosted several sectarian practices that pervaded various state institutions, fragmented the institutional framework of the state by leading to distortions in executive and legislative authorities (Leenders 2012), and required politicians to dispense favors to their supporters in return for their votes during electoral rounds (Cammet 2014). Even though the FPM appeared quite vocal in opposing the pre-existing order in the initial post-2005 phase, the debate on how far it should head in combating this pre-existing system while attempting its revision preoccupied the minds of FPM members.

Subsequently, several FPM members found themselves obliged to adopt some aspects of electoral practices in order to maintain an edge during parliamentary elections. Therefore, the issue of having to abide by the parameters of this distorted political system was externally imposed on the FPM, which, in turn, contributed to its vitality by adopting some of its practices. This is quite similar to game theory dilemmas in which the players find themselves cheating or committing violations lest their counterparts do so first and beat them. Yet, even though all parties to the game in Lebanon are aware of the detrimental effects of sectarianism (cheating in game theory), no party seems intent on dropping sectarian practices as a strategy and will make only slight reforms when pressured by civil society organizations and the financial condition of the Lebanese economy, implying that the secular state will not dock on Lebanese shores any time soon.

Another point meriting scrutiny is Bassil's consolidation of power within the FPM at the expense of other party contenders. Back in 2009, mounting political rejection of Bassil's continued role as minister by the March 14 alliance not only contributed to a nine-month delay in government formation, but also consolidated his position within the FPM. Bassil may have enjoyed a privileged relationship with Aoun as his son-in-law, but Bassil's political performance, which clearly annoyed some politicians, must have received Aoun's blessing. We do not know whether the tide of Aoun's support would have shifted against Bassil had he been passive rather than outspoken and confrontational. But as an active politician,

Bassil received the backing and support of his father-in-law, which, in turn, strengthened his position in the FPM vis-à-vis other party members.

Yet, Bassil's outspoken character earned him the reputation of a confrontational politician. His occasional disagreements with Lebanese politicians portray him as an undiplomatic and confrontational political figure in Lebanese politics. For instance, his tardy reception of Sleiman Frangiyeh by making the latter wait unattended for 10 minutes in the salon of his residence in Batroun must have been perceived by Frangiyeh as an offensive move; this deepened the divide among the two men, who were still allies at the time. Political disagreement between Bassil and Speaker of the House Nabih Berri caused the former to dub the latter a thug, which enraged Berri's supporters, whose armed onslaught on FPM headquarters risked tossing the country into sectarian sedition before political mediation resolved matters (Haboush, January 29, 2018). While Bassil can show some signs of diplomatic behavior, he exhibits no qualms about relapsing to confrontational behavior, which can result in political deadlock in a number of dossiers in Lebanese politics.

Bassil also quarreled with his FPM colleagues over the shape and form of the FPM party, preferring an organizational structure relying on a powerful party president enjoying centralized authority and decentralization of administrative tasks, instead of a system obliging the party president to yield to checks by vesting power in internal party committees. However, FPM members opposed to Bassil's leadership style voiced their concerns at some practices carried out by their party's leadership, most notably the positioning of newcomers to the FPM in national politics instead of loyal FPM members; they felt that the role of veteran activists was shrinking in the party. When these members, who included Naim Aoun and Antoine Nasrallah among others, voiced their concerns in media outlets, they were expelled by their party's leadership for attempting to drive a wedge within the party.

Following the expulsion of this FPM group in 2015, no effort to lead a political movement in opposition to the FPM leadership took place until the political declaration of April 6, 2019 (Tayyar Declaration 2019). The very same group of former FPM activists declared that they had decided to upgrade their organizational efforts in response to the dire political and economic situation of the country. In extremely nebulous language, this group pointed the finger of blame at the current FPM leadership embodied in Gebran Bassil for its political practices.

Therefore, the charisma deficit resulting in the post-Aoun phase is unlikely to be filled by any political figure within the FPM, be it Bassil or others. Although the impact of charisma has not been adequately analyzed in this book, the FPM activists interviewed unanimously agreed that no politician can replace Aoun in leadership charisma. The proposed solution to overcome this issue was to institute a solid FPM structure with clear party mechanisms to replace appointments or the preferential treatment of members within the party.

In fact, several rounds of internal party elections for the selection of FPM nominees to the 2018 parliamentary elections occurred after 2015, but the negotiations happening prior to the formation of parliamentary electoral slates often disqualified FPM party favorites. FPM party members selected their preferred candidates for parliamentary elections in every district across Lebanon. However, last minute horse-trading often brought in new non-partisan candidates to the FPM electoral slate at the expense of party activists; the most evident example of this was the replacement of long-time FPM activist Tanious Hobeika with millionaire businessman Sarkis Sarkis on the FPM electoral slate for the Matn district in the 2018 parliamentary elections. This reality points to the ineffectiveness of institutional mechanisms alone in ordering party affairs if such mechanisms are not coupled with practices that seek to render party politics a transparent affair.

In all honesty, it is highly doubtful that anyone, whether Bassil or other party cohorts, facing the same constraints and challenges in the management of the FPM amid an intensifying sectarian political environment in Lebanon would have emerged unscathed from the harsh critique of journalists and commentators. Lebanese elections had been an expensive ordeal ever since the 1960s (Hudson 1968), but the failure of the FPM to contribute to change in that field or to avoid election spending altogether is what disgruntles some FPM supporters. Given the fierce competition fought between various political parties during electoral rounds, FPM leadership is likely to depend more heavily on businesspeople and to attempt to attract more sources of funding into the ranks of the party in the future.

Perhaps Bassil can be faulted for not adopting more diplomatic overtures with other Lebanese politicians or for being quite so confrontational with other party cohorts. The dissension of some party members continues to be a topic of disrepute for the party leader in media pieces; the FPM would do well to resolve such party disputes and reunite veteran party activists in the ranks of the party. The occasional ousting of party members from the ranks of the FPM, such as the recent eviction of Hobeika in April 2019, compromises democratic debate within the party and encourages members to simply rubberstamp their party leadership's decisions.

However, party longevity not only depends on Bassil's ability to steer the FPM toward success, but also on reinterpreting the aims and dreams of the FPM in line with the realities of Lebanese politics. Therefore, has the "FPM dream" been lost in translation or does it merely require some fine-tuning?

Part III: Dreams Face off Against Reality

Activism, change and sectarianism have been defining features of the FPM's 30-year trajectory, which marked the group out as struggling toward a secular society and state in the period up to 2005, before its relapse into sectarian modes of political subjectification and mobilization. While the FPM leadership consciously adopted the new sectarian discourse and approach after 2005, the prevailing political factors in Lebanese and regional politics dictated these moves.

As noted in the previous sections, Michel Aoun, Gebran Bassil and the FPM adopted a more sectarian discourse following 2005 because of the prevailing conditions in Lebanese politics. They regularly pointed out their willingness to work toward a secular society and state, although such an end goal is hardly in reach due to the institutionalization of sectarianism across all walks of society and state policies. For instance, the adoption of the 2018 parliamentary electoral law based on proportional representation intended to represent various segments of society in line with their corresponding base of support. However, the intensifying sectarian mobilization of supporters turned what could have been an opportunity for secular change into another opportunity to assert popularity among the Christian community of Lebanon.

This begs the question of whether the dreams of a secular state, corrupt-free politics and the representation of the interests of youth as opposed to those of the traditional political elite, which were voiced by the young people gathering in front of the Baabda Palace as early as 1989, can still be attained, or are they banished by the sectarian nature of Lebanese politics? Over the years, FPM activists believed that their leader, Michel Aoun, carried the keys to change in several dossiers. The reason for this perception lay in Aoun's persuasive talents and his firm promises to better conditions when at the helm of the state.

Much to the chagrin of FPM activists, some of these promises can be met, whereas others require the cooperation of a wide array of the political, economic and religious elite, especially in matters concerning the secular transformation of a sectarian system. Therefore, Aoun alone cannot propose, enact and forcefully implement civil marriage laws, for instance, without the cooperation of spiritual leaders from across the country's 17 officially endorsed sects. These promises will require much time and consistent effort, even when driven by a politician of Aoun's stature.

In a country where a basketball match can relapse into episodes of sectarian violence, the financial-economic elite display a vested interest in the persistence of sectarian balances and farmers seek the support of those in the political sectarian elite, this mutually reinforcing system has various beneficiaries, despite their being members of society who sometimes voice their opposition to it. Therefore, any major change to the pre-existing political order in Lebanon will require a root-and-branch transformation of multiple layers of politics, starting from the laws and practices that form amenable sectarian subjects (marriage laws, system of employment, dispensing public goods, etc.) and moving to the legal and institutional order that preserves sectarian identification with the state and the political entrepreneurs (politicians) who lubricate sectarian state–society relationships in line with their interests.

Seeing that such a radical transformation of society is hardly attainable given Lebanon's circumstances, the FPM party would do well to redefine its political priorities and avoid deluding supporters. It should divide its goals into long-term objectives that require the collaboration of society at large and short-term to middle-range goals, which require consistent efforts, but may generate results in the short run.

Again, these long-term goals are matters related to the secular transformation of society, which requires the cooperation of multiple actors within Lebanon. This cannot be an FPM goal because the movement alone cannot possibly score any successes on that front, even if it manages to promote a Shia, Sunni or Druze FPM member to Parliament. Various political parties could resort to strategies of co-optation, which could be explored in future research, to maintain the support of their sectarian community.

The FPM party will have to inform its activists that the implementation of these long-term goals will be tabled as topics for discussion in party meetings in order to determine the best method of implementation. Perhaps the secularization of Lebanese society and state could become part of the party's philosophical orientation and not an end in itself. By shelving it as a philosophical orientation, party leadership and activists alike would become less obliged to deliver on these goals according to a specific timetable and thus would not have to bear the brunt of incisive questions from the press during interviews.

Many of the short- to middle-range goals, to Gebran Bassil's credit, occupy an important order of priority on the political agenda of FPM ministers. Combating corruption, introducing reform plans and delivering outcomes are three aims that FPM ministers and MPs are encouraged by their leadership to execute. As a goal-oriented politician, Bassil inspires many of his colleagues within the FPM to adopt a hands-on approach and demonstrate their productivity to Lebanese society at large.

Even though FPM ministers are encumbered by the dire economic conditions of the Lebanese economy—a stalling housing market, slow growth, rising unemployment, high banking interest rates to shore up money supplies, poor infrastructure, the world's highest refugee-to-population ratio, the ongoing war in neighboring Syria and the unsettled conditions of members in the Lebanese diaspora whose remittances provide stable financial inflows (see Atallah et al. 2018; Zoughaib and Garrote Sanchez 2019)—they have the opportunity to fulfill their party's goals by introducing reforms in several ministerial portfolios. The enactment of proper monitoring mechanisms, structural adjustments and the legal infrastructure for better financial management than was the case in 1991 are requirements imposed on Lebanon by international donors at the Cedar conference on April 6, 2018, whose US$11 billion pledges promise to inject investments into a slowing economy (Perry and Melander, April 6, 2018). Of course, they will have to cooperate with politicians of diverse persuasions in order to carry out those goals effectively.

However, the FPM can only ensure its longevity and preserve its goals if it maintains ethical practices without resorting to the adoption of double standards or convoluted practices in national politics and with party members. While Bassil's role in national politics is welcomed on many fronts, his performance within the FPM points to undemocratic practices, especially when expelling party activists who oppose his opinion. The expulsion of various activists from party ranks from 2015 to date speaks to this reality.

Although this author will shy away from predicting the FPM's fate in the post-Aoun phase with any certainty, the research conducted for this book shows that the movement already possesses ample resources to persist in Lebanese politics. However, the potential downfall of the party, if it occurs, will result from undemocratic practices against party members, double standards in the implementation of mechanisms to ensure progression within party ranks and preferential treatment of members by the leadership at the expense of veteran activists. Indeed, only time will tell whether the FPM dream will get lost in translation, or whether the FPM leadership will institute what will turn out to be a powerful political party that outlives its founding father.

References

Abdallah, H. 2008. "Lebanese Rivals Set to Elect President After Historic Agreement." *Daily Star*, May 22. Accessed April 4, 2019. http://www.dailystar.com.lb/News/Lebanon-News/2008/May-22/51877-lebanese-rivals-set-to-elect-president-after-historic-accord.ashx.

Abou Rizk, T. 2018. "Generator Mafias Profit from Lebanese Power Supply Gap." By the East, August 30. Accessed April 4, 2019. https://www.bytheeast.com/2018/08/30/generator-mafias-profit-from-lebanese-power-supply-gap/.

Abs, Z. Interview by this author. 2014. Beirut, October 31.

Ajroudi, A., and A. Chughtai. 2018. "Lebanon Elections 2018: Politics as Usual." Al Jazeera, May 2. Accessed April 27, 2019. https://www.aljazeera.com/indepth/features/lebanon-elections-2018-politics-usual-180501091710689.html.

Al-Jazeera. 2006. "Sixth Lebanese Cabinet Member Quits." Al Jazeera, November 13. Accessed April 5, 2019. https://www.aljazeera.com/archive/2006/11/2008410147714l654.html.

———. 2017. "Michel Aoun: Nothing Justifies Saad Hariri's Detention." Al Jazeera, November 15. Accessed April 4, 2019. https://www.aljazeera.com/news/2017/11/michel-aoun-justifies-saad-hariri-detention-171115150827644.html.

Annahar. 2016. "Jeajea Endorses Aoun's Candidacy for Presidency." *Annahar-English*, January 18. Accessed March 30, 2019. https://en.annahar.com/article/303102-geagea-to-nominate-aoun-for-presidency-bid-riachi.

Asharq Al-awsat. 2019. "Lebanon Approves Electricity Sector Reform Plan." *Asharq Al-awsat*, April 8. https://aawsat.com/english/home/article/1670506/lebanon-approves-electricity-sector-reform-plan.

Assi, A. 2016. "Lebanon's Consociational Model: Christian Parties and the Struggle for Political Power in Post-2005 Period." *Global Discourse* 6 (4): 650–672.

Atallah, S., M. Mahmalat, and S. Zoughaib. 2018. "Cedre Reform Program: Learning from Paris III." Policy Brief (Lebanese Center for Policy Studies).

Accessed April 27, 2019. http://www.lcps-lebanon.org/publication.php?id=322&category=700&title=700.

Bakri, N., and A. Cowell. 2008. "Lebanese Reach Agreement to Resolve 18-Month Political Crisis." *The New York Times*, May 21. Accessed April 18, 2019. https://www.nytimes.com/2008/05/21/world/africa/21iht-lebanon.4.13105564.html.

Bassil, G. Interview by The Business Year. 2016. HE Gebran Bassil: Home and Away. https://www.thebusinessyear.com/lebanon-2016/home-and-away/interview.

BBC. 2008. "Lebanon Rivals Agree Crisis Deal." BBC, May 21. Accessed March 25, 2019. http://news.bbc.co.uk/2/hi/7411835.stm.

Cammet, M. 2014. *Compassionate Communalism: Welfare and Sectarianism in Lebanon*. Ithaca: Cornell University Press.

Chamoun, M. Interview by this author. 2014. Beirut, October 15.

CNN. 2006. "Protestors Burn Consulate Over Cartoons." CNN, February 5. Accessed April 22, 2019. http://edition.cnn.com/2006/WORLD/asiapcf/02/05/cartoon.protests/.

Elghossain, A. 2017. "One Step Forward for Lebanon's Elections." Carnegie Endowment for International Peace, July 11. Accessed April 22, 2019. https://carnegieendowment.org/sada/71496.

El-Khazen, F. 2003. "The Postwar Political Process: Authoritarianism by Diffusion." In *Lebanon in Limbo: Postwar Society and State in an Uncertain Regional Environment*, edited by T. Hanf and N. Salam, Chap. 3. Baden-Baden: Nomos.

France24. 2008. "General Aoun Visits Old Foe Syria." France24, December 4. Accessed April 4, 2019. https://www.france24.com/en/20081204-general-aoun-visits-old-foe-syria.

Habib, O., and F.-S. Kanaan. 2019. "Lebanon Offshore Drilling to Start 'Before End of Year'." *Daily Star*, April 3. http://www.dailystar.com.lb/default.aspx/Arts-and-Ent/Opinion/Opinion/Life/News/Business/Local/2019/Apr-03/480278-lebanon-offshore-drilling-to-start-before-end-of-year.ashx.

Haboush, J. 2018. "Berri Demands TV Apology for Bassil's 'Thug' Comment." *Daily Star*, January 29. http://www.dailystar.com.lb/News/Lebanon-News/2018/Jan-29/435907-bassil-calls-berri-a-thug-in-leaked-video-tensions-flare.ashx.

Haddad, S. 2010. "Michel Aoun: La visite à Brad n'a rien à voir avec la politique." *L'Orient le Jour*, February 13. Accessed April 5, 2019. https://www.lorientlejour.com/article/646951/Michel_Aoun%2B%253A_La_visite_a_Brad_n%2527a_rien_a_voir_avec_la_politique.html.

Hage Ali, M. 2010. "Lebanon: The Greed Factor." *Guardian*, December 8. Accessed April 25, 2019. https://www.theguardian.com/commentisfree/2010/dec/08/lebanon-funding.

Helou, J. 2017. "Revising Lebanon's Foreign Policy After Hariri Crisis." Beirut-Today, December 11. Accessed April 26, 2019. http://beirut-today.com/2017/12/11/revising-lebanons-foreign-policy-strategy-hariri-crisis/.

Hudson, M. C. 1968. *The Precarious Republic: Political Modernization in Lebanon*. New York: Random House.

Ilias, F. 2010. *The Evolving Patterns of Lebanese Politics in Post-Syria Lebanon*. Genève: Graduate Institute Publications. Accessed April 13, 2019. https://books.openedition.org/iheid/245?lang=en.

LDE. 2019. *www.lde-leb.com*. Accessed April 27, 2019. http://www.lde-leb.com/.

Leenders, R. 2012. *Spoils of Truce: Corruption and State-Building in Postwar Lebanon*. Ithaca: Cornell University Press.

Mahdi, D., and D. Garrote Sanchez. 2019. "How Do People in Lebanon Perceive Corruption?" Policy Brief (Lebanese Center for Policy Studies). http://lcps-lebanon.org/publication.php?id=329.

Ministry of Economy and Trade. 2018. "Regarding the Necessary Measures and Procedures to Be Taken to Control the Private Generators Electricity Tariff." Ministry of Economy and Trade, October 8. Accessed April 26, 2019. https://www.economy.gov.lb/en/announcements/regarding-the-necessary-measures-and-procedures-to-be-taken-to-control-the-private-electricity-generators–tariff.

Mourad, J., and D. Garrote Sanchez. 2019. "Voter Turnout and Vote Buying in the 2018 Parliamentary Elections." Policy Brief (Lebanese Center for Policy Studies). Accessed April 25, 2019. http://www.lcps-lebanon.org/publication.php?id=328.

Perry, T. 2016. "Old Enemies Set to Elect Aoun as Lebanon's President." Reuters, October 30. Accessed April 20, 2019. https://www.reuters.com/article/us-lebanon-presidency/old-enemies-set-to-elect-aoun-as-lebanons-president-idUSKBN12U0M3.

Perry, T., and I. Melander. 2018. "Lebanon Wins Pledges Exceeding $11 Billion in Paris." Reuters, April 6. Accessed April 10, 2019. https://www.reuters.com/article/us-lebanon-economy-france/lebanon-wins-pledges-exceeding-11-billion-in-paris-idUSKCN1HD0UU.

Qazi, L. 2013. "Al-liqa Al-Masihi: Aoun Mutahadithan bism Al-Mashriqiya. 'The Christian Gathering: Aoun Represents Orientalist'." Elnashra, October 31. Accessed March 30, 2019. https://www.elnashra.com/news/show/678108.

Rida, N. 2010. "Feltman Green 'Op. Disfigure Hezbollah'... Typical Flop." Alahed News. Accessed March 19, 2019. https://english.alahednews.com.lb/11470/385.

———. 2019. "Pompeo Offered to Help Resolve Maritime Dispute Between Lebanon Israel." *Asharq Al-awsat*, March 24. Accessed April 26, 2019.

https://aawsat.com/english/home/article/1648241/pompeo-offered-help-resolve-maritime-dispute-between-lebanon-israel.

Salloukh, B. F., R. Barakat, J. S. Al-Habbal, L. W. Khattab, S. Mikaelian, and A. Nerguizian. 2015. *The Politics of Sectarianism in Postwar Lebanon*. London: Pluto Press.

Schenker, D. 2016. "A New President for Lebanon." The Washington Institute for Near East Policy, October 31. Accessed April 3, 2019. https://www.washingtoninstitute.org/policy-analysis/view/a-new-president-for-lebanon1.

Stel, N., and W. Naudé. 2016. "'Public–Private Entanglement': Entrepreneurship in Lebanon's Hybrid Political Order." *The Journal of Development Studies* 52 (2): 254–268.

Tayyar Declaration. 2019. "Declaration by Former FPM Activists Instituting the 'Tayyar' Movement." Beirut, April 6.

UNSCR 1595. 2005. United Nations S/Res/1595. New York, April 7.

Yacoubian, M. 2009. *Lebanon's Parliamentary Elections: Anticipating Opportunities and Challenges*. Working Paper. Washington, DC: United States Institute of Peace. Accessed April 22, 2019.

Zoughaib, S., and D. Garrote Sanchez. 2019. "Growing Pessimism and Concern over the State of Lebanon's Economy." Policy Brief, Accessed April 27, 2019. http://www.lcps-lebanon.org/publication.php?id=330&category=700&title=700.

Index

J. P. Helou, *Activism, Change and Sectarianism in the Free Patriotic Movement in Lebanon*, Reform and Transition in the Mediterranean, https://doi.org/10.1007/978-3-030-25704-0

G

H

9783030257033